YOUR MOST COMPREHENSIVE AND
REVEALING INDIVIDUAL FORECAST

SUPER HOROSCOPE

SAGITTARIUS

20 00

November 23 - December 20

BERKLEY BOOKS, NEW YORK

The publishers regret that they cannot answer
individual letters requesting personal horoscope information.

2000 SUPER HOROSCOPE SAGITTARIUS

PRINTING HISTORY
Berkley Trade Edition / August 1999

The Penguin Putnam Inc. World Wide Web site address is
http://www.penguinputnam.com

ISBN: 0-425-16889-1

BERKLEY®
Berkley Books are published by The Berkley Publishing Group,
a division of Penguin Putnam Inc.,
375 Hudson Street, New York, New York 10014.
"BERKLEY" and the "B" logo
are trademarks belonging to Penguin Putnam Inc.

PRINTED IN THE UNITED STATES OF AMERICA

10 9 8 7 6 5 4 3 2 1

CONTENTS

THE CUSP-BORN SAGITTARIUS

Are you *really* a Sagittarius? If your birthday falls around the fourth week in November, at the very beginning of Sagittarius, will you still retain the traits of Scorpio, the sign of the Zodiac before Sagittarius? And what if you were born near Christmas— are you more Capricorn than Sagittarius? Many people born at the edge, or cusp, of a sign have great difficulty determining exactly what sign they are. If you are one of these people, here's how you can figure it out once and for all.

Consult the cusp table on the facing page, then locate the year of your birth. The table will tell you the precise days on which the Sun entered and left your sign for the year of your birth. In that way you can determine if you are a true Sagittarius—or whether you are a Scorpio or Capricorn—according to the variations in cusp dates from year to year (see also page 17).

If you were born at the beginning or end of Sagittarius, yours is a lifetime reflecting a process of subtle transformation. Your life on Earth will symbolize a significant change in consciousness, for you are about to enter a whole new way of living or are leaving one behind.

If you were born at the beginning of Sagittarius, you may want to read the horoscope for Scorpio as well as Sagittarius, for Scorpio holds the key to many of your hidden weaknesses, sexual uncertainties, wishes, fantasies, and spiritual potentials. You are the symbol of the human mind awakening to its higher capabilities. You are preparing the way for the liberation of your soul into the realms of wisdom and truth. You leave behind greed, blind desire, and shallow lust, as you learn to create and understand yourself. You travel, see new places, see how people live, figure yourself out, acquire knowledge.

You may hide a stubborn and dangerous extremism and you may rely too much on luck, but at some crisis point in your life a change of consciousness will occur to shift your behavior patterns. New worlds open up, as you become aware of immortality and the infinite possibilities of your own mind.

If you were born at the end of Sagittarius, you may want to read the horoscope book for Capricorn as well as Sagittarius, for Capricorn is a deep part of your materialistic values. You were

4

born with the need to bring your dreams into reality and put your talents and ambitions to practical use.

You need to conquer worry and depression and inhibition. You will learn to take life seriously, but without losing your sense of humor and hope. You must find a balance between believing nothing and believing too much. You need to find the firm middle ground between cynicism and idealism.

THE CUSPS OF SAGITTARIUS

DATES SUN ENTERS SAGITTARIUS (LEAVES SCORPIO)

November 22 every year from 1900 to 2000,
except for the following:

November 21		November 23		
1976	1992	1902	1915	1931
80	93	03	19	35
84	96	07	23	39
88	2000	10	27	43
		11		

DATES SUN LEAVES SAGITTARIUS (ENTERS CAPRICORN)

December 22 every year from 1900 to 2000,
except for the following:

December 21				
1912	1944	1964	1977	1989
16	48	65	80	92
20	52	68	81	93
23	53	69	84	94
28	56	72	85	96
32	57	73	86	97
36	60	76	88	98
40	61			2000

THE ASCENDANT: SAGITTARIUS RISING

Could you be a "double" Sagittarius? That is, could you have Sagittarius as your Rising sign as well as your Sun sign? The tables on pages 8–9 will tell you Sagittarius what your Rising sign happens to be. Just find the hour of your birth, then find the day of your birth, and you will see which sign of the Zodiac is your Ascendant, as the Rising sign is called. The Ascendant is called that because it is the sign rising on the eastern horizon at the time of your birth. For a more detailed discussion of the Rising sign and the twelve houses of the Zodiac, see pages 17–20.

The Ascendant, or Rising sign, is placed on the 1st house in a horoscope, of which there are twelve houses. The 1st house represents your response to the environment—your unique response. Call it identity, personality, ego, self-image, facade, come-on, body-mind-spirit—whatever term best conveys to you the meaning of the you that acts and reacts in the world. It is a you that is always changing, discovering a new you. Your identity started with birth and early environment, over which you had little conscious control, and continues to experience, to adjust, to express itself. The 1st house also represents how others see you. Has anyone ever guessed your sign to be your Rising sign? People may respond to that personality, that facade, that body type governed by your Rising sign.

Your Ascendant, or Rising sign, modifies your basic Sun sign personality, and it affects the way you act out the daily predictions for your Sun sign. If your Rising sign indeed is Sagittarius, what follows is a description of its effects on your horoscope. If your Rising sign is not Sagittarius, but some other sign of the Zodiac, you may wish to read the horoscope book for that sign.

With Sagittarius on the Ascendant, the planet rising in the 1st house is Jupiter, ruler of Sagittarius. In this position Jupiter confers good health, a pleasing personality, a generous disposition, and an increased vitality. It also confers honors or wealth at some point in your lifetime. You may reap unexpected good fortune in times of hardship. At some point, too, you may exile yourself from everyday life to serve a larger dedication. You will sacrifice for your ideals. Because you are zealous in your beliefs, you could

6

make enemies behind your back. Again, the influence of Jupiter works to overcome the opposition.

You are the student, the idealist. Your need for wisdom is boundless. And you think big! You are not satisfied gathering concrete facts or analyzing practical information. You want to infer the grand patterns, to abstract, to generalize, and finally to generate new ideas. You are a visionary, a dreamer, a futurist. Philosophy, law, and religion attract you, for their truths go beyond the limits of everyday experience. Though you firmly hold your beliefs, you are not dogmatic. Rather, you romanticize them, and your method of persuasion is more seductive than shrill. You restless types are very adaptable, changing your ideas with each new discovery. Your mind is completely open.

With Sagittarius Rising you can be attracted to great causes. Your ideas are not generated merely to erect an impressive intellectual framework. Enlightened by your deep compassion, they become ideals in the service of humanity. There may be an inspirational quality to the causes you join or to the ideals you generate for a cause. Justice and mercy are concepts to be translated into action. You work hard to do that, but you are not rebellious or bossy or demanding. You are brave and forthright, without being reckless or combative. Cooperation and communication are important goals. You like working in groups; your friendly good humor is a model for all social relationships.

There is another you, a private you, that people do not necessarily know very well but may glimpse when you have gone out of their lives. That you is restless, opportunistic, seemingly rootless. You live so much in your mind that you don't want to be tied down by mundane obligations. In fact, you will escape from situations that limit your freedom of choice or action, even if you must dishonor a commitment to do so. You could shirk responsibility by flying off to some greener pasture, yet be no richer for the new experience. Carried to extremes, your quest for adventure could be self-indulgent, yet wasteful of yourself and selfish to the people around you.

Like the Archer, the zodiacal symbol of Sagittarius, you like to roam and hunt, though ideas and people may be your terrain and game. But some of you really prefer the outdoor life and sports. You certainly like to travel. Change recharges your happy-go-lucky nature. You like to get around but not get stuck in a rut, so just as swiftly as you appear on a scene, you disappear. Many jobs and places of residence are outcomes of your journeys.

The key words for Sagittarius Rising are buoyancy and expansiveness. Channel these forces into modes of industriousness so you do not waste your noble visions.

RISING SIGNS FOR SAGITTARIUS

Hour of Birth	Day of Birth		
	November 21–25	November 26–30	December 1–5
Midnight	Virgo	Virgo	Virgo
1 AM	Virgo	Virgo	Virgo
2 AM	Libra	Libra	Libra
3 AM	Libra	Libra	Libra
4 AM	Libra	Libra; Scorpio 11/29	Libra
5 AM	Scorpio	Scorpio	Scorpio
6 AM	Scorpio	Scorpio	Scorpio
7 AM	Sagittarius	Sagittarius	Sagittarius
8 AM	Sagittarius	Sagittarius	Sagittarius
9 AM	Sagittarius	Capricorn	Capricorn
10 AM	Capricorn	Capricorn	Capricorn
11 AM	Capricorn; Aquarius 11/25	Aquarius	Aquarius
Noon	Aquarius	Aquarius	Aquarius; Pisces 12/3
1 PM	Pisces	Pisces	Pisces
2 PM	Aries	Aries	Aries
3 PM	Aries	Taurus	Taurus
4 PM	Taurus	Taurus	Taurus; Gemini 12/2
5 PM	Gemini	Gemini	Gemini
6 PM	Gemini	Gemini	Gemini; Cancer 12/2
7 PM	Cancer	Cancer	Cancer
8 PM	Cancer	Cancer	Cancer
9 PM	Leo	Leo	Leo
10 PM	Leo	Leo	Leo
11 PM	Leo	Leo; Virgo 11/30	Virgo

Hour of Birth	Day of Birth		
	December 6–10	December 11–16	December 17–22
Midnight	Virgo	Virgo	Virgo; Libra 12/22
1 AM	Libra	Libra	Libra
2 AM	Libra	Libra	Libra
3 AM	Libra	Libra; Scorpio 12/14	Scorpio
4 AM	Scorpio	Scorpio	Scorpio
5 AM	Scorpio	Scorpio	Scorpio; Sagittarius 12/21
6 AM	Sagittarius	Sagittarius	Sagittarius
7 AM	Sagittarius	Sagittarius	Sagittarius
8 AM	Sagittarius	Capricorn	Capricorn
9 AM	Capricorn	Capricorn	Capricorn
10 AM	Capricorn; Aquarius 12/10	Aquarius	Aquarius
11 AM	Aquarius	Aquarius	Aquarius; Pisces 12/18
Noon	Pisces	Pisces	Pisces; Aries 12/22
1 PM	Aries	Aries	Aries
2 PM	Aries	Taurus	Taurus
3 PM	Taurus	Taurus	Taurus; Gemini 12/19
4 PM	Gemini	Gemini	Gemini
5 PM	Gemini	Gemini	Cancer
6 PM	Cancer	Cancer	Cancer
7 PM	Cancer	Cancer	Cancer; Leo 12/22
8 PM	Leo	Leo	Leo
9 PM	Leo	Leo	Leo
10 PM	Leo	Leo; Virgo 12/15	Virgo
11 PM	Virgo	Virgo	Virgo

THE PLACE OF ASTROLOGY IN TODAY'S WORLD

Does astrology have a place in the fast-moving, ultra-scientific world we live in today? Can it be justified in a sophisticated society whose outriders are already preparing to step off the moon into the deep space of the planets themselves? Or is it just a hangover of ancient superstition, a psychological dummy for neurotics and dreamers of every historical age?

These are the kind of questions that any inquiring person can be expected to ask when they approach a subject like astrology which goes beyond, but never excludes, the materialistic side of life.

The simple, single answer is that astrology works. It works for many millions of people in the western world alone. In the United States there are 10 million followers and in Europe, an estimated 25 million. America has more than 4000 practicing astrologers, Europe nearly three times as many. Even down-under Australia has its hundreds of thousands of adherents. In the eastern countries, astrology has enormous followings, again, because it has been proved to work. In India, for example, brides and grooms for centuries have been chosen on the basis of their astrological compatibility.

Astrology today is more vital than ever before, more practicable because all over the world the media devotes much space and time to it, more valid because science itself is confirming the precepts of astrological knowledge with every new exciting step. The ordinary person who daily applies astrology intelligently does not have to wonder whether it is true nor believe in it blindly. He can see it working for himself. And, if he can use it—and this book is designed to help the reader to do just that—he can make living a far richer experience, and become a more developed personality and a better person.

Astrology and Relationships

Astrology is the science of relationships. It is not just a study of planetary influences on man and his environment. It is the study of man himself.

We are at the center of our personal universe, of all our relationships. And our happiness or sadness depends on how we act, how we relate to the people and things that surround us. The emotions that we generate have a distinct effect—for better or worse—on the world around us. Our friends and our enemies will confirm this. Just look in the mirror the next time you are angry. In other words, each of us is a kind of sun or planet or star radiating our feelings on the environment around us. Our influence on our personal universe, whether loving, helpful, or destructive, varies with our changing moods, expressed through our individual character.

Our personal "radiations" are potent in the way they affect our moods and our ability to control them. But we usually are able to throw off our emotion in some sort of action—we have a good cry, walk it off, or tell someone our troubles—before it can build up too far and make us physically ill. Astrology helps us to understand the universal forces working on us, and through this understanding, we can become more properly adjusted to our surroundings so that we find ourselves coping where others may flounder.

The Challenge of Love

The challenge of love lies in recognizing the difference between infatuation, emotion, sex, and, sometimes, the intentional deceit of the other person. Mankind, with its record of broken marriages, despair, and disillusionment, is obviously not very good at making these distinctions.

Can astrology help?

Yes. In the same way that advance knowledge can usually help in any human situation. And there is probably no situation as human, as poignant, as pathetic and universal, as the failure of man's love.

Love, of course, is not just between man and woman. It involves love of children, parents, home, and friends. But the big problems usually involve the choice of partner.

Astrology has established degrees of compatibility that exist between people born under the various signs of the Zodiac. Because people are individuals, there are numerous variations and modifications. So the astrologer, when approached on mate and marriage matters, makes allowances for them. But the fact remains that some groups of people are suited for each other and some are not, and astrology has expressed this in terms of characteristics we all can study and use as a personal guide.

No matter how much enjoyment and pleasure we find in the different aspects of each other's character, if it is not an overall compatibility, the chances of our finding fulfillment or enduring happiness in each other are pretty hopeless. And astrology can help us to find someone compatible.

Astrology and Science

Closely related to our emotions is the "other side" of our personal universe, our physical welfare. Our body, of course, is largely influenced by things around us over which we have very little control. The phone rings, we hear it. The train runs late. We snag our stocking or cut our face shaving. Our body is under a constant bombardment of events that influence our daily lives to varying degrees.

The question that arises from all this is, what makes each of us act so that we have to involve other people and keep the ball of activity and evolution rolling? This is the question that both science and astrology are involved with. The scientists have attacked it from different angles: anthropology, the study of human evolution as body, mind and response to environment; anatomy, the study of bodily structure; psychology, the science of the human mind; and so on. These studies have produced very impressive classifications and valuable information, but because the approach to the problem is fragmented, so is the result. They remain "branches" of science. Science generally studies effects. It keeps turning up wonderful answers but no lasting solutions. Astrology, on the other hand, approaches the question from the broader viewpoint. Astrology began its inquiry with the totality of human experience and saw it as an effect. It then looked to find the cause, or at least the prime movers, and during thousands of years of observation of man and his *universal* environment came up with the extraordinary principle of planetary influence—or astrology, which, from the Greek, means the science of the stars.

Modern science, as we shall see, has confirmed much of astrology's foundations—most of it unintentionally, some of it reluctantly, but still, indisputably.

It is not difficult to imagine that there must be a connection between outer space and Earth. Even today, scientists are not too sure how our Earth was created, but it is generally agreed that it is only a tiny part of the universe. And as a part of the universe, people on Earth see and feel the influence of heavenly bodies in almost every aspect of our existence. There is no doubt that the Sun has the greatest influence on life on this planet. Without it there would be no life, for without it there would be no warmth, no division into day and night, no cycles of time or season at all. This is clear and easy to see. The influence of the Moon, on the other hand, is more subtle, though no less definite.

There are many ways in which the influence of the Moon manifests itself here on Earth, both on human and animal life. It is a well-known fact, for instance, that the large movements of water on our planet—that is the ebb and flow of the tides—are caused by the Moon's gravitational pull. Since this is so, it follows that these water movements do not occur only in the oceans, but that all bodies of water are affected, even down to the tiniest puddle.

The human body, too, which consists of about 70 percent water, falls within the scope of this lunar influence. For example the menstrual cycle of most women corresponds to the 28-day lunar month; the period of pregnancy in humans is 273 days, or equal to nine lunar months. Similarly, many illnesses reach a crisis at the change of the Moon, and statistics in many countries have shown that the crime rate is highest at the time of the Full Moon. Even human sexual desire has been associated with the phases of the Moon. But it is in the movement of the tides that we get the clearest demonstration of planetary influence, which leads to the irresistible correspondence between the so-called metaphysical and the physical.

Tide tables are prepared years in advance by calculating the future positions of the Moon. Science has known for a long time that the Moon is the main cause of tidal action. But only in the last few years has it begun to realize the possible extent of this influence on mankind. To begin with, the ocean tides do not rise and fall as we might imagine from our personal observations of them. The Moon as it orbits around Earth sets up a circular wave of attraction which pulls the oceans of the world after it, broadly in an east to west direction. This influence is like a phantom wave crest, a loop of power stretching from pole to pole which passes over and around the Earth like an invisible shadow. It travels with equal effect across the land masses and, as scientists were recently amazed to observe, caused oysters placed in the dark in the middle of the United States where there is no sea to open their shells to receive the nonexistent tide. If the land-locked oysters react to this invisible signal, what effect does it have on us who not so long ago in evolutionary time came out of the sea and still have its salt in our blood and sweat?

Less well known is the fact that the Moon is also the primary force behind the circulation of blood in human beings and animals, and the movement of sap in trees and plants. Agriculturists have established that the Moon has a distinct influence on crops, which explains why for centuries people have planted according to Moon cycles. The habits of many animals, too, are directed by the movement of the Moon. Migratory birds, for instance, depart only at or near the time of the Full Moon. And certain sea creatures, eels in particular, move only in accordance with certain phases of the Moon.

Know Thyself—Why?

In today's fast-changing world, everyone still longs to know what the future holds. It is the one thing that everyone has in common: rich and poor, famous and infamous, all are deeply concerned about tomorrow.

But the key to the future, as every historian knows, lies in the past. This is as true of individual people as it is of nations. You cannot understand your future without first understanding your past, which is simply another way of saying that you must first of all know yourself.

The motto "know thyself" seems obvious enough nowadays, but it was originally put forward as the foundation of wisdom by the ancient Greek philosophers. It was then adopted by the "mystery religions" of the ancient Middle East, Greece, Rome, and is still used in all genuine schools of mind training or mystical discipline, both in those of the East, based on yoga, and those of the West. So it is universally accepted now, and has been through the ages.

But how do you go about discovering what sort of person you are? The first step is usually classification into some sort of system of types. Astrology did this long before the birth of Christ. Psychology has also done it. So has modern medicine, in its way.

One system classifies people according to the source of the impulses they respond to most readily: the muscles, leading to direct bodily action; the digestive organs, resulting in emotion; or the brain and nerves, giving rise to thinking. Another such system says that character is determined by the endocrine glands, and gives us such labels as "pituitary," "thyroid," and "hyperthyroid" types. These different systems are neither contradictory nor mutually exclusive. In fact, they are very often different ways of saying the same thing.

Very popular, useful classifications were devised by Carl Jung, the eminent disciple of Freud. Jung observed among the different faculties of the mind, four which have a predominant influence on character. These four faculties exist in all of us without exception, but not in perfect balance. So when we say, for instance, that someone is a "thinking type," it means that in any situation he or she tries to be rational. Emotion, which may be the opposite of thinking, will be his or her weakest function. This thinking type can be sensible and reasonable, or calculating and unsympathetic. The emotional type, on the other hand, can often be recognized by exaggerated language—everything is either marvelous or terrible—and in extreme cases they even invent dramas and quarrels out of nothing just to make life more interesting.

The other two faculties are intuition and physical sensation. The sensation type does not only care for food and drink, nice clothes and furniture; he or she is also interested in all forms of physical experience. Many scientists are sensation types as are athletes and nature-lovers. Like sensation, intuition is a form of perception and we all possess it. But it works through that part of the mind which is not under conscious control—consequently it sees meanings and connections which are not obvious to thought or emotion. Inventors and original thinkers are always intuitive, but so, too, are superstitious people who see meanings where none exist.

Thus, sensation tells us what is going on in the world, feeling (that is, emotion) tells us how important it is to ourselves, thinking enables us to interpret it and work out what we should do about it, and intuition tells us what it means to ourselves and others. All four faculties are essential, and all are present in every one of us. But some people are guided chiefly by one, others by another. In addition, Jung also observed a division of the human personality into the extrovert and the introvert, which cuts across these four types.

A disadvantage of all these systems of classification is that one cannot tell very easily where to place oneself. Some people are reluctant to admit that they act to please their emotions. So they deceive themselves for years by trying to belong to whichever type they think is the "best." Of course, there is no best; each has its faults and each has its good points.

The advantage of the signs of the Zodiac is that they simplify classification. Not only that, but your date of birth is personal—it is unarguably yours. What better way to know yourself than by going back as far as possible to the very moment of your birth? And this is precisely what your horoscope is all about, as we shall see in the next section.

WHAT IS A HOROSCOPE?

If you had been able to take a picture of the skies at the moment of your birth, that photograph would be your horoscope. Lacking such a snapshot, it is still possible to recreate the picture—and this is at the basis of the astrologer's art. In other words, your horoscope is a representation of the skies with the planets in the exact positions they occupied at the time you were born.

The year of birth tells an astrologer the positions of the distant, slow-moving planets Jupiter, Saturn, Uranus, Neptune, and Pluto. The month of birth indicates the Sun sign, or birth sign as it is commonly called, as well as indicating the positions of the rapidly moving planets Venus, Mercury, and Mars. The day and time of birth will locate the position of our Moon. And the moment—the exact hour and minute—of birth determines the houses through what is called the Ascendant, or Rising sign.

With this information the astrologer consults various tables to calculate the specific positions of the Sun, Moon, and other planets relative to your birthplace at the moment you were born. Then he or she locates them by means of the Zodiac.

The Zodiac

The Zodiac is a band of stars (constellations) in the skies, centered on the Sun's apparent path around the Earth, and is divided into twelve equal segments, or signs. What we are actually dividing up is the Earth's path around the Sun. But from our point of view here on Earth, it seems as if the Sun is making a great circle around our planet in the sky, so we say it is the Sun's apparent path. This twelvefold division, the Zodiac, is a reference system for the astrologer. At any given moment the planets—and in astrology both the Sun and Moon are considered to be planets—can all be located at a specific point along this path.

Now where in all this are you, the subject of the horoscope? Your character is largely determined by the sign the Sun is in. So that is where the astrologer looks first in your horoscope, at your Sun sign.

The Sun Sign and the Cusp

There are twelve signs in the Zodiac, and the Sun spends approximately one month in each sign. But because of the motion of the Earth around the Sun—the Sun's apparent motion—the dates when the Sun enters and leaves each sign may change from year to year. Some people born near the cusp, or edge, of a sign have difficulty determining which is their Sun sign. But in this book a Table of Cusps is provided for the years 1900 to 2000 (page 5) so you can find out what your true Sun sign is.

Here are the twelve signs of the Zodiac, their ancient zodiacal symbol, and the dates when the Sun enters and leaves each sign for the year 2000. Remember, these dates may change from year to year.

ARIES	Ram	March 20–April 19
TAURUS	Bull	April 19–May 20
GEMINI	Twins	May 20–June 20
CANCER	Crab	June 20–July 22
LEO	Lion	July 22–August 22
VIRGO	Virgin	August 22–September 22
LIBRA	Scales	September 22–October 22
SCORPIO	Scorpion	October 22–November 21
SAGITTARIUS	Archer	November 21–December 21
CAPRICORN	Sea Goat	December 21–January 20
AQUARIUS	Water Bearer	January 20–February 19
PISCES	Fish	February 19–March 20

It is possible to draw significant conclusions and make meaningful predictions based simply on the Sun sign of a person. There are many people who have been amazed at the accuracy of the description of their own character based only on the Sun sign. But an astrologer needs more information than just your Sun sign to interpret the photograph that is your horoscope.

The Rising Sign and the Zodiacal Houses

An astrologer needs the exact time and place of your birth in order to construct and interpret your horoscope. The illustration on the next page shows the flat chart, or natural wheel, an astrologer uses. Note the inner circle of the wheel labeled 1 through 12. These 12 divisions are known as the houses of the Zodiac.

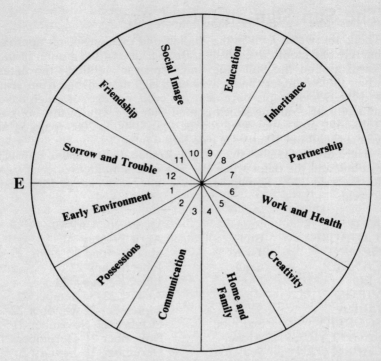

The 1st house always starts from the position marked E, which corresponds to the eastern horizon. The rest of the houses 2 through 12 follow around in a "counterclockwise" direction. The point where each house starts is known as a cusp, or edge.

The cusp, or edge, of the 1st house (point E) is where an astrologer would place your Rising sign, the Ascendant. And, as already noted, the exact time of your birth determines your Rising sign. Let's see how this works.

As the Earth rotates on its axis once every 24 hours, each one of the twelve signs of the Zodiac appears to be "rising" on the horizon, with a new one appearing about every 2 hours. Actually it is the turning of the Earth that exposes each sign to view, but in our astrological work we are discussing apparent motion. This Rising sign marks the Ascendant, and it colors the whole orientation of a horoscope. It indicates the sign governing the 1st house of the chart, and will thus determine which signs will govern all the other houses.

To visualize this idea, imagine two color wheels with twelve divisions superimposed upon each other. For just as the Zodiac is divided into twelve constellations that we identify as the signs, another twelvefold division is used to denote the houses. Now imagine one wheel (the signs) moving slowly while the other wheel (the houses) remains still. This analogy may help you see how the signs keep shifting the "color" of the houses as the Rising sign continues to change every two hours. To simplify things, a Table of Rising Signs has been provided (pages 8–9) for your specific Sun sign.

Once your Rising sign has been placed on the cusp of the 1st house, the signs that govern the rest of the 11 houses can be placed on the chart. In any individual's horoscope the signs do not necessarily correspond with the houses. For example, it could be that a sign covers part of two adjacent houses. It is the interpretation of such variations in an individual's horoscope that marks the professional astrologer.

But to gain a workable understanding of astrology, it is not necessary to go into great detail. In fact, we just need a description of the houses and their meanings, as is shown in the illustration above and in the table below.

THE 12 HOUSES OF THE ZODIAC

1st	Individuality, body appearance, general outlook on life	Personality house
2nd	Finance, possessions, ethical principles, gain or loss	Money house
3rd	Relatives, communication, short journeys, writing, education	Relatives house
4th	Family and home, parental ties, land and property, security	Home house
5th	Pleasure, children, creativity, entertainment, risk	Pleasure house
6th	Health, harvest, hygiene, work and service, employees	Health house
7th	Marriage and divorce, the law, partnerships and alliances	Marriage house
8th	Inheritance, secret deals, sex, death, regeneration	Inheritance house
9th	Travel, sports, study, philosophy and religion	Travel house
10th	Career, social standing, success and honor	Business house
11th	Friendship, social life, hopes and wishes	Friends house
12th	Troubles, illness, secret enemies, hidden agendas	Trouble house

The Planets in the Houses

An astrologer, knowing the exact time and place of your birth, will use tables of planetary motion in order to locate the planets in your horoscope chart. He or she will determine which planet or planets are in which sign and in which house. It is not uncommon, in an individual's horoscope, for there to be two or more planets in the same sign and in the same house.

The characteristics of the planets modify the influence of the Sun according to their natures and strengths.

Sun: Source of life. Basic temperament according to the Sun sign. The conscious will. Human potential.

Moon: Emotions. Moods. Customs. Habits. Changeable. Adaptive. Nurturing.

Mercury: Communication. Intellect. Reasoning power. Curiosity. Short travels.

Venus: Love. Delight. Charm. Harmony. Balance. Art. Beautiful possessions.

Mars: Energy. Initiative. War. Anger. Adventure. Courage. Daring. Impulse.

Jupiter: Luck. Optimism. Generous. Expansive. Opportunities. Protection.

Saturn: Pessimism. Privation. Obstacles. Delay. Hard work. Research. Lasting rewards after long struggle.

Uranus: Fashion. Electricity. Revolution. Independence. Freedom. Sudden changes. Modern science.

Neptune: Sensationalism. Theater. Dreams. Inspiration. Illusion. Deception.

Pluto: Creation and destruction. Total transformation. Lust for power. Strong obsessions.

Superimpose the characteristics of the planets on the functions of the house in which they appear. Express the result through the character of the Sun sign, and you will get the basic idea.

Of course, many other considerations have been taken into account in producing the carefully worked out predictions in this book: the aspects of the planets to each other; their strength according to position and sign; whether they are in a house of exaltation or decline; whether they are natural enemies or not; whether a planet occupies its own sign; the position of a planet in relation to its own house or sign; whether the sign is male or female; whether the sign is a fire, earth, water, or air sign. These are only a few of the colors on the astrologer's pallet which he or she must mix with the inspiration of the artist and the accuracy of the mathematician.

How To Use These Predictions

A person reading the predictions in this book should understand that they are produced from the daily position of the planets for a group of people and are not, of course, individually specialized. To get the full benefit of them our readers should relate the predictions to their own character and circumstances, coordinate them, and draw their own conclusions from them.

If you are a serious observer of your own life, you should find a definite pattern emerging that will be a helpful and reliable guide.

The point is that we always retain our free will. The stars indicate certain directional tendencies but we are not compelled to follow. We can do or not do, and wisdom must make the choice.

We all have our good and bad days. Sometimes they extend into cycles of weeks. It is therefore advisable to study daily predictions in a span ranging from the day before to several days ahead.

Daily predictions should be taken very generally. The word "difficult" does not necessarily indicate a whole day of obstruction or inconvenience. It is a warning to you to be cautious. Your caution will often see you around the difficulty before you are involved. This is the correct use of astrology.

In another section (pages 78–84), detailed information is given about the influence of the Moon as it passes through each of the twelve signs of the Zodiac. There are instructions on how to use the Moon Tables (pages 85–92), which provide Moon Sign Dates throughout the year as well as the Moon's role in health and daily affairs. This information should be used in conjunction with the daily forecasts to give a fuller picture of the astrological trends.

HISTORY OF ASTROLOGY

The origins of astrology have been lost far back in history, but we do know that reference is made to it as far back as the first written records of the human race. It is not hard to see why. Even in primitive times, people must have looked for an explanation for the various happenings in their lives. They must have wanted to know why people were different from one another. And in their search they turned to the regular movements of the Sun, Moon, and stars to see if they could provide an answer.

It is interesting to note that as soon as man learned to use his tools in any type of design, or his mind in any kind of calculation, he turned his attention to the heavens. Ancient cave dwellings reveal dim crescents and circles representative of the Sun and Moon, rulers of day and night. Mesopotamia and the civilization of Chaldea, in itself the foundation of those of Babylonia and Assyria, show a complete picture of astronomical observation and well-developed astrological interpretation.

Humanity has a natural instinct for order. The study of anthropology reveals that primitive people—even as far back as prehistoric times—were striving to achieve a certain order in their lives. They tried to organize the apparent chaos of the universe. They had the desire to attach meaning to things. This demand for order has persisted throughout the history of man. So that observing the regularity of the heavenly bodies made it logical that primitive peoples should turn heavenward in their search for an understanding of the world in which they found themselves so random and alone.

And they did find a significance in the movements of the stars. Shepherds tending their flocks, for instance, observed that when the cluster of stars now known as the constellation Aries was in sight, it was the time of fertility and they associated it with the Ram. And they noticed that the growth of plants and plant life corresponded with different phases of the Moon, so that certain times were favorable for the planting of crops, and other times were not. In this way, there grew up a tradition of seasons and causes connected with the passage of the Sun through the twelve signs of the Zodiac.

Astrology was valued so highly that the king was kept informed of the daily and monthly changes in the heavenly bodies, and the results of astrological studies regarding events of the future. Head astrologers were clearly men of great rank and position, and the office was said to be a hereditary one.

Omens were taken, not only from eclipses and conjunctions of

the Moon or Sun with one of the planets, but also from storms
and earthquakes. In the eastern civilizations, particularly, the rev-
erence inspired by astrology appears to have remained unbroken
since the very earliest days. In ancient China, astrology, astron-
omy, and religion went hand in hand. The astrologer, who was
also an astronomer, was part of the official government service
and had his own corner in the Imperial Palace. The duties of the
Imperial astrologer, whose office was one of the most important
in the land, were clearly defined, as this extract from early records
shows:

> This exalted gentleman must concern himself with the stars in
> the heavens, keeping a record of the changes and movements
> of the Planets, the Sun and the Moon, in order to examine the
> movements of the terrestrial world with the object of prognos-
> ticating good and bad fortune. He divides the territories of the
> nine regions of the empire in accordance with their dependence
> on particular celestial bodies. All the fiefs and principalities are
> connected with the stars and from this their prosperity or mis-
> fortune should be ascertained. He makes prognostications ac-
> cording to the twelve years of the Jupiter cycle of good and evil
> of the terrestrial world. From the colors of the five kinds of
> clouds, he determines the coming of floods or droughts, abun-
> dance or famine. From the twelve winds, he draws conclusions
> about the state of harmony of heaven and earth, and takes note
> of good and bad signs that result from their accord or disaccord.
> In general, he concerns himself with five kinds of phenomena
> so as to warn the Emperor to come to the aid of the government
> and to allow for variations in the ceremonies according to their
> circumstances.

The Chinese were also keen observers of the fixed stars, giving
them such unusual names as Ghost Vehicle, Sun of Imperial Con-
cubine, Imperial Prince, Pivot of Heaven, Twinkling Brilliance,
Weaving Girl. But, great astrologers though they may have been,
the Chinese lacked one aspect of mathematics that the Greeks
applied to astrology—deductive geometry. Deductive geometry
was the basis of much classical astrology in and after the time of
the Greeks, and this explains the different methods of prognos-
tication used in the East and West.

Down through the ages the astrologer's art has depended, not
so much on the uncovering of new facts, though this is important,
as on the interpretation of the facts already known. This is the
essence of the astrologer's skill.

But why should the signs of the Zodiac have any effect at all
on the formation of human character? It is easy to see why people

thought they did, and even now we constantly use astrological expressions in our everyday speech. The thoughts of "lucky star," "ill-fated," "star-crossed," "mooning around," are interwoven into the very structure of our language.

Wherever the concept of the Zodiac is understood and used, it could well appear to have an influence on the human character. Does this mean, then, that the human race, in whose civilization the idea of the twelve signs of the Zodiac has long been embedded, is divided into only twelve types? Can we honestly believe that it is really as simple as that? If so, there must be pretty wide ranges of variation within each type. And if, to explain the variation, we call in heredity and environment, experiences in early childhood, the thyroid and other glands, and also the four functions of the mind together with extroversion and introversion, then one begins to wonder if the original classification was worth making at all. No sensible person believes that his favorite system explains everything. But even so, he will not find the system much use at all if it does not even save him the trouble of bothering with the others.

In the same way, if we were to put every person under only one sign of the Zodiac, the system becomes too rigid and unlike life. Besides, it was never intended to be used like that. It may be convenient to have only twelve types, but we know that in practice there is every possible gradation between aggressiveness and timidity, or between conscientiousness and laziness. How, then, do we account for this?

A person born under any given Sun sign can be mainly influenced by one or two of the other signs that appear in their individual horoscope. For instance, famous persons born under the sign of Gemini include Henry VIII, whom nothing and no one could have induced to abdicate, and Edward VIII, who did just that. Obviously, then, the sign Gemini does not fully explain the complete character of either of them.

Again, under the opposite sign, Sagittarius, were both Stalin, who was totally consumed with the notion of power, and Charles V, who freely gave up an empire because he preferred to go into a monastery. And we find under Scorpio many uncompromising characters such as Luther, de Gaulle, Indira Gandhi, and Montgomery, but also Petain, a successful commander whose name later became synonymous with collaboration.

A single sign is therefore obviously inadequate to explain the differences between people; it can only explain resemblances, such as the combativeness of the Scorpio group, or the far-reaching devotion of Charles V and Stalin to their respective ideals—the Christian heaven and the Communist utopia.

But very few people have only one sign in their horoscope chart. In addition to the month of birth, the day and, even more, the hour to the nearest minute if possible, ought to be considered. Without this, it is impossible to have an actual horoscope, for the word horoscope literally means "a consideration of the hour."

The month of birth tells you only which sign of the Zodiac was occupied by the Sun. The day and hour tell you what sign was occupied by the Moon. And the minute tells you which sign was rising on the eastern horizon. This is called the Ascendant, and, as some astrologers believe, it is supposed to be the most important thing in the whole horoscope.

The Sun is said to signify one's heart, that is to say, one's deepest desires and inmost nature. This is quite different from the Moon, which signifies one's superficial way of behaving. When the ancient Romans referred to the Emperor Augustus as a Capricorn, they meant that he had the Moon in Capricorn. Or, to take another example, a modern astrologer would call Disraeli a Scorpion because he had Scorpio Rising, but most people would call him Sagittarius because he had the Sun there. The Romans would have called him Leo because his Moon was in Leo.

So if one does not seem to fit one's birth month, it is always worthwhile reading the other signs, for one may have been born at a time when any of them were rising or occupied by the Moon. It also seems to be the case that the influence of the Sun develops as life goes on, so that the month of birth is easier to guess in people over the age of forty. The young are supposed to be influenced mainly by their Ascendant, the Rising sign, which characterizes the body and physical personality as a whole.

It is nonsense to assume that all people born at a certain time will exhibit the same characteristics, or that they will even behave in the same manner. It is quite obvious that, from the very moment of its birth, a child is subject to the effects of its environment, and that this in turn will influence its character and heritage to a decisive extent. Also to be taken into account are education and economic conditions, which play a very important part in the formation of one's character as well.

People have, in general, certain character traits and qualities which, according to their environment, develop in either a positive or a negative manner. Therefore, selfishness (inherent selfishness, that is) might emerge as unselfishness; kindness and consideration as cruelty and lack of consideration toward others. In the same way, a naturally constructive person may, through frustration, become destructive, and so on. The latent characteristics with which people are born can, therefore, through environment and good or bad training, become something that would appear to be its opposite, and so give the lie to the astrologer's description of their character. But this is not the case. The true character is still there, but it is buried deep beneath these external superficialities.

Careful study of the character traits of various signs of the Zodiac are of immeasurable help, and can render beneficial service to the intelligent person. Undoubtedly, the reader will already have discovered that, while he is able to get on very well with some people, he just "cannot stand" others. The causes sometimes seem inexplicable. At times there is intense dislike, at other times immediate sympathy. And there is, too, the phenomenon of love at first sight, which is also apparently inexplicable. People appear to be either sympathetic or unsympathetic toward each other for no apparent reason.

Now if we look at this in the light of the Zodiac, we find that people born under different signs are either compatible or incompatible with each other. In other words, there are good and bad interrelating factors among the various signs. This does not, of course, mean that humanity can be divided into groups of hostile camps. It would be quite wrong to be hostile or indifferent toward people who happen to be born under an incompatible sign. There is no reason why everybody should not, or cannot, learn to control and adjust their feelings and actions, especially after they are aware of the positive qualities of other people by studying their character analyses, among other things.

Every person born under a certain sign has both positive and negative qualities, which are developed more or less according to our free will. Nobody is entirely good or entirely bad, and it is up to each of us to learn to control ourselves on the one hand and at the same time to endeavor to learn about ourselves and others.

It cannot be emphasized often enough that it is free will that determines whether we will make really good use of our talents and abilities. Using our free will, we can either overcome our failings or allow them to rule us. Our free will enables us to exert sufficient willpower to control our failings so that they do not harm ourselves or others.

Astrology can reveal our inclinations and tendencies. Astrology can tell us about ourselves so that we are able to use our free will to overcome our shortcomings. In this way astrology helps us do our best to become needed and valuable members of society as well as helpmates to our family and our friends. Astrology also can save us a great deal of unhappiness and remorse.

Yet it may seem absurd that an ancient philosophy could be a prop to modern men and women. But below the materialistic surface of modern life, there are hidden streams of feeling and thought. Symbology is reappearing as a study worthy of the scholar; the psychosomatic factor in illness has passed from the writings of the crank to those of the specialist; spiritual healing in all its forms is no longer a pious hope but an accepted phenomenon. And it is into this context that we consider astrology, in the sense that it is an analysis of human types.

Astrology and medicine had a long journey together, and only parted company a couple of centuries ago. There still remain in medical language such astrological terms as "saturnine," "choleric," and "mercurial," used in the diagnosis of physical tendencies. The herbalist, for long the handyman of the medical profession, has been dominated by astrology since the days of the Greeks. Certain herbs traditionally respond to certain planetary influences, and diseases must therefore be treated to ensure harmony between the medicine and the disease.

But the stars are expected to foretell and not only to diagnose.

Astrological forecasting has been remarkably accurate, but often it is wide of the mark. The brave person who cares to predict world events takes dangerous chances. Individual forecasting is less clear cut; it can be a help or a disillusionment. Then we come to the nagging question: if it is possible to foreknow, is it right to foretell? This is a point of ethics on which it is hard to pronounce judgment. The doctor faces the same dilemma if he finds that symptoms of a mortal disease are present in his patient and that he can only prognosticate a steady decline. How much to tell an individual in a crisis is a problem that has perplexed many distinguished scholars. Honest and conscientious astrologers in this modern world, where so many people are seeking guidance, face the same problem.

Five hundred years ago it was customary to call in a learned man who was an astrologer who was probably also a doctor and a philosopher. By his knowledge of astrology, his study of planetary influences, he felt himself qualified to guide those in distress. The world has moved forward at a fantastic rate since then, and yet people are still uncertain of themselves. At first sight it seems fantastic in the light of modern thinking that they turn to the most ancient of all studies, and get someone to calculate a horoscope for them. But is it *really* so fantastic if you take a second look? For astrology is concerned with tomorrow, with survival. And in a world such as ours, tomorrow and survival are the keywords for the twenty-first century.

ASTROLOGICAL BRIDGE TO THE 21st CENTURY

As the last decade of the twentieth century comes to a close, planetary aspects for its final years connect you with the future. Major changes completed in 1995 and 1996 give rise to new planetary cycles that form the bridge to the twenty-first century and new horizons. The years 1996 through 1999 and into the year 2000 reveal hidden paths and personal hints for achieving your potential, for making the most of your message from the planets.

All the major planets begin new cycles in the late 1990s. Jupiter, planet of good fortune, transits four zodiacal signs from 1996 through 1999 and goes through a complete cycle in each of the elements earth, air, fire, and water. Jupiter is in Capricorn, then in Aquarius, next in Pisces, and finally in Aries as the century turns. With the dawning of the twenty-first century, each new yearly Jupiter cycle follows the natural progression of the Zodiac, from Aries in 2000, then Taurus in 2001, next Gemini in 2002, and so on through Pisces in 2011. The beneficent planet Jupiter promotes your professional and educational goals while urging informed choice and deliberation. Jupiter sharpens your focus and hones your skills. And while safeguarding good luck, Jupiter can turn unusual risks into achievable aims.

Saturn, planet of reason and responsibility, has begun a new cycle in the spring of 1996 when it entered fiery Aries. Saturn in Aries through March 1999 heightens a longing for independence. Your movements are freed from everyday restrictions, allowing you to travel, to explore, to act on a variety of choices. With Saturn in Aries you get set to blaze a new trail. Saturn enters earthy Taurus in March 1999 for a three-year stay over the turn of the century into the year 2002. Saturn in Taurus inspires industry and affection. Practicality, perseverance, and planning can reverse setbacks and minimize risk. Saturn in Taurus lends beauty, order, and structure to your life. In order to take advantage of opportunity through responsibility, to persevere against adversity, look to beautiful planet Saturn.

Uranus, planet of innovation and surprise, started an important new cycle in January of 1996. At that time Uranus entered its natural home in airy Aquarius. Uranus in Aquarius into the year 2003 has a profound effect on your personality and the lens through which you see the world. A basic change in the way you project yourself is just one impact of Uranus in Aquarius. More significantly, a whole new consciousness is evolving. Winds of change blowing your way emphasize movement and freedom. Uranus in Aquarius poses involvement in the larger community beyond self, family, friends, lovers, associates. Radical ideas and progressive thought signal a journey of liberation. As the century turns, follow Uranus on the path of humanitarianism. While you carve a prestigious niche in public life, while you preach social reform and justice, you will be striving to make the world a better place for all people.

Neptune, planet of vision and mystery, is in earthy Capricorn until late 1998. Neptune in Capricorn excites creativity while restraining fanciful thinking. Wise use of resources helps you build persona and prestige. Then Neptune enters airy Aquarius during November 1998 and is there into the year 2011. Neptune in Aquarius, the sign of the Water Bearer, represents two sides of the coin of wisdom: inspiration and reason. Here Neptune stirs powerful currents bearing a rich and varied harvest, the fertile breeding ground for idealistic aims and practical considerations. Neptune's fine intuition tunes in to your dreams, your imagination, your spirituality. You can never turn your back on the mysteries of life. Uranus and Neptune, the planets of enlightenment and renewed idealism both in the sign of Aquarius, give you glimpses into the future, letting you peek through secret doorways into the twenty-first century.

Pluto, planet of beginnings and endings, has completed one cycle of growth November 1995 in the sign of Scorpio. Pluto in Scorpio marked a long period of experimentation and rejuvenation. Then Pluto entered the fiery sign of Sagittarius on November 10, 1995 and is there into the year 2007. Pluto in Sagittarius during its long stay of twelve years can create significant change. The great power of Pluto in Sagittarius may already be starting its transformation of your character and lifestyle. Pluto in Sagittarius takes you on a new journey of exploration and learning. The awakening you experience on intellectual and artistic levels heralds a new cycle of growth. Uncompromising Pluto, seeker of truth, challenges your identity, persona, and self-expression. Uncovering the real you, Pluto holds the key to understanding and meaningful communication. Pluto in Sagittarius can be the guiding light illuminating the first decade of the twenty-first century. Good luck is riding on the waves of change.

THE SIGNS OF THE ZODIAC

Dominant Characteristics

Aries: March 21–April 20

The Positive Side of Aries

The Aries has many positive points to his character. People born under this first sign of the Zodiac are often quite strong and enthusiastic. On the whole, they are forward-looking people who are not easily discouraged by temporary setbacks. They know what they want out of life and they go out after it. Their personalities are strong. Others are usually quite impressed by the Ram's way of doing things. Quite often they are sources of inspiration for others traveling the same route. Aries men and women have a special zest for life that can be contagious; for others, they are a fine example of how life should be lived.

The Aries person usually has a quick and active mind. He is imaginative and inventive. He enjoys keeping busy and active. He generally gets along well with all kinds of people. He is interested in mankind, as a whole. He likes to be challenged. Some would say he thrives on opposition, for it is when he is set against that he often does his best. Getting over or around obstacles is a challenge he generally enjoys. All in all, Aries is quite positive and young-thinking. He likes to keep abreast of new things that are happening in the world. Aries are often fond of speed. They like things to be done quickly, and this sometimes aggravates their slower colleagues and associates.

The Aries man or woman always seems to remain young. Their whole approach to life is youthful and optimistic. They never say die, no matter what the odds. They may have an occasional setback, but it is not long before they are back on their feet again.

The Negative Side of Aries

Everybody has his less positive qualities—and Aries is no exception. Sometimes the Aries man or woman is not very tactful in communicating with others; in his hurry to get things done he is apt to be a little callous or inconsiderate. Sensitive people are likely to find him somewhat sharp-tongued in some situations. Often in his eagerness to get the show on the road, he misses the mark altogether and cannot achieve his aims.

At times Aries can be too impulsive. He can occasionally be stubborn and refuse to listen to reason. If things do not move quickly enough to suit the Aries man or woman, he or she is apt to become rather nervous or irritable. The uncultivated Aries is not unfamiliar with moments of doubt and fear. He is capable of being destructive if he does not get his way. He can overcome some of his emotional problems by steadily trying to express himself as he really is, but this requires effort.

Taurus: April 21–May 20

The Positive Side of Taurus

The Taurus person is known for his ability to concentrate and for his tenacity. These are perhaps his strongest qualities. The Taurus man or woman generally has very little trouble in getting along with others; it's his nature to be helpful toward people in need. He can always be depended on by his friends, especially those in trouble.

Taurus generally achieves what he wants through his ability to persevere. He never leaves anything unfinished but works on something until it has been completed. People can usually take him at his word; he is honest and forthright in most of his dealings. The Taurus person has a good chance to make a success of his life because of his many positive qualities. The Taurus who aims high seldom falls short of his mark. He learns well by experience. He is thorough and does not believe in shortcuts of any kind. The Bull's thoroughness pays off in the end, for through his deliberateness he learns how to rely on himself and what he has learned. The Taurus person tries to get along with others, as a rule. He is not overly critical and likes people to be themselves. He is a tolerant person and enjoys peace and harmony—especially in his home life.

Taurus is usually cautious in all that he does. He is not a person who believes in taking unnecessary risks. Before adopting any one line of action, he will weigh all of the pros and cons. The Taurus person is steadfast. Once his mind is made up it seldom changes. The person born under this sign usually is a good family person—reliable and loving.

The Negative Side of Taurus

Sometimes the Taurus man or woman is a bit too stubborn. He won't listen to other points of view if his mind is set on something. To others, this can be quite annoying. Taurus also does not like to be told what to do. He becomes rather angry if others think him not too bright. He does not like to be told he is wrong, even when he is. He dislikes being contradicted.

Some people who are born under this sign are very suspicious of others—even of those persons close to them. They find it difficult to trust people fully. They are often afraid of being deceived or taken advantage of. The Bull often finds it difficult to forget or forgive. His love of material things sometimes makes him rather avaricious and petty.

Gemini: May 21–June 20

The Positive Side of Gemini

The person born under this sign of the Heavenly Twins is usually quite bright and quick-witted. Some of them are capable of doing many different things. The Gemini person very often has many different interests. He keeps an open mind and is always anxious to learn new things.

Gemini is often an analytical person. He is a person who enjoys making use of his intellect. He is governed more by his mind than by his emotions. He is a person who is not confined to one view; he can often understand both sides to a problem or question. He knows how to reason, how to make rapid decisions if need be.

He is an adaptable person and can make himself at home almost anywhere. There are all kinds of situations he can adapt to. He is a person who seldom doubts himself; he is sure of his talents and his ability to think and reason. Gemini is generally most satisfied

when he is in a situation where he can make use of his intellect. Never short of imagination, he often has strong talents for invention. He is rather a modern person when it comes to life; Gemini almost always moves along with the times—perhaps that is why he remains so youthful throughout most of his life.

Literature and art appeal to the person born under this sign. Creativity in almost any form will interest and intrigue the Gemini man or woman.

The Gemini is often quite charming. A good talker, he often is the center of attraction at any gathering. People find it easy to like a person born under this sign because he can appear easygoing and usually has a good sense of humor.

The Negative Side of Gemini

Sometimes the Gemini person tries to do too many things at one time—and as a result, winds up finishing nothing. Some Twins are easily distracted and find it rather difficult to concentrate on one thing for too long a time. Sometimes they give in to trifling fancies and find it rather boring to become too serious about any one thing. Some of them are never dependable, no matter what they promise.

Although the Gemini man or woman often appears to be well-versed on many subjects, this is sometimes just a veneer. His knowledge may be only superficial, but because he speaks so well he gives people the impression of erudition. Some Geminis are sharp-tongued and inconsiderate; they think only of themselves and their own pleasure.

Cancer: June 21–July 20

The Positive Side of Cancer

The Moon Child's most positive point is his understanding nature. On the whole, he is a loving and sympathetic person. He would never go out of his way to hurt anyone. The Cancer man or woman is often very kind and tender; they give what they can to others. They hate to see others suffering and will do what they can to help someone in less fortunate circumstances than themselves. They are often very concerned about the world. Their interest in people generally goes beyond that of just their own families and close friends; they have a deep sense of community and respect humanitarian values. The Moon Child means what he says, as a rule; he is honest about his feelings.

The Cancer man or woman is a person who knows the art of patience. When something seems difficult, he is willing to wait until the situation becomes manageable again. He is a person who knows how to bide his time. Cancer knows how to concentrate on one thing at a time. When he has made his mind up he generally sticks with what he does, seeing it through to the end.

Cancer is a person who loves his home. He enjoys being surrounded by familiar things and the people he loves. Of all the signs, Cancer is the most maternal. Even the men born under this sign often have a motherly or protective quality about them. They like to take care of people in their family—to see that they are well loved and well provided for. They are usually loyal and faithful. Family ties mean a lot to the Cancer man or woman. Parents and in-laws are respected and loved. Young Cancer responds very well to adults who show faith in him. The Moon Child has a strong sense of tradition. He is very sensitive to the moods of others.

The Negative Side of Cancer

Sometimes Cancer finds it rather hard to face life. It becomes too much for him. He can be a little timid and retiring, when things don't go too well. When unfortunate things happen, he is apt to just shrug and say, "Whatever will be will be." He can be fatalistic to a fault. The uncultivated Cancer is a bit lazy. He doesn't have very much ambition. Anything that seems a bit difficult he'll gladly leave to others. He may be lacking in initiative. Too sensitive, when he feels he's been injured, he'll crawl back into his shell and nurse his imaginary wounds. The immature Moon Child often is given to crying when the smallest thing goes wrong.

Some Cancers find it difficult to enjoy themselves in environments outside their homes. They make heavy demands on others, and need to be constantly reassured that they are loved. Lacking such reassurance, they may resort to sulking in silence.

Leo: July 21–August 21

The Positive Side of Leo

Often Leos make good leaders. They seem to be good organizers and administrators. Usually they are quite popular with others. Whatever group it is that they belong to, the Leo man or woman is almost sure to be or become the leader. Loyalty, one of the Lion's noblest traits, enables him or her to maintain this leadership position.

Leo is generous·most of the time. It is his best characteristic. He or she likes to give gifts and presents. In making others happy, the Leo person becomes happy himself. He likes to splurge when spending money on others. In some instances it may seem that the Lion's generosity knows no boundaries. A hospitable person, the Leo man or woman is very fond of welcoming people to his house and entertaining them. He is never short of company.

Leo has plenty of energy and drive. He enjoys working toward some specific goal. When he applies himself correctly, he gets what he wants most often. The Leo person is almost never unsure of himself. He has plenty of confidence and aplomb. He is a person who is direct in almost everything he does. He has a quick mind and can make a decision in a very short time.

He usually sets a good example for others because of his ambitious manner and positive ways. He knows how to stick to something once he's started. Although Leo may be good at making a joke, he is not superficial or glib. He is a loving person, kind and thoughtful.

There is generally nothing small or petty about the Leo man or woman. He does what he can for those who are deserving. He is a person others can rely upon at all times. He means what he says. An honest person, generally speaking, he is a friend who is valued and sought out.

The Negative Side of Leo

Leo, however, does have his faults. At times, he can be just a bit too arrogant. He thinks that no one deserves a leadership position except him. Only he is capable of doing things well. His opinion of himself is often much too high. Because of his conceit, he is

sometimes rather unpopular with a good many people. Some Leos are too materialistic; they can only think in terms of money and profit.

Some Leos enjoy lording it over others—at home or at their place of business. What is more, they feel they have the right to. Egocentric to an impossible degree, this sort of Leo cares little about how others think or feel. He can be rude and cutting.

Virgo: August 22–September 22

The Positive Side of Virgo

The person born under the sign of Virgo is generally a busy person. He knows how to arrange and organize things. He is a good planner. Above all, he is practical and is not afraid of hard work.

Often called the sign of the Harvester, Virgo knows how to attain what he desires. He sticks with something until it is finished. He never shirks his duties, and can always be depended upon. The Virgo person can be thoroughly trusted at all times.

The man or woman born under this sign tries to do everything to perfection. He doesn't believe in doing anything halfway. He always aims for the top. He is the sort of a person who is always learning and constantly striving to better himself—not because he wants more money or glory, but because it gives him a feeling of accomplishment.

The Virgo man or woman is a very observant person. He is sensitive to how others feel, and can see things below the surface of a situation. He usually puts this talent to constructive use.

It is not difficult for the Virgo to be open and earnest. He believes in putting his cards on the table. He is never secretive or underhanded. He's as good as his word. The Virgo person is generally plainspoken and down to earth. He has no trouble in expressing himself.

The Virgo person likes to keep up to date on new developments in his particular field. Well-informed, generally, he sometimes has a keen interest in the arts or literature. What he knows, he knows well. His ability to use his critical faculties is well-developed and sometimes startles others because of its accuracy.

Virgos adhere to a moderate way of life; they avoid excesses. Virgo is a responsible person and enjoys being of service.

The Negative Side of Virgo

Sometimes a Virgo person is too critical. He thinks that only he can do something the way it should be done. Whatever anyone else does is inferior. He can be rather annoying in the way he quibbles over insignificant details. In telling others how things should be done, he can be rather tactless and mean.

Some Virgos seem rather emotionless and cool. They feel emotional involvement is beneath them. They are sometimes too tidy, too neat. With money they can be rather miserly. Some Virgos try to force their opinions and ideas on others.

Libra: September 23–October 22

The Positive Side of Libra

Libras love harmony. It is one of their most outstanding character traits. They are interested in achieving balance; they admire beauty and grace in things as well as in people. Generally speaking, they are kind and considerate people. Libras are usually very sympathetic. They go out of their way not to hurt another person's feelings. They are outgoing and do what they can to help those in need.

People born under the sign of Libra almost always make good friends. They are loyal and amiable. They enjoy the company of others. Many of them are rather moderate in their views; they believe in keeping an open mind, however, and weighing both sides of an issue fairly before making a decision.

Alert and intelligent, Libra, often known as the Lawgiver, is always fair-minded and tries to put himself in the position of the other person. They are against injustice; quite often they take up for the underdog. In most of their social dealings, they try to be tactful and kind. They dislike discord and bickering, and most Libras strive for peace and harmony in all their relationships.

The Libra man or woman has a keen sense of beauty. They appreciate handsome furnishings and clothes. Many of them are artistically inclined. Their taste is usually impeccable. They know how to use color. Their homes are almost always attractively arranged and inviting. They enjoy entertaining people and see to it that their guests always feel at home and welcome.

Libra gets along with almost everyone. He is well-liked and socially much in demand.

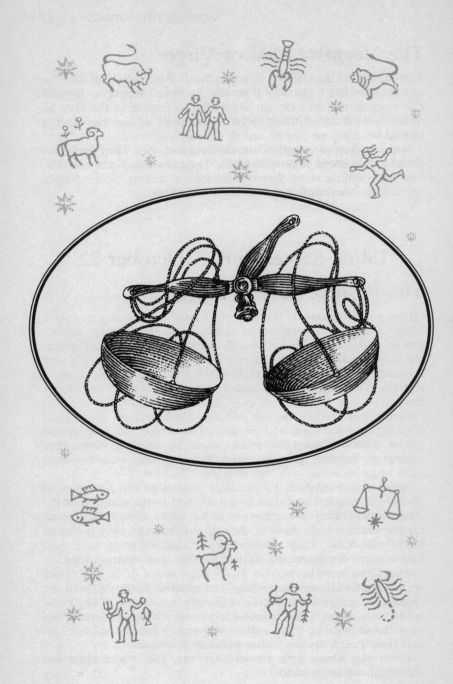

The Negative Side of Libra

Some people born under this sign tend to be rather insincere. So eager are they to achieve harmony in all relationships that they will even go so far as to lie. Many of them are escapists. They find facing the truth an ordeal and prefer living in a world of make-believe.

In a serious argument, some Libras give in rather easily even when they know they are right. Arguing, even about something they believe in, is too unsettling for some of them.

Libras sometimes care too much for material things. They enjoy possessions and luxuries. Some are vain and tend to be jealous.

Scorpio: October 23–November 22

The Positive Side of Scorpio

The Scorpio man or woman generally knows what he or she wants out of life. He is a determined person. He sees something through to the end. Scorpio is quite sincere, and seldom says anything he doesn't mean. When he sets a goal for himself he tries to go about achieving it in a very direct way.

The Scorpion is brave and courageous. They are not afraid of hard work. Obstacles do not frighten them. They forge ahead until they achieve what they set out for. The Scorpio man or woman has a strong will.

Although Scorpio may seem rather fixed and determined, inside he is often quite tender and loving. He can care very much for others. He believes in sincerity in all relationships. His feelings about someone tend to last; they are profound and not superficial.

The Scorpio person is someone who adheres to his principles no matter what happens. He will not be deterred from a path he believes to be right.

Because of his many positive strengths, the Scorpion can often achieve happiness for himself and for those that he loves.

He is a constructive person by nature. He often has a deep understanding of people and of life, in general. He is perceptive and unafraid. Obstacles often seem to spur him on. He is a positive person who enjoys winning. He has many strengths and resources; challenge of any sort often brings out the best in him.

The Negative Side of Scorpio

The Scorpio person is sometimes hypersensitive. Often he imagines injury when there is none. He feels that others do not bother to recognize him for his true worth. Sometimes he is given to excessive boasting in order to compensate for what he feels is neglect.

Scorpio can be proud, arrogant, and competitive. They can be sly when they put their minds to it and they enjoy outwitting persons or institutions noted for their cleverness.

Their tactics for getting what they want are sometimes devious and ruthless. They don't care too much about what others may think. If they feel others have done them an injustice, they will do their best to seek revenge. The Scorpion often has a sudden, violent temper; and this person's interest in sex is sometimes quite unbalanced or excessive.

Sagittarius: November 23–December 20

The Positive Side of Sagittarius

People born under this sign are honest and forthright. Their approach to life is earnest and open. Sagittarius is often quite adult in his way of seeing things. They are broad-minded and tolerant people. When dealing with others the person born under the sign of the Archer is almost always open and forthright. He doesn't believe in deceit or pretension. His standards are high. People who associate with Sagittarius generally admire and respect his tolerant viewpoint.

The Archer trusts others easily and expects them to trust him. He is never suspicious or envious and almost always thinks well of others. People always enjoy his company because he is so friendly and easygoing. The Sagittarius man or woman is often good-humored. He can always be depended upon by his friends, family, and co-workers.

The person born under this sign of the Zodiac likes a good joke every now and then. Sagittarius is eager for fun and laughs, which makes him very popular with others.

A lively person, he enjoys sports and outdoor life. The Archer is fond of animals. Intelligent and interesting, he can begin an

animated conversation with ease. He likes exchanging ideas and discussing various views.

He is not selfish or proud. If someone proposes an idea or plan that is better than his, he will immediately adopt it. Imaginative yet practical, he knows how to put ideas into practice.

The Archer enjoys sport and games, and it doesn't matter if he wins or loses. He is a forgiving person, and never sulks over something that has not worked out in his favor.

He is seldom critical, and is almost always generous.

The Negative Side of Sagittarius

Some Sagittarius are restless. They take foolish risks and seldom learn from the mistakes they make. They don't have heads for money and are often mismanaging their finances. Some of them devote much of their time to gambling.

Some are too outspoken and tactless, always putting their feet in their mouths. They hurt others carelessly by being honest at the wrong time. Sometimes they make promises which they don't keep. They don't stick close enough to their plans and go from one failure to another. They are undisciplined and waste a lot of energy.

Capricorn: December 21–January 19

The Positive Side of Capricorn

The person born under the sign of Capricorn, known variously as the Mountain Goat or Sea Goat, is usually very stable and patient. He sticks to whatever tasks he has and sees them through. He can always be relied upon and he is not averse to work.

An honest person, Capricorn is generally serious about whatever he does. He does not take his duties lightly. He is a practical person and believes in keeping his feet on the ground.

Quite often the person born under this sign is ambitious and knows how to get what he wants out of life. The Goat forges ahead and never gives up his goal. When he is determined about something, he almost always wins. He is a good worker—a hard worker. Although things may not come easy to him, he will not complain, but continue working until his chores are finished.

He is usually good at business matters and knows the value of money. He is not a spendthrift and knows how to put something away for a rainy day; he dislikes waste and unnecessary loss.

Capricorn knows how to make use of his self-control. He can apply himself to almost anything once he puts his mind to it. His ability to concentrate sometimes astounds others. He is diligent and does well when involved in detail work.

The Capricorn man or woman is charitable, generally speaking, and will do what is possible to help others less fortunate. As a friend, he is loyal and trustworthy. He never shirks his duties or responsibilities. He is self-reliant and never expects too much of the other fellow. He does what he can on his own. If someone does him a good turn, then he will do his best to return the favor.

The Negative Side of Capricorn

Like everyone, Capricorn, too, has faults. At times, the Goat can be overcritical of others. He expects others to live up to his own high standards. He thinks highly of himself and tends to look down on others.

His interest in material things may be exaggerated. The Capricorn man or woman thinks too much about getting on in the world and having something to show for it. He may even be a little greedy.

He sometimes thinks he knows what's best for everyone. He is too bossy. He is always trying to organize and correct others. He may be a little narrow in his thinking.

Aquarius: January 20–February 18

The Positive Side of Aquarius

The Aquarius man or woman is usually very honest and forthright. These are his two greatest qualities. His standards for himself are generally very high. He can always be relied upon by others. His word is his bond.

Aquarius is perhaps the most tolerant of all the Zodiac personalities. He respects other people's beliefs and feels that everyone is entitled to his own approach to life.

He would never do anything to injure another's feelings. He is never unkind or cruel. Always considerate of others, the Water

Bearer is always willing to help a person in need. He feels a very strong tie between himself and all the other members of mankind.

The person born under this sign, called the Water Bearer, is almost always an individualist. He does not believe in teaming up with the masses, but prefers going his own way. His ideas about life and mankind are often quite advanced. There is a saying to the effect that the average Aquarius is fifty years ahead of his time.

Aquarius is community-minded. The problems of the world concern him greatly. He is interested in helping others no matter what part of the globe they live in. He is truly a humanitarian sort. He likes to be of service to others.

Giving, considerate, and without prejudice, Aquarius have no trouble getting along with others.

The Negative Side of Aquarius

Aquarius may be too much of a dreamer. He makes plans but seldom carries them out. He is rather unrealistic. His imagination has a tendency to run away with him. Because many of his plans are impractical, he is always in some sort of a dither.

Others may not approve of him at all times because of his unconventional behavior. He may be a bit eccentric. Sometimes he is so busy with his own thoughts that he loses touch with the realities of existence.

Some Aquarius feel they are more clever and intelligent than others. They seldom admit to their own faults, even when they are quite apparent. Some become rather fanatic in their views. Their criticism of others is sometimes destructive and negative.

Pisces: February 19–March 20

The Positive Side of Pisces

Known as the sign of the Fishes, Pisces has a sympathetic nature. Kindly, he is often dedicated in the way he goes about helping others. The sick and the troubled often turn to him for advice and assistance. Possessing keen intuition, Pisces can easily understand people's deepest problems.

He is very broad-minded and does not criticize others for their faults. He knows how to accept people for what they are. On the whole, he is a trustworthy and earnest person. He is loyal to his friends and will do what he can to help them in time of need. Generous and good-natured, he is a lover of peace; he is often willing to help others solve their differences. People who have taken a wrong turn in life often interest him and he will do what he can to persuade them to rehabilitate themselves.

He has a strong intuitive sense and most of the time he knows how to make it work for him. Pisces is unusually perceptive and often knows what is bothering someone before that person, himself, is aware of it. The Pisces man or woman is an idealistic person, basically, and is interested in making the world a better place in which to live. Pisces believes that everyone should help each other. He is willing to do more than his share in order to achieve cooperation with others.

The person born under this sign often is talented in music or art. He is a receptive person; he is able to take the ups and downs of life with philosophic calm.

The Negative Side of Pisces

Some Pisces are often depressed; their outlook on life is rather glum. They may feel that they have been given a bad deal in life and that others are always taking unfair advantage of them. Pisces sometimes feel that the world is a cold and cruel place. The Fishes can be easily discouraged. The Pisces man or woman may even withdraw from the harshness of reality into a secret shell of his own where he dreams and idles away a good deal of his time.

Pisces can be lazy. He lets things happen without giving the least bit of resistance. He drifts along, whether on the high road or on the low. He can be lacking in willpower.

Some Pisces people seek escape through drugs or alcohol. When temptation comes along they find it hard to resist. In matters of sex, they can be rather permissive.

Sun Sign Personalities

ARIES: Hans Christian Andersen, Pearl Bailey, Marlon Brando, Wernher Von Braun, Charlie Chaplin, Joan Crawford, Da Vinci, Bette Davis, Doris Day, W. C. Fields, Alec Guinness, Adolf Hitler, William Holden, Thomas Jefferson, Nikita Khrushchev, Elton John, Arturo Toscanini, J. P. Morgan, Paul Robeson, Gloria Steinem, Sarah Vaughn, Vincent van Gogh, Tennessee Williams

TAURUS: Fred Astaire, Charlotte Brontë, Carol Burnett, Irving Berlin, Bing Crosby, Salvador Dali, Tchaikovsky, Queen Elizabeth II, Duke Ellington, Ella Fitzgerald, Henry Fonda, Sigmund Freud, Orson Welles, Joe Louis, Lenin, Karl Marx, Golda Meir, Eva Peron, Bertrand Russell, Shakespeare, Kate Smith, Benjamin Spock, Barbra Streisand, Shirley Temple, Harry Truman

GEMINI: Ruth Benedict, Josephine Baker, Rachel Carson, Carlos Chavez, Walt Whitman, Bob Dylan, Ralph Waldo Emerson, Judy Garland, Paul Gauguin, Allen Ginsberg, Benny Goodman, Bob Hope, Burl Ives, John F. Kennedy, Peggy Lee, Marilyn Monroe, Joe Namath, Cole Porter, Laurence Olivier, Harriet Beecher Stowe, Queen Victoria, John Wayne, Frank Lloyd Wright

CANCER: "Dear Abby," Lizzie Borden, David Brinkley, Yul Brynner, Pearl Buck, Marc Chagall, Princess Diana, Babe Didrikson, Mary Baker Eddy, Henry VIII, John Glenn, Ernest Hemingway, Lena Horne, Oscar Hammerstein, Helen Keller, Ann Landers, George Orwell, Nancy Reagan, Rembrandt, Richard Rodgers, Ginger Rogers, Rubens, Jean-Paul Sartre, O. J. Simpson

LEO: Neil Armstrong, James Baldwin, Lucille Ball, Emily Brontë, Wilt Chamberlain, Julia Child, William J. Clinton, Cecil B. De Mille, Ogden Nash, Amelia Earhart, Edna Ferber, Arthur Goldberg, Alfred Hitchcock, Mick Jagger, George Meany, Annie Oakley, George Bernard Shaw, Napoleon, Jacqueline Onassis, Henry Ford, Francis Scott Key, Andy Warhol, Mae West, Orville Wright

VIRGO: Ingrid Bergman, Warren Burger, Maurice Chevalier, Agatha Christie, Sean Connery, Lafayette, Peter Falk, Greta Garbo, Althea Gibson, Arthur Godfrey, Goethe, Buddy Hackett, Michael Jackson, Lyndon Johnson, D. H. Lawrence, Sophia Loren, Grandma Moses, Arnold Palmer, Queen Elizabeth I, Walter Reuther, Peter Sellers, Lily Tomlin, George Wallace

LIBRA: Brigitte Bardot, Art Buchwald, Truman Capote, Dwight D. Eisenhower, William Faulkner, F. Scott Fitzgerald, Gandhi, George Gershwin, Micky Mantle, Helen Hayes, Vladimir Horowitz, Doris Lessing, Martina Navratalova, Eugene O'Neill, Luciano Pavarotti, Emily Post, Eleanor Roosevelt, Bruce Springsteen, Margaret Thatcher, Gore Vidal, Barbara Walters, Oscar Wilde

SCORPIO: Vivien Leigh, Richard Burton, Art Carney, Johnny Carson, Billy Graham, Grace Kelly, Walter Cronkite, Marie Curie, Charles de Gaulle, Linda Evans, Indira Gandhi, Theodore Roosevelt, Rock Hudson, Katherine Hepburn, Robert F. Kennedy, Billie Jean King, Martin Luther, Georgia O'Keeffe, Pablo Picasso, Jonas Salk, Alan Shepard, Robert Louis Stevenson

SAGITTARIUS: Jane Austen, Louisa May Alcott, Woody Allen, Beethoven, Willy Brandt, Mary Martin, William F. Buckley, Maria Callas, Winston Churchill, Noel Coward, Emily Dickinson, Walt Disney, Benjamin Disraeli, James Doolittle, Kirk Douglas, Chet Huntley, Jane Fonda, Chris Evert Lloyd, Margaret Mead, Charles Schulz, John Milton, Frank Sinatra, Steven Spielberg

CAPRICORN: Muhammad Ali, Isaac Asimov, Pablo Casals, Dizzy Dean, Marlene Dietrich, James Farmer, Ava Gardner, Barry Goldwater, Cary Grant, J. Edgar Hoover, Howard Hughes, Joan of Arc, Gypsy Rose Lee, Martin Luther King, Jr., Rudyard Kipling, Mao Tse-tung, Richard Nixon, Gamal Nasser, Louis Pasteur, Albert Schweitzer, Stalin, Benjamin Franklin, Elvis Presley

AQUARIUS: Marian Anderson, Susan B. Anthony, Jack Benny, John Barrymore, Mikhail Baryshnikov, Charles Darwin, Charles Dickens, Thomas Edison, Clark Gable, Jascha Heifetz, Abraham Lincoln, Yehudi Menuhin, Mozart, Jack Nicklaus, Ronald Reagan, Jackie Robinson, Norman Rockwell, Franklin D. Roosevelt, Gertrude Stein, Charles Lindbergh, Margaret Truman

PISCES: Edward Albee, Harry Belafonte, Alexander Graham Bell, Chopin, Adelle Davis, Albert Einstein, Golda Meir, Jackie Gleason, Winslow Homer, Edward M. Kennedy, Victor Hugo, Mike Mansfield, Michelangelo, Edna St. Vincent Millay, Liza Minelli, John Steinbeck, Linus Pauling, Ravel, Renoir, Diana Ross, William Shirer, Elizabeth Taylor, George Washington

The Signs and Their Key Words

		POSITIVE	NEGATIVE
ARIES	self	courage, initiative, pioneer instinct	brash rudeness, selfish impetuosity
TAURUS	money	endurance, loyalty, wealth	obstinacy, gluttony
GEMINI	mind	versatility	capriciousness, unreliability
CANCER	family	sympathy, homing instinct	clannishness, childishness
LEO	children	love, authority, integrity	egotism, force
VIRGO	work	purity, industry, analysis	faultfinding, cynicism
LIBRA	marriage	harmony, justice	vacillation, superficiality
SCORPIO	sex	survival, regeneration	vengeance, discord
SAGITTARIUS	travel	optimism, higher learning	lawlessness
CAPRICORN	career	depth	narrowness, gloom
AQUARIUS	friends	human fellowship, genius	perverse unpredictability
PISCES	confinement	spiritual love, universality	diffusion, escapism

The Elements and Qualities of The Signs

Every sign has both an *element* and a *quality* associated with it. The element indicates the basic makeup of the sign, and the quality describes the kind of activity associated with each.

Element	Sign	Quality	Sign
FIRE	ARIES	CARDINAL	ARIES
	LEO		LIBRA
	SAGITTARIUS		CANCER
			CAPRICORN
EARTH	TAURUS		
	VIRGO		
	CAPRICORN	FIXED	TAURUS
			LEO
			SCORPIO
AIR.........	GEMINI		AQUARIUS
	LIBRA		
	AQUARIUS		
		MUTABLE	GEMINI
WATER....	CANCER		VIRGO
	SCORPIO		SAGITTARIUS
	PISCES		PISCES

Signs can be grouped together according to their element and quality. Signs of the same element share many basic traits in common. They tend to form stable configurations and ultimately harmonious relationships. Signs of the same quality are often less harmonious, but they share many dynamic potentials for growth as well as profound fulfillment.

Further discussion of each of these sign groupings is provided on the following pages.

The Fire Signs

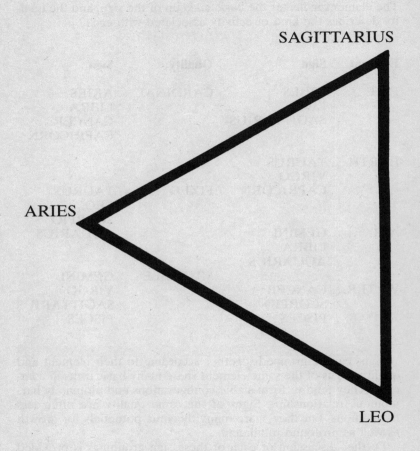

This is the fire group. On the whole these are emotional, volatile types, quick to anger, quick to forgive. They are adventurous, powerful people and act as a source of inspiration for everyone. They spark into action with immediate exuberant impulses. They are intelligent, self-involved, creative, and idealistic. They all share a certain vibrancy and glow that outwardly reflects an inner flame and passion for living.

The Earth Signs

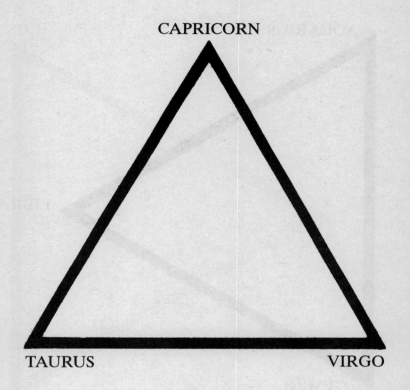

CAPRICORN

TAURUS

VIRGO

This is the earth group. They are in constant touch with the material world and tend to be conservative. Although they are all capable of spartan self-discipline, they are earthy, sensual people who are stimulated by the tangible, elegant, and luxurious. The thread of their lives is always practical, but they do fantasize and are often attracted to dark, mysterious, emotional people. They are like great cliffs overhanging the sea, forever married to the ocean but always resisting erosion from the dark, emotional forces that thunder at their feet.

The Air Signs

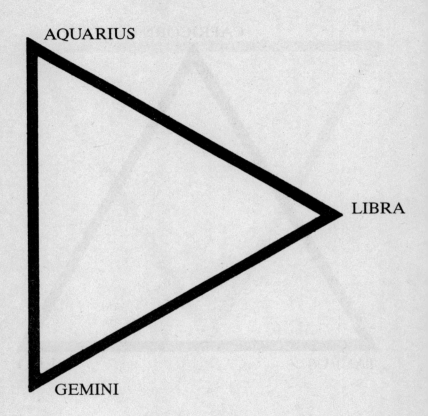

AQUARIUS

LIBRA

GEMINI

This is the air group. They are light, mental creatures desirous of contact, communication, and relationship. They are involved with people and the forming of ties on many levels. Original thinkers, they are the bearers of human news. Their language is their sense of word, color, style, and beauty. They provide an atmosphere suitable and pleasant for living. They add change and versatility to the scene, and it is through them that we can explore new territory of human intelligence and experience.

The Water Signs

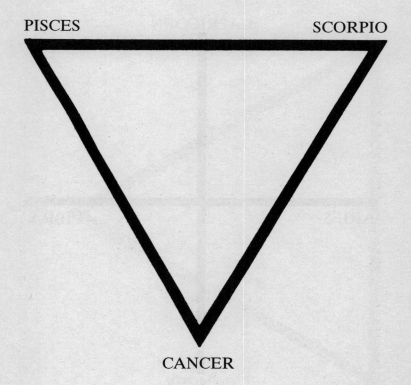

PISCES

SCORPIO

CANCER

This is the water group. Through the water people, we are all joined together on emotional, nonverbal levels. They are silent, mysterious types whose magic hypnotizes even the most determined realist. They have uncanny perceptions about people and are as rich as the oceans when it comes to feeling, emotion, or imagination. They are sensitive, mystical creatures with memories that go back beyond time. Through water, life is sustained. These people have the potential for the depths of darkness or the heights of mysticism and art.

The Cardinal Signs

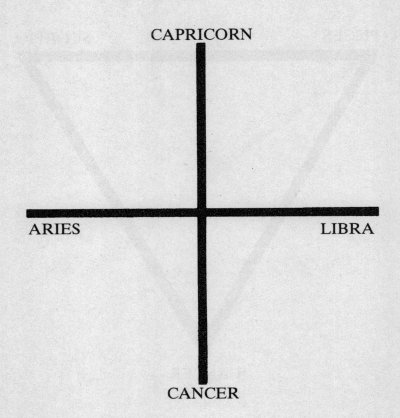

Put together, this is a clear-cut picture of dynamism, activity, tremendous stress, and remarkable achievement. These people know the meaning of great change since their lives are often characterized by significant crises and major successes. This combination is like a simultaneous storm of summer, fall, winter, and spring. The danger is chaotic diffusion of energy; the potential is irrepressible growth and victory.

The Fixed Signs

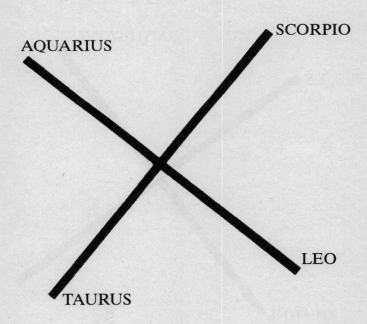

Fixed signs are always establishing themselves in a given place or area of experience. Like explorers who arrive and plant a flag, these people claim a position from which they do not enjoy being deposed. They are staunch, stalwart, upright, trusty, honorable people, although their obstinacy is well-known. Their contribution is fixity, and they are the angels who support our visible world.

The Mutable Signs

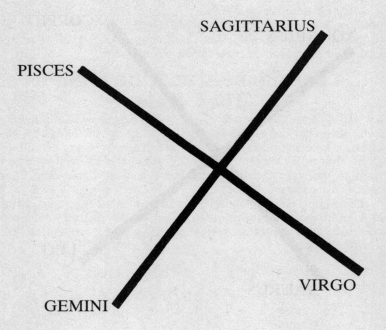

Mutable people are versatile, sensitive, intelligent, nervous, and deeply curious about life. They are the translators of all energy. They often carry out or complete tasks initiated by others. Combinations of these signs have highly developed minds; they are imaginative and jumpy and think and talk a lot. At worst their lives are a Tower of Babel. At best they are adaptable and ready creatures who can assimilate one kind of experience and enjoy it while anticipating coming changes.

THE PLANETS
OF THE SOLAR SYSTEM

This section describes the planets of the solar system, In astrology, both the Sun and the Moon are considered to be planets. Because of the Moon's influence in our day-to-day lives, the Moon is described in a separate section following this one.

The Planets and the Signs They Rule

The signs of the Zodiac are linked to the planets in the following way. Each sign is governed or ruled by one or more planets. No matter where the planets are located in the sky at any given moment, they still rule their respective signs, and when they travel through the signs they rule, they have special dignity and their effects are stronger.

Following is a list of the planets and the signs they rule. After looking at the list, read the definitions of the planets and see if you can determine how the planet ruling *your* Sun sign has affected your life.

SIGNS	RULING PLANETS
Aries	Mars, Pluto
Taurus	Venus
Gemini	Mercury
Cancer	Moon
Leo	Sun
Virgo	Mercury
Libra	Venus
Scorpio	Mars, Pluto
Sagittarius	Jupiter
Capricorn	Saturn
Aquarius	Saturn, Uranus
Pisces	Jupiter, Neptune

Characteristics of the Planets

The following pages give the meaning and characteristics of the planets of the solar system. They all travel around the Sun at different speeds and different distances. Taken with the Sun, they all distribute individual intelligence and ability throughout the entire chart.

The planets modify the influence of the Sun in a chart according to their own particular natures, strengths, and positions. Their positions must be calculated for each year and day, and their function and expression in a horoscope will change as they move from one area of the Zodiac to another.

We start with a description of the sun.

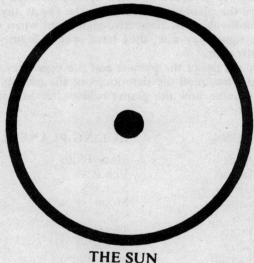

THE SUN

SUN

This is the center of existence. Around this flaming sphere all the planets revolve in endless orbits. Our star is constantly sending out its beams of light and energy without which no life on Earth would be possible. In astrology it symbolizes everything we are trying to become, the center around which all of our activity in life will always revolve. It is the symbol of our basic nature and describes the natural and constant thread that runs through everything that we do from birth to death on this planet.

To early astrologers, the Sun seemed to be another planet because it crossed the heavens every day, just like the rest of the bodies in the sky.

It is the only star near enough to be seen well—it is, in fact, a dwarf star. Approximately 860,000 miles in diameter, it is about ten times as wide as the giant planet Jupiter. The next nearest star is nearly 300,000 times as far away, and if the Sun were located as far away as most of the bright stars, it would be too faint to be seen without a telescope.

Everything in the horoscope ultimately revolves around this singular body. Although other forces may be prominent in the charts of some individuals, still the Sun is the total nucleus of being and symbolizes the complete potential of every human being alive. It is vitality and the life force. Your whole essence comes from the position of the Sun.

You are always trying to express the Sun according to its position by house and sign. Possibility for all development is found in the Sun, and it marks the fundamental character of your personal radiations all around you.

It is the symbol of strength, vigor, wisdom, dignity, ardor, and generosity, and the ability for a person to function as a mature individual. It is also a creative force in society. It is consciousness of the gift of life.

The underdeveloped solar nature is arrogant, pushy, undependable, and proud, and is constantly using force.

MERCURY

Mercury is the planet closest to the Sun. It races around our star, gathering information and translating it to the rest of the system. Mercury represents your capacity to understand the desires of your own will and to translate those desires into action.

In other words it is the planet of mind and the power of communication. Through Mercury we develop an ability to think, write, speak, and observe—to become aware of the world around us. It colors our attitudes and vision of the world, as well as our capacity to communicate our inner responses to the outside world. Some people who have serious disabilities in their power of verbal communication have often wrongly been described as people lacking intelligence.

Although this planet (and its position in the horoscope) indicates your power to communicate your thoughts and perceptions to the world, intelligence is something deeper. Intelligence is distributed throughout all the planets. It is the relationship of the planets to each other that truly describes what we call intelligence. Mercury rules speaking, language, mathematics, draft and design, students, messengers, young people, offices, teachers, and any pursuits where the mind of man has wings.

VENUS

Venus is beauty. It symbolizes the harmony and radiance of a rare and elusive quality: beauty itself. It is refinement and delicacy, softness and charm. In astrology it indicates grace, balance, and the aesthetic sense. Where Venus is we see beauty, a gentle drawing in of energy and the need for satisfaction and completion. It is a special touch that finishes off rough edges. It is sensitivity, and affection, and it is always the place for that other elusive phenomenon: love. Venus describes our sense of what is beautiful and loving. Poorly developed, it is vulgar, tasteless, and self-indulgent. But its ideal is the flame of spiritual love—Aphrodite, goddess of love, and the sweetness and power of personal beauty.

MARS

Mars is raw, crude energy. The planet next to Earth but outward from the Sun is a fiery red sphere that charges through the horoscope with force and fury. It represents the way you reach out for new adventure and new experience. It is energy and drive, initiative, courage, and daring. It is the power to start something and see it through. It can be thoughtless, cruel and wild, angry and hostile, causing cuts, burns, scalds, and wounds. It can stab its way through a chart, or it can be the symbol of healthy spirited adventure, well-channeled constructive power to begin and keep up the drive. If you have trouble starting things, if you lack the get-up-and-go to start the ball rolling, if you lack aggressiveness and self-confidence, chances are there's another planet influencing your Mars. Mars rules soldiers, butchers, surgeons, salesmen—any field that requires daring, bold skill, operational technique, or self-promotion.

JUPITER

This is the largest planet of the solar system. Scientists have recently learned that Jupiter reflects more light than it receives from the Sun. In a sense it is like a star itself. In astrology it rules good luck and good cheer, health, wealth, optimism, happiness, success, and joy. It is the symbol of opportunity and always opens the way for new possibilities in your life. It rules exuberance, enthusiasm, wisdom, knowledge, generosity, and all forms of expansion in general. It rules actors, statesmen, clerics, professional people, religion, publishing, and the distribution of many people over large areas.

Sometimes Jupiter makes you think you deserve everything, and you become sloppy, wasteful, careless and rude, prodigal and lawless, in the illusion that nothing can ever go wrong. Then there is the danger of overconfidence, exaggeration, undependability, and overindulgence.

Jupiter is the minimization of limitation and the emphasis on spirituality and potential. It is the thirst for knowledge and higher learning.

SATURN

Saturn circles our system in dark splendor with its mysterious rings, forcing us to be awakened to whatever we have neglected in the past. It will present real puzzles and problems to be solved, causing delays, obstacles, and hindrances. By doing so, Saturn stirs our own sensitivity to those areas where we are laziest.

Here we must patiently develop *method*, and only through painstaking effort can our ends be achieved. It brings order to a horoscope and imposes reason just where we are feeling least reasonable. By creating limitations and boundary, Saturn shows the consequences of being human and demands that we accept the changing cycles inevitable in human life. Saturn rules time, old age, and sobriety. It can bring depression, gloom, jealousy, and greed, or serious acceptance of responsibilities out of which success will develop. With Saturn there is nothing to do but face facts. It rules laborers, stones, granite, rocks, and crystals of all kinds.

THE OUTER PLANETS:
URANUS, NEPTUNE, PLUTO

Uranus, Neptune, Pluto are the outer planets. They liberate human beings from cultural conditioning, and in that sense are the lawbreakers. In early times it was thought that Saturn was the last planet of the system—the outer limit beyond which we could never go. The discovery of the next three planets ushered in new phases of human history, revolution, and technology.

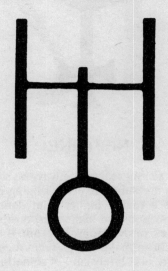

URANUS

Uranus rules unexpected change, upheaval, revolution. It is the symbol of total independence and asserts the freedom of an individual from all restriction and restraint. It is a breakthrough planet and indicates talent, originality, and genius in a horoscope. It usually causes last-minute reversals and changes of plan, unwanted separations, accidents, catastrophes, and eccentric behavior. It can add irrational rebelliousness and perverse bohemianism to a personality or a streak of unaffected brilliance in science and art. It rules technology, aviation, and all forms of electrical and electronic advancement. It governs great leaps forward and topsy-turvy situations, and *always* turns things around at the last minute. Its effects are difficult to predict, since it rules sudden last-minute decisions and events that come like lightning out of the blue.

NEPTUNE

Neptune dissolves existing reality the way the sea erodes the cliffs beside it. Its effects are subtle like the ringing of a buoy's bell in the fog. It suggests a reality higher than definition can usually describe. It awakens a sense of higher responsibility often causing guilt, worry, anxieties, or delusions. Neptune is associated with all forms of escape and can make things seem a certain way so convincingly that you are absolutely sure of something that eventually turns out to be quite different.

It is the planet of illusion and therefore governs the invisible realms that lie beyond our ordinary minds, beyond our simple factual ability to prove what is "real." Treachery, deceit, disillusionment, and disappointment are linked to Neptune. It describes a vague reality that promises eternity and the divine, yet in a manner so complex that we cannot really fathom it at all. At its worst Neptune is a cheap intoxicant; at its best it is the poetry, music, and inspiration of the higher planes of spiritual love. It has dominion over movies, photographs, and much of the arts.

PLUTO

Pluto lies at the outpost of our system and therefore rules finality in a horoscope—the final closing of chapters in your life, the passing of major milestones and points of development from which there is no return. It is a final wipeout, a closeout, an evacuation. It is a distant, subtle but powerful catalyst in all transformations that occur. It creates, destroys, then recreates. Sometimes Pluto starts its influence with a minor event or insignificant incident that might even go unnoticed. Slowly but surely, little by little, everything changes, until at last there has been a total transformation in the area of your life where Pluto has been operating. It rules mass thinking and the trends that society first rejects, then adopts, and finally outgrows.

Pluto rules the dead and the underworld—all the powerful forces of creation and destruction that go on all the time beneath, around, and above us. It can bring a lust for power with strong obsessions.

It is the planet that rules the metamorphosis of the caterpillar into a butterfly, for it symbolizes the capacity to change totally and forever a person's lifestyle, way of thought, and behavior.

THE MOON IN EACH SIGN

The Moon is the nearest planet to the Earth. It exerts more observable influence on us from day to day than any other planet. The effect is very personal, very intimate, and if we are not aware of how it works it can make us quite unstable in our ideas. And the annoying thing is that at these times we often see our own instability but can do nothing about it. A knowledge of what can be expected may help considerably. We can then be prepared to stand strong against the Moon's negative influences and use its positive ones to help us to get ahead. Who has not heard of going with the tide?

The Moon reflects, has no light of its own. It reflects the Sun—the life giver—in the form of vital movement. The Moon controls the tides, the blood rhythm, the movement of sap in trees and plants. Its nature is inconstancy and change so it signifies our moods, our superficial behavior—walking, talking, and especially thinking. Being a true reflector of other forces, the Moon is cold, watery like the surface of a still lake, brilliant and scintillating at times, but easily ruffled and disturbed by the winds of change.

The Moon takes about 27⅓ days to make a complete transit of the Zodiac. It spends just over 2¼ days in each sign. During that time it reflects the qualities, energies, and characteristics of the sign and, to a degree, the planet which rules the sign. When the Moon in its transit occupies a sign incompatible with our own birth sign, we can expect to feel a vague uneasiness, perhaps a touch of irritableness. We should not be discouraged nor let the feeling get us down, or, worse still, allow ourselves to take the discomfort out on others. Try to remember that the Moon has to change signs within 55 hours and, provided you are not physically ill, your mood will probably change with it. It is amazing how frequently depression lifts with the shift in the Moon's position. And, of course, when the Moon is transiting a sign compatible or sympathetic to yours, you will probably feel some sort of stimulation or just be plain happy to be alive.

In the horoscope, the Moon is such a powerful indicator that competent astrologers often use the sign it occupied at birth as the birth sign of the person. This is done particularly when the Sun is on the cusp, or edge, of two signs. Most experienced astrologers, however, coordinate both Sun and Moon signs by reading and confirming from one to the other and secure a far more accurate and personalized analysis.

For these reasons, the Moon tables which follow this section (see pages 86–92) are of great importance to the individual. They show the days and the exact times the Moon will enter each sign of the Zodiac for the year. Remember, you have to adjust the indicated times to local time. The corrections, already calculated for most of the main cities, are at the beginning of the tables. What follows now is a guide to the influences that will be reflected to the Earth by the Moon while it transits each of the twelve signs. The influence is at its peak about 26 hours after the Moon enters a sign. As you read the daily forecast, check the Moon sign for any given day and glance back at this guide.

MOON IN ARIES
This is a time for action, for reaching out beyond the usual self-imposed limitations and faint-hearted cautions. If you have plans in your head or on your desk, put them into practice. New ventures, applications, new jobs, new starts of any kind—all have a good chance of success. This is the period when original and dynamic impulses are being reflected onto Earth. Such energies are extremely vital and favor the pursuit of pleasure and adventure in practically every form. Sick people should feel an improvement. Those who are well will probably find themselves exuding confidence and optimism. People fond of physical exercise should find their bodies growing with tone and well-being. Boldness, strength, determination should characterize most of your activities with a readiness to face up to old challenges. Yesterday's problems may seem petty and exaggerated—so deal with them. Strike out alone. Self-reliance will attract others to you. This is a good time for making friends. Business and marriage partners are more likely to be impressed with the man and woman of action. Opposition will be overcome or thrown aside with much less effort than usual. CAUTION: Be dominant but not domineering.

MOON IN TAURUS
The spontaneous, action-packed person of yesterday gives way to the cautious, diligent, hardworking "thinker." In this period ideas will probably be concentrated on ways of improving finances. A great deal of time may be spent figuring out and going over schemes and plans. It is the right time to be careful with detail.

People will find themselves working longer than usual at their desks. Or devoting more time to serious thought about the future. A strong desire to put order into business and financial arrangements may cause extra work. Loved ones may complain of being neglected and may fail to appreciate that your efforts are for their ultimate benefit. Your desire for system may extend to criticism of arrangements in the home and lead to minor upsets. Health may be affected through overwork. Try to secure a reasonable amount of rest and relaxation, although the tendency will be to "keep going" despite good advice. Work done conscientiously in this period should result in a solid contribution to your future security. CAUTION: Try not to be as serious with people as the work you are engaged in.

MOON IN GEMINI
The humdrum of routine and too much work should suddenly end. You are likely to find yourself in an expansive, quicksilver world of change and self-expression. Urges to write, to paint, to experience the freedom of some sort of artistic outpouring, may be very strong. Take full advantage of them. You may find yourself finishing something you began and put aside long ago. Or embarking on something new which could easily be prompted by a chance meeting, a new acquaintance, or even an advertisement. There may be a yearning for a change of scenery, the feeling to visit another country (not too far away), or at least to get away for a few days. This may result in short, quick journeys. Or, if you are planning a single visit, there may be some unexpected changes or detours on the way. Familiar activities will seem to give little satisfaction unless they contain a fresh element of excitement or expectation. The inclination will be toward untried pursuits, particularly those that allow you to express your inner nature. The accent is on new faces, new places. CAUTION: Do not be too quick to commit yourself emotionally.

MOON IN CANCER
Feelings of uncertainty and vague insecurity are likely to cause problems while the Moon is in Cancer. Thoughts may turn frequently to the warmth of the home and the comfort of loved ones. Nostalgic impulses could cause you to bring out old photographs and letters and reflect on the days when your life seemed to be much more rewarding and less demanding. The love and understanding of parents and family may be important, and, if it is not forthcoming, you may have to fight against bouts of self-pity. The cordiality of friends and the thought of good times with them that are sure to be repeated will help to restore you to a happier frame

of mind. The desire to be alone may follow minor setbacks or rebuffs at this time, but solitude is unlikely to help. Better to get on the telephone or visit someone. This period often causes peculiar dreams and upsurges of imaginative thinking which can be helpful to authors of occult and mystical works. Preoccupation with the personal world of simple human needs can overshadow any material strivings. CAUTION: Do not spend too much time thinking—seek the company of loved ones or close friends.

MOON IN LEO
New horizons of exciting and rather extravagant activity open up. This is the time for exhilarating entertainment, glamorous and lavish parties, and expensive shopping sprees. Any merrymaking that relies upon your generosity as a host has every chance of being a spectacular success. You should find yourself right in the center of the fun, either as the life of the party or simply as a person whom happy people like to be with. Romance thrives in this heady atmosphere and friendships are likely to explode unexpectedly into serious attachments. Children and younger people should be attracted to you and you may find yourself organizing a picnic or a visit to a fun-fair, the movies, or the beach. The sunny company and vitality of youthful companions should help you to find some unsuspected energy. In career, you could find an opening for promotion or advancement. This should be the time to make a direct approach. The period favors those engaged in original research. CAUTION: Bask in popularity, not in flattery.

MOON IN VIRGO
Off comes the party cap and out steps the busy, practical worker. He wants to get his personal affairs straight, to rearrange them, if necessary, for more efficiency, so he will have more time for more work. He clears up his correspondence, pays outstanding bills, makes numerous phone calls. He is likely to make inquiries, or sign up for some new insurance and put money into gilt-edged investment. Thoughts probably revolve around the need for future security—to tie up loose ends and clear the decks. There may be a tendency to be "finicky," to interfere in the routine of others, particularly friends and family members. The motive may be a genuine desire to help with suggestions for updating or streamlining their affairs, but these will probably not be welcomed. Sympathy may be felt for less fortunate sections of the community and a flurry of some sort of voluntary service is likely. This may be accompanied by strong feelings of responsibility on several fronts and health may suffer from extra efforts made. CAUTION: Everyone may not want your help or advice.

MOON IN LIBRA

These are days of harmony and agreement and you should find yourself at peace with most others. Relationships tend to be smooth and sweet-flowing. Friends may become closer and bonds deepen in mutual understanding. Hopes will be shared. Progress by cooperation could be the secret of success in every sphere. In business, established partnerships may flourish and new ones get off to a good start. Acquaintances could discover similar interests that lead to congenial discussions and rewarding exchanges of some sort. Love, as a unifying force, reaches its optimum. Marriage partners should find accord. Those who wed at this time face the prospect of a happy union. Cooperation and tolerance are felt to be stronger than dissension and impatience. The argumentative are not quite so loud in their bellowings, nor as inflexible in their attitudes. In the home, there should be a greater recognition of the other point of view and a readiness to put the wishes of the group before selfish insistence. This is a favorable time to join an art group. CAUTION: Do not be too independent—let others help you if they want to.

MOON IN SCORPIO

Driving impulses to make money and to economize are likely to cause upsets all around. No area of expenditure is likely to be spared the ax, including the household budget. This is a time when the desire to cut down on extravagance can become near fanatical. Care must be exercised to try to keep the aim in reasonable perspective. Others may not feel the same urgent need to save and may retaliate. There is a danger that possessions of sentimental value will be sold to realize cash for investment. Buying and selling of stock for quick profit is also likely. The attention turns to organizing, reorganizing, tidying up at home and at work. Neglected jobs could suddenly be done with great bursts of energy. The desire for solitude may intervene. Self-searching thoughts could disturb. The sense of invisible and mysterious energies in play could cause some excitability. The reassurance of loves ones may help. CAUTION: Be kind to the people you love.

MOON IN SAGITTARIUS

These are days when you are likely to be stirred and elevated by discussions and reflections of a religious and philosophical nature. Ideas of faraway places may cause unusual response and excitement. A decision may be made to visit someone overseas, perhaps a person whose influence was important to your earlier character development. There could be a strong resolution to get away from present intellectual patterns, to learn new subjects, and to meet more interesting people. The superficial may be rejected in all its forms. An impatience with old ideas and unimaginative contacts could lead to a change of companions and interests. There may be an upsurge of religious feeling and metaphysical inquiry. Even a new insight into the significance of astrology and other occult studies is likely under the curious stimulus of the Moon in Sagittarius. Physically, you may express this need for fundamental change by spending more time outdoors: sports, gardening, long walks appeal. CAUTION: Try to channel any restlessness into worthwhile study.

MOON IN CAPRICORN

Life in these hours may seem to pivot around the importance of gaining prestige and honor in the career, as well as maintaining a spotless reputation. Ambitious urges may be excessive and could be accompanied by quite acquisitive drives for money. Effort should be directed along strictly ethical lines where there is no possibility of reproach or scandal. All endeavors are likely to be characterized by great earnestness, and an air of authority and purpose which should impress those who are looking for leadership or reliability. The desire to conform to accepted standards may extend to sharp criticism of family members. Frivolity and unconventional actions are unlikely to amuse while the Moon is in Capricorn. Moderation and seriousness are the orders of the day. Achievement and recognition in this period could come through community work or organizing for the benefit of some amateur group. CAUTION: Dignity and esteem are not always self-awarded.

MOON IN AQUARIUS

Moon in Aquarius is in the second last sign of the Zodiac where ideas can become disturbingly fine and subtle. The result is often a mental "no-man's land" where imagination cannot be trusted with the same certitude as other times. The dangers for the individual are the extremes of optimism and pessimism. Unless the imagination is held in check, situations are likely to be misread, and rosy conclusions drawn where they do not exist. Consequences for the unwary can be costly in career and business. Best to think twice and not speak or act until you think again. Pessimism can be a cruel self-inflicted penalty for delusion at this time. Between the two extremes are strange areas of self-deception which, for example, can make the selfish person think he is actually being generous. Eerie dreams which resemble the reality and even seem to continue into the waking state are also possible. CAUTION: Look for the fact and not just for the image in your mind.

MOON IN PISCES

Everything seems to come to the surface now. Memory may be crystal clear, throwing up long-forgotten information which could be valuable in the career or business. Flashes of clairvoyance and intuition are possible along with sudden realizations of one's own nature, which may be used for self-improvement. A talent, never before suspected, may be discovered. Qualities not evident before in friends and marriage partners are likely to be noticed. As this is a period in which the truth seems to emerge, the discovery of false characteristics is likely to lead to disenchantment or a shift in attachments. However, when qualities are accepted, it should lead to happiness and deeper feeling. Surprise solutions could bob up for old problems. There may be a public announcement of the solving of a crime or mystery. People with secrets may find someone has "guessed" correctly. The secrets of the soul or the inner self also tend to reveal themselves. Religious and philosophical groups may make some interesting discoveries. CAUTION: Not a time for activities that depend on secrecy.

NOTE: When you read your daily forecasts, use the Moon Sign Dates that are provided in the following section of Moon Tables. Then you may want to glance back here for the Moon's influence in a given sign.

MOON TABLES

CORRECTION FOR NEW YORK TIME, FIVE HOURS WEST OF GREENWICH

Atlanta, Boston, Detroit, Miami, Washington, Montreal, Ottawa, Quebec, Bogota, Havana, Lima, Santiago .. Same time

Chicago, New Orleans, Houston, Winnipeg, Churchill, Mexico City .... Deduct 1 hour

Albuquerque, Denver, Phoenix, El Paso, Edmonton, Helena .... Deduct 2 hours

Los Angeles, San Francisco, Reno, Portland, Seattle, Vancouver .... Deduct 3 hours

Honolulu, Anchorage, Fairbanks, Kodiak .... Deduct 5 hours

Nome, Samoa, Tonga, Midway.................... Deduct 6 hours

Halifax, Bermuda, San Juan, Caracas, La Paz, Barbados ....Add 1 hour

St. John's, Brasilia, Rio de Janeiro, Sao Paulo, Buenos Aires, Montevideo..........................Add 2 hours

Azores, Cape Verde Islands...........................Add 3 hours

Canary Islands, Madeira, Reykjavik ....Add 4 hours

London, Paris, Amsterdam, Madrid, Lisbon, Gibraltar, Belfast, Rabat ....Add 5 hours

Frankfurt, Rome, Oslo, Stockholm, Prague, Belgrade...Add 6 hours

Bucharest, Beirut, Tel Aviv, Athens, Istanbul, Cairo, Alexandria, Cape Town, Johannesburg ....Add 7 hours

Moscow, Leningrad, Baghdad, Dhahran, Addis Ababa, Nairobi, Teheran, Zanzibar.........Add 8 hours

Bombay, Calcutta, Sri Lanka..................... Add 10 ½ hours

Hong Kong, Shanghai, Manila, Peking, Perth...... Add 13 hours

Tokyo, Okinawa, Darwin, Pusan.................... Add 14 hours

Sydney, Melbourne, Port Moresby, Guam.......... Add 15 hours

Auckland, Wellington, Suva, Wake.................. Add 17 hours

2000 MOON SIGN DATES— NEW YORK TIME

JANUARY		FEBRUARY		MARCH	
Day Moon Enters		**Day Moon Enters**		**Day Moon Enters**	
1. Scorp.		1. Capric.	0:11 pm	1. Capric.	
2. Sagitt.	4:33 pm	2. Capric.		2. Aquar.	8:15 am
3. Sagitt.		3. Capric.		3. Aquar.	
4. Sagitt.		4. Aquar.	0:32 am	4. Pisces	6:31 pm
5. Capric.	5:25 am	5. Aquar.		5. Pisces	
6. Capric.		6. Pisces	11:03 am	6. Pisces	
7. Aquar.	5:54 pm	7. Pisces		7. Aries	1:55 am
8. Aquar.		8. Aries	7:18 pm	8. Aries	
9. Aquar.		9. Aries		9. Taurus	7:02 am
10. Pisces	5:00 am	10. Aries		10. Taurus	
11. Pisces		11. Taurus	1:22 am	11. Gemini	10:47 am
12. Aries	1:49 pm	12. Taurus		12. Gemini	
13. Aries		13. Gemini	5:24 am	13. Cancer	1:52 pm
14. Taurus	7:39 pm	14. Gemini		14. Cancer	
15. Taurus		15. Cancer	7:46 am	15. Leo	4:44 pm
16. Gemini	10:26 pm	16. Cancer		16. Leo	
17. Gemini		17. Leo	9:12 am	17. Virgo	7:49 pm
18. Cancer	11:02 pm	18. Leo		18. Virgo	
19. Cancer		19. Virgo	10:54 am	19. Libra	11:58 pm
20. Leo	10:59 pm	20. Virgo		20. Libra	
21. Leo		21. Libra	2:22 pm	21. Libra	
22. Leo		22. Libra		22. Scorp.	6:19 am
23. Virgo	0:08 am	23. Scorp.	8:59 pm	23. Scorp.	
24. Virgo		24. Scorp.		24. Sagitt.	3:44 pm
25. Libra	4:10 am	25. Scorp.		25. Sagitt.	
26. Libra		26. Sagitt.	7:11 am	26. Sagitt.	
27. Scorp.	0:02 pm	27. Sagitt.		27. Capric.	3:52 am
28. Scorp.		28. Capric.	7:46 pm	28. Capric.	
29. Sagitt.	11:19 pm	29. Capric.		29. Aquar.	4:35 pm
30. Sagitt.				30. Aquar.	
31. Sagitt.				31. Aquar.	

Summer time to be considered where applicable.

2000 MOON SIGN DATES—
NEW YORK TIME

APRIL			MAY			JUNE		
Day	Moon Enters		Day	Moon Enters		Day	Moon Enters	
1.	Pisces	3:13 am	1.	Aries		1.	Gemini	11:35 am
2.	Pisces		2.	Taurus	11:55 pm	2.	Gemini	
3.	Aries	10:23 am	3.	Taurus		3.	Cancer	11:31 am
4.	Aries		4.	Taurus		4.	Cancer	
5.	Taurus	2:30 pm	5.	Gemini	1:24 am	5.	Leo	11:47 am
6.	Taurus		6.	Gemini		6.	Leo	
7.	Gemini	4:59 pm	7.	Cancer	2:15 am	7.	Virgo	1:58 pm
8.	Gemini		8.	Cancer		8.	Virgo	
9.	Cancer	7:17 pm	9.	Leo	4:02 am	9.	Libra	7:00 pm
10.	Cancer		10.	Leo		10.	Libra	
11.	Leo	10:17 pm	11.	Virgo	7:42 am	11.	Libra	
12.	Leo		12.	Virgo		12.	Scorp.	0:56 am
13.	Leo		13.	Libra	1:28 pm	13.	Scorp.	
14.	Virgo	2:20 am	14.	Libra		14.	Sagitt.	1:19 pm
15.	Virgo		15.	Scorp.	9:17 pm	15.	Sagitt.	
16.	Libra	7:37 am	16.	Scorp.		16.	Sagitt.	
17.	Libra		17.	Scorp.		17.	Capric.	1:28 am
18.	Scorp.	2:36 pm	18.	Sagitt.	7:10 am	18.	Capric.	
19.	Scorp.		19.	Sagitt.		19.	Aquar.	2:27 pm
20.	Sagitt.	11:59 pm	20.	Capric.	7:02 pm	20.	Aquar.	
21.	Sagitt.		21.	Capric.		21.	Aquar.	
22.	Sagitt.		22.	Capric.		22.	Pisces	2:53 am
23.	Capric.	11:48 am	23.	Aquar.	8:01 am	23.	Pisces	
24.	Capric.		24.	Aquar.		24.	Aries	0:56 pm
25.	Capric.		25.	Pisces	8:08 pm	25.	Aries	
26.	Aquar.	0:43 am	26.	Pisces		26.	Taurus	7:20 pm
27.	Aquar.		27.	Pisces		27.	Taurus	
28.	Pisces	0:07 pm	28.	Aries	5:09 am	28.	Gemini	10:00 pm
29.	Pisces		29.	Aries		29.	Gemini	
30.	Aries	7:56 pm	30.	Taurus	10:03 am	30.	Cancer	10:10 pm
			31.	Taurus				

Summer time to be considered where applicable.

2000 MOON SIGN DATES—
NEW YORK TIME

JULY		AUGUST		SEPTEMBER	
Day Moon Enters		**Day Moon Enters**		**Day Moon Enters**	
1. Cancer		1. Virgo	8:28 am	1. Libra	
2. Leo	9:39 pm	2. Virgo		2. Scorp.	0:56 am
3. Leo		3. Libra	10:32 am	3. Scorp.	
4. Virgo	10:20 pm	4. Libra		4. Sagitt.	9:09 am
5. Virgo		5. Scorp.	4:05 pm	5. Sagitt.	
6. Virgo		6. Scorp.		6. Capric.	8:48 pm
7. Libra	1:48 am	7. Scorp.		7. Capric.	
8. Libra		8. Sagitt.	1:31 am	8. Capric.	
9. Scorp.	8:49 am	9. Sagitt.		9. Aquar.	9:45 am
10. Scorp.		10. Capric.	1:45 pm	10. Aquar.	
11. Sagitt.	7:07 pm	11. Capric.		11. Pisces	9:35 pm
12. Sagitt.		12. Capric.		12. Pisces	
13. Sagitt.		13. Aquar.	2:44 am	13. Pisces	
14. Capric.	7:29 am	14. Aquar.		14. Aries	7:01 am
15. Capric.		15. Pisces	2:42 pm	15. Aries	
16. Aquar.	8:28 pm	16. Pisces		16. Taurus	2:06 pm
17. Aquar.		17. Pisces		17. Taurus	
18. Aquar.		18. Aries	0:45 am	18. Gemini	7:23 pm
19. Pisces	8:45 am	19. Aries		19. Gemini	
20. Pisces		20. Taurus	8:32 am	20. Cancer	11:17 pm
21. Aries	7:10 pm	21. Taurus		21. Cancer	
22. Aries		22. Gemini	1:56 pm	22. Cancer	
23. Aries		23. Gemini		23. Leo	2:01 am
24. Taurus	2:45 am	24. Cancer	5:01 pm	24. Leo	
25. Taurus		25. Cancer		25. Virgo	4:03 am
26. Gemini	7:02 am	26. Leo	6:18 pm	26. Virgo	
27. Gemini		27. Leo		27. Libra	6:23 am
28. Cancer	8:31 am	28. Virgo	6:56 pm	28. Libra	
29. Cancer		29. Virgo		29. Scorp.	10:31 am
30. Leo	8:25 am	30. Libra	8:34 pm	30. Scorp.	
31. Leo		31. Libra			

Summer time to be considered where applicable.

2000 MOON SIGN DATES—
NEW YORK TIME

OCTOBER		NOVEMBER		DECEMBER	
Day Moon Enters		**Day Moon Enters**		**Day Moon Enters**	
1. Sagitt.	5:51 pm	1. Capric.		1. Aquar.	
2. Sagitt.		2. Capric.		2. Pisces	10:24 pm
3. Sagitt.		3. Aquar.	1:42 am	3. Pisces	
4. Capric.	4:43 am	4. Aquar.		4. Pisces	
5. Capric.		5. Pisces	2:14 pm	5. Aries	9:18 am
6. Aquar.	5:34 pm	6. Pisces		6. Aries	
7. Aquar.		7. Pisces		7. Taurus	4:28 pm
8. Aquar.		8. Aries	0:03 am	8. Taurus	
9. Pisces	5:37 am	9. Aries		9. Gemini	7:51 pm
10. Pisces		10. Taurus	6:13 am	10. Gemini	
11. Aries	2:52 pm	11. Taurus		11. Cancer	8:50 pm
12. Aries		12. Gemini	9:28 am	12. Cancer	
13. Taurus	9:07 pm	13. Gemini		13. Leo	9:10 pm
14. Taurus		14. Cancer	11:22 am	14. Leo	
15. Taurus		15. Cancer		15. Virgo	10:31 pm
16. Gemini	1:20 am	16. Leo	1:20 pm	16. Virgo	
17. Gemini		17. Leo		17. Virgo	
18. Cancer	4:38 am	18. Virgo	4:16 pm	18. Libra	2:02 am
19. Cancer		19. Virgo		19. Libra	
20. Leo	7:43 am	20. Libra	8:36 pm	20. Scorp.	8:13 am
21. Leo		21. Libra		21. Scorp.	
22. Virgo	10:53 am	22. Libra		22. Sagitt.	4:58 pm
23. Virgo		23. Scorp.	2:34 am	23. Sagitt.	
24. Libra	2:31 pm	24. Scorp.		24. Sagitt.	
25. Libra		25. Sagitt.	10:34 am	25. Capric.	3:55 am
26. Scorp.	7:24 pm	26. Sagitt.		26. Capric.	
27. Scorp.		27. Capric.	8:58 pm	27. Aquar.	4:26 pm
28. Scorp.		28. Capric.		28. Aquar.	
29. Sagitt.	2:41 am	29. Capric.		29. Aquar.	
30. Sagitt.		30. Aquar.	9:28 am	30. Pisces	5:28 am
31. Capric.	1:03 pm			31. Pisces	

Summer time to be considered where applicable.

2000 PHASES OF THE MOON—
NEW YORK TIME

New Moon	First Quarter	Full Moon	Last Quarter
Jan. 6	Jan. 14	Jan. 20	Jan. 28
Feb. 5	Feb. 12	Feb. 19	Feb. 26
March 5	March 13	March 19	March 27
April 4	April 11	April 18	April 26
May 3	May 10	May 18	May 26
June 2	June 8	June 16	June 24
July 1	July 8	July 16	July 24
July 30	Aug. 6	Aug. 15	Aug. 22
Aug. 29	Sept. 5	Sept. 13	Sept. 20
Sept. 27	Oct. 5	Oct. 13	Oct. 20
Oct. 27	Nov. 4	Nov. 11	Nov. 18
Nov. 25	Dec. 3	Dec. 11	Dec. 17
Dec. 25	Jan. 2 ('01)	Jan. 9 ('01)	Jan. 17 ('01)

Each phase of the Moon lasts approximately seven to eight days, during which the Moon's shape gradually changes as it comes out of one phase and goes into the next.

There will be a partial solar eclipse during the New Moon phase on February 5, July 1, July 30, and December 25.

There will be a lunar eclipse during the Full Moon phase on January 20 and July 16.

2000 FISHING GUIDE

	Good	Best
January	14-18-21-22-23-24	6-19-20-28
February	5-17-18-19-20-21-27	12-16-22
March	13-17-18-19	6-20-21-22-23-28
April	4-15-16-21-26	11-17-18-19-20
May	10-18-19-20	4-15-16-17-21-26
June	2-9-14-15-16-19-25	13-17-18
July	13-14-17-18-19-31	1-8-15-16-24
August	13-14-15-18-22-29	7-12-16-17
September	5-10-11-14-15-16-27	12-13-21
October	11-12-13-16-20	5-10-14-15-27
November	4-8-9-10-12-13-14	11-18-25
December	10-11-14	4-8-9-12-13-18-25

2000 PLANTING GUIDE

	Aboveground Crops	Root Crops
January	7-10-11-15-16-19-20	1-25-26-27-28-29
February	7-8-11-12-16	2-3-22-23-24-25-29
March	6-10-14	1-5-20-21-22-23-27-28
April	6-10-11-17	1-2-19-20-24-25-29-30
May	4-7-8-14-15-16-17	3-21-22-26-27-31
June	4-10-11-12-13	17-18-22-23-27-28
July	2-7-8-9-10-11-15	20-21-24-25-29
August	4-5-6-7-11-12-31	16-17-21-25-26
September	1-2-3-7-8-12-28-29-30	17-18-21-22
October	1-4-5-6-10-27-28	14-15-18-19-25-26
November	1-2-6-7-28-29	11-15-21-22-23-24
December	3-4-8-9-26-31	12-13-18-19-20-21
	Pruning	Weeds and Pests
January	1-28-29	3-4-21-22-23-24-30-31
February	24-25	4-20-27-28
March	5-23	3-4-25-26-30-31
April	1-2-19-20-29-30	21-22-26-27
May	26-27	1-2-19-20-24-25-29
June	22-23	20-21-25-26-29-30
July	20-21-29	17-18-22-23-27
August	16-17-25-26	18-19-23-24-27-28
September	21-22	15-19-20-23-24-25-26
October	18-19	13-16-17-21-22-23
November	15-23-24	13-17-18-19-20
December	12-13-21	11-14-15-16-17-23-24

MOON'S INFLUENCE OVER PLANTS

Centuries ago it was established that seeds planted when the Moon is in signs and phases called Fruitful will produce more growth than seeds planted when the Moon is in a Barren sign.

Fruitful Signs: Taurus, Cancer, Libra, Scorpio, Capricorn, Pisces
Barren Signs: Aries, Gemini, Leo, Virgo, Sagittarius, Aquarius
Dry Signs: Aries, Gemini, Sagittarius, Aquarius

Activity	Moon In
Mow lawn, trim plants	**Fruitful sign:** 1st & 2nd quarter
Plant flowers	**Fruitful sign:** 2nd quarter; best in Cancer and Libra
Prune	**Fruitful sign:** 3rd & 4th quarter
Destroy pests; spray	**Barren sign:** 4th quarter
Harvest potatoes, root crops	**Dry sign:** 3rd & 4th quarter; Taurus, Leo, and Aquarius

MOON'S INFLUENCE OVER YOUR HEALTH

ARIES   Head, brain, face, upper jaw
TAURUS   Throat, neck, lower jaw
GEMINI   Hands, arms, lungs, shoulders, nervous system
CANCER   Esophagus, stomach, breasts, womb, liver
LEO   Heart, spine
VIRGO   Intestines, liver
LIBRA   Kidneys, lower back
SCORPIO   Sex and eliminative organs
SAGITTARIUS   Hips, thighs, liver
CAPRICORN   Skin, bones, teeth, knees
AQUARIUS   Circulatory system, lower legs
PISCES   Feet, tone of being

Try to avoid work being done on that part of the body when the
Moon is in the sign governing that part.

MOON'S INFLUENCE OVER DAILY AFFAIRS

The Moon makes a complete transit of the Zodiac every 27 days
7 hours and 43 minutes. In making this transit the Moon forms
different aspects with the planets and consequently has favorable
or unfavorable bearings on affairs and events for persons according to the sign of the Zodiac under which they were born.

When the Moon is in conjunction with the Sun it is called a
New Moon; when the Moon and Sun are in opposition it is called
a Full Moon. From New Moon to Full Moon, first and second
quarter—which takes about two weeks—the Moon is increasing
or waxing. From Full Moon to New Moon, third and fourth quarter, the Moon is decreasing or waning.

Activity	Moon In
Business: buying and selling	Sagittarius, Aries, Gemini, Virgo
new, requiring public support	1st and 2nd quarter
meant to be kept quiet	3rd and 4th quarter
Investigation	3rd and 4th quarter
Signing documents	1st & 2nd quarter, Cancer, Scorpio, Pisces
Advertising	2nd quarter, Sagittarius
Journeys and trips	1st & 2nd quarter, Gemini, Virgo
Renting offices, etc.	Taurus, Leo, Scorpio, Aquarius
Painting of house/apartment	3rd & 4th quarter, Taurus, Scorpio, Aquarius
Decorating	Gemini, Libra, Aquarius
Buying clothes and accessories	Taurus, Virgo
Beauty salon or barber shop visit	1st & 2nd quarter, Taurus, Leo, Libra, Scorpio, Aquarius
Weddings	1st & 2nd quarter

SAGITTARIUS

SAGITTARIUS

Character Analysis

People born under this ninth sign of the Zodiac are quite often self-reliant and intelligent. Generally, they are quite philosophical in their outlook on life. They know how to make practical use of their imagination.

There is seldom anything narrow about a Sagittarius man or woman. He or she is generally very tolerant and considerate. They would never consciously do anything that would hurt another's feelings. They are gifted with a good sense of humor and believe in being honest in relationships with others. At times Sagittarius is a little short of tact. They are so intent on telling the truth that sometimes they can be blunt.

Nevertheless, Sagittarius men and women mean well, and people who enjoy a relationship with them are often willing to overlook this flaw. Sagittarius may even tell people true things about themselves that they do not wish to hear. At times this can cause a strain in the relationship. Sagittarius often wishes that others were as forthright and honest as he or she is—no matter what the consequences.

Sagittarius men and women are positive and optimistic and love life. They often help others to snap out of an ill mood. Their joie de vivre is often infectious. People enjoy being around Sagittarius because they are almost always in a good mood.

Quite often people born under the sign of Sagittarius are fond of the outdoors. They enjoy sporting events and often excel in them. Like the Archer, the zodiacal symbol of the sign, Sagittarius men and women are fond of animals, especially horses and dogs.

Generally, the Archer is healthy—in mind and in body. They have pluck. They enjoy the simple things of life. Fresh air and good comradeship are important to them. On the other hand, they are fond of developing their minds. Many Sagittarius cannot read or study enough. They like to keep abreast of things. They are interested in theater and the arts in general. Some of them are quite religious. Some choose a religious life.

Because they are outgoing for the most part, they sometimes come in touch with situations that others are never confronted with. In the long run this tends to make their life experiences quite rich and varied. They are well-balanced. They like to be active. And they enjoy using their intellects.

It is important to the person born under this sign that justice prevails. They dislike seeing anyone treated unfairly. If Sagittarius feels that the old laws are out of date or unrealistic, he or she will fight to have them changed. At times they can be true rebels. It is important to the Archer that law is carried out impartially. In matters of law, they often excel.

Sagittarius are almost always fond of travel. It seems to be imbedded in their natures. At times, they feel impelled to get away from familiar surroundings and people. Faraway places have a magical attraction for someone born under this sign. They enjoy reading about foreign lands and strange customs.

Many people who are Sagittarius are not terribly fond of living in big cities; they prefer the quiet and greenery of the countryside. Of all the signs of the Zodiac the sign of Sagittarius is closest to mother nature. They can usually build a trusting relationship with animals. They respect wildlife in all its forms.

Sagittarius is quite clever in conversation. He or she has a definite way with words. They like a good argument. They know how to phrase things exactly. Their sense of humor often has a cheerful effect on their manner of speech. They are seldom without a joke.

At times, the Sagittarius wit is apt to hurt someone's feelings, but this is never intentional. A slip of the tongue sometimes gets the Archer into social difficulties. As a result, there can be argumentative and angry scenes. But Sagittarius men and women cool down quickly. They are not given to holding grudges. They are willing to forgive and forget.

On the whole, Sagittarius is good-natured and fun-loving. They find it easy to take up with all sorts of people. In most cases, their social circle is large. People enjoy their company and their parties. Many friends share the Sagittarius interest in the outdoor life as well as intellectual pursuits.

Sagittarius sometimes can be impulsive. They are not afraid of risk. On the contrary, they can be foolhardy in the way they court danger. But Sagittarius men and women are very sporting in all they that do. If they should wind up the loser, they will not waste time grieving about it. They are fairly optimistic—they believe in good luck.

Health

Often people born under the sign of Sagittarius are quite athletic. They are healthy-looking—quite striking in a robust way. Often they are rather tall and well-built. They are enthusiastic people and like being active or involved. Exercise and sports may interest them a great deal.

Sagittarius cannot stand not being active. They have to be on the go. As they grow older, they seem to increase in strength and physical ability. At times they may have worries, but they never allow them to affect humor or health.

It is important to Sagittarius men and women to remain physically sound. They are usually very physically fit, but their nervous system may be somewhat sensitive. Too much activity—even while they find action attractive—may put a severe strain on them after a time. The Archer should try to concentrate their energies on as few objects as possible. However, usually they have many projects scattered here and there, and can be easily exhausted.

At times, illnesses fall upon the Archer suddenly or strangely. Some Sagittarius are accident-prone. They are not afraid of taking risks and as a result are sometimes careless in the way they do things. Injuries often come to them by way of sports or other vigorous activities.

Sometimes men and women of this sign try to ignore signs of illness—especially if they are engaged in some activity that has captured their interest. This results in a severe setback at times.

In later life, Sagittarius sometimes suffers from stomach disorders. High blood pressure is another ailment that might affect them. They should also be on guard for signs of arthritis and sciatica. In spite of these possible dangers, the average Sagittarius manages to stay quite youthful and alert through their many interests and pastimes.

Occupation

Sagittarius is someone who can be relied upon in a work situation. They are loyal and dependable. They are energetic workers, anxious to please superiors. They are forward-looking by nature and enjoy working in modern surroundings and toward progressive goals.

Challenges do not frighten Sagittarius. They are flexible and can work in confining situations even though they may not enjoy it. Work that gives them a chance to move around and meet new people is well suited to their character. If they have to stay in one locale, they become sad and ill-humored. They can take orders but they would rather be in a situation where they do not have to. They are difficult to please at times, and may hop from job to job before feeling that it is really time to settle down. Sagittarius do their best work when they are allowed to work on their own.

Sagittarius individuals are interested in expressing themselves in the work they do. If they occupy a position that does not allow them to be creative, they will seek outside activities. Such hobbies or pastimes give them a chance to develop and broaden their talents.

Some Sagittarius do well in the field of journalism. Others make good teachers and public speakers. They are generally quite flexible and would do well in many different positions. Some excel as foreign ministers or in music. Others do well in government work or in publishing.

Men and women born under this ninth sign are often more

intelligent than the average person. The cultivated Sagittarius knows how to employ intellectual gifts to their best advantage. In politics and religion, Sagittarius often displays brilliance.

The Sagittarius man or woman is pleasant to work with. They are considerate of colleagues and would do nothing that might upset the working relationship. Because they are so self-reliant, they often inspire teammates. Sagittarius likes to work with detail. Their ideas are both practical and idealistic. Sagittarius is curious by nature and is always looking for ways of expanding their knowledge.

Sagittarius are almost always generous. They rarely refuse someone in need, but are always willing to share what they have. Whether they are up or down, Sagittarius can always be relied upon to help someone in dire straits. Their attitude toward life may be happy-go-lucky in general. They are difficult to depress no matter what the situation. They are optimistic and forward-looking. Money always seems to fall into their hands.

The average Sagittarius is interested in expansion and promotion. Sometimes these concerns weaken their projects rather than strengthen them. Also, the average Sagittarius is more interested in contentment and joy than in material gain. However, they will do their best to make the most of any profit that comes their way.

When Sagittarius does get hooked on a venture, he or she is often willing to take risks to secure a profit. In the long run they are successful. They have a flair for carrying off business deals. It is the cultivated Sagittarius who prepares in advance for any business contingency. In that way he or she can bring knowledge and experience to bear on their professional and financial interests.

Home and Family

Not all Sagittarius are very interested in home life. Many of them set great store in being mobile. Their activities outside the home may attract them more than those inside the home. Not exactly homebodies, Sagittarius, however, can adjust themselves to a stable domestic life if they put their minds to it.

People born under this sign are not keen on luxuries and other displays of wealth. They prefer the simple things. Anyone entering their home should be able to discern this. They are generally neat. They like a place that has plenty of space—not too cluttered with imposing furniture.

Even when they settle down, Sagittarius men and women like to keep a small corner of their life just for themselves. Independence is important to them. If necessary, they will insist upon it, no matter what the situation. They like a certain amount of beauty in the home, but they may not be too interested in keeping things looking nice. Their interests lead them elsewhere. Housekeeping may bore them to distraction. When forced to stick to a domestic routine, they can become somewhat disagreeable.

Children bring Sagittarius men and women a great deal of happiness. They are fond of family life. Friends generally drop in any old time to visit for they know they will always be welcomed and properly entertained. The Archer's love for their fellow man is well known.

The Sagittarius parent may be bewildered at first by a newborn baby. They may worry about holding such a tiny tot for fear of injuring the little one. Although some Sagittarius may be clumsy, they do have a natural touch with small children and should not worry about handling them properly. As soon as the infant begins to grow up and develop a definite personality, Sagittarius can relax and relate. There is always a strong tie between children and the Sagittarius parent.

Children are especially drawn to Sagittarius because they seem to understand them better than other adults.

One is apt to find children born under this sign a little restless and disorganized at times. They are usually quite independent in their ways and may ask for quite a bit of freedom while still young. They don't like being fussed over by adults. They like to feel that their parents believe in them and trust them on their own.

Social Relationships

Sagittarius enjoys having people around. It is not difficult for them to make friends. They are very sociable by nature. Most of the friends they make they keep for life.

Sagittarius men and women are broad-minded, so they have all sorts of pals and casual acquaintances. They appreciate people for their good qualities, however few a person might have. Sagittarius are not quick to judge and are usually very forgiving. They are not impressed by what a friend has in the way of material goods.

Sagittarius men and women are generally quite popular. They are much in demand socially. People like their easy disposition and good humor. Their friendship is valued by others. Quite often in spite of their chumminess, Sagittarius is rather serious. Light conversation may be somewhat difficult for them.

Sagittarius men and women believe in speaking their minds, in saying what they feel. Yet at times, they can appear quiet and retiring. It all depends on their mood. Some people feel that there are two sides to the Sagittarius personality. This characteristic is reflected in the zodiacal symbol for the sign—a double symbol: the hunter and the horse intertwined, denoting two different natures.

It may be difficult for some people to get to know a Sagittarius man or woman. In some instances Sagittarius employ silence as a sort of protection. When people pierce through, however, and will not leave him or her in peace, Sagittarius can become quite angry.

On the whole, Sagittarius is kind and considerate. Their nature is gentle and unassuming. With the wrong person, though, they can become somewhat disagreeable. They do become angry, but they cool down quickly and are willing to let bygones be bygones. Sagittarius individuals never hold a grudge against anyone.

Companionship and harmony in all social relationships is necessary for Sagittarius. They are willing to make some sacrifices for it. Any partner, friend, or mate must be a good listener. There are times when Sagittarius feel it necessary to pour their hearts out. They are willing to listen to someone's problems and want the same considerate treatment in return.

A partner, friend, or lover should also be able to take an interest in any hobbies, pastimes, or sports a Sagittarius wants to pursue. If not, Sagittarius men and women will be tempted to go their own way even more so than their nature dictates.

Sagittarius individuals do not beat around the bush. They do say what they mean. Being direct is one of their strongest qualities. Sometimes it pays off, sometimes it doesn't. They often forget that the one they love may be very sensitive and can take offhand remarks personally.

Sagittarius has a tendency to be too blunt and to reveal secrets, innocently or otherwise, that hurt people's feelings. A friend or partner may not be able to overlook this flaw or may not be able to correct it either in a subtle or direct way. When making jokes or casual comments, Sagittarius sometimes strikes a sensitive chord in a companion, which can result in a serious misunderstanding.

But the cultivated Sagittarius learns the boundaries of social behavior. They know when not to go too far. Understanding a partner's viewpoint is the first step toward assuring a good relationship down the road.

Love and Marriage

Sagittarius individuals are faithful to their loved ones. They are affectionate and not at all possessive. Love is important for them spiritually as well as physically. For some Sagittarius, romance is a chance to escape reality—a chance for adventure.

Quite often a mate or lover finds it difficult to keep up with Sagittarius—they are so active and energetic. When Sagittarius men and women fall in love, however, they are quite easy to handle.

Sagittarius do like having freedom. They will make concessions in a steady relationship. Still there will be a part of themselves that they keep from others. He or she is very intent on preserving their individual rights, no matter what sort of relationship they are engaged in. Sagittarius ideals are generally high, and they are important. Sagittarius is looking for someone with similar standards, not someone too lax or too conventional.

In love, Sagittarius men and women may be a bit childlike at times. As a result of this they are apt to encounter various disappointments before they find the one meant for them. At times he or she says things they really shouldn't, and this causes the end of a romantic relationship.

Men and women born under this sign may have many love affairs before they feel ready to settle down with just one person. If the person they love does not exactly measure up to their standards, they are apt to overlook this—depending on how strong their love is—and accept the person for what that person is.

On the whole, Sagittarius men and women are not envious. They are willing to allow a partner needed freedoms—within reason. Sagittarius does this so they will not have to jeopardize their own liberties. Live and let live could easily be their motto. If their ideals and freedom are threatened, Sagittarius fights hard to protect what they believe is just and fair.

They do not want to make any mistakes in love, so they take their time when choosing someone to settle down with. They are direct and positive when they meet the right one. They do not waste time.

The average Sagittarius may be a bit altar-shy. It may take a bit of convincing before Sagittarius agree that married life is right for them. This is generally because they do not want to lose their freedom. Sagittarius is an active person who enjoys being around a lot of other people. Sitting quietly at home does not interest them at all. At times it may seem that he or she wants to have things their own way, even in marriage. It may take some doing to get Sagittarius to realize that in marriage, as in other things, give-and-take plays a great role.

Romance and the Sagittarius Woman

The Sagittarius woman is kind and gentle. Most of the time she is very considerate of others and enjoys being of help in some way to her friends. She can be quite active and, as a result, be rather difficult to catch. On the whole, she is optimistic and friendly. She believes in looking on the bright side of things. She knows how to make the best of situations that others feel are not worth salvaging. She has plenty of pluck.

Men generally like her because of her easygoing manner. Quite often she becomes friends with a man before venturing on to romance. There is something about her that makes her more of a companion than a lover. The woman Archer can best be described as sporting and broad-minded.

She is almost never possessive. She enjoys her own freedom too much to want to make demands on that of another person.

She is always youthful in her disposition. She may seem naive or guileless at times. Generally it takes her longer really to mature than it does others. She tends to be impulsive and may easily jump from one thing to another. If she has an unfortunate experience in love early in life, she may shy away from fast or intimate contacts for a while. She is usually very popular. Not all the men who are attracted to her see her as a possible lover, but more as a friend or companion.

The woman born under the sign of the Archer generally believes in true love. She may have several romances before she decides to settle down. For her there is no particular rush. She is willing to have a long romantic relationship with the man she loves before making marriage plans.

The Sagittarius woman is often the outdoors type and has a strong liking for animals—especially dogs and horses. Quite often she excels in sports. She is not generally someone who is content to stay at home and cook and take care of the house. She would rather be out attending to her other interests. When she does household work, however, she does it well.

She makes a good companion as well as a wife. She usually enjoys participating with her husband in his various interests and affairs. Her sunny disposition often brightens up the dull moments of a love affair.

At times her temper may flare, but she is herself again after a few moments. She would never butt into her husband's business affairs, but she does enjoy being asked for her opinion from time to time. Generally she is up to date on all that her husband is doing and can offer him some pretty sound advice.

The Sagittarius woman is seldom jealous of her husband's interest in other people—even if some of them are of the opposite sex. If she has no reason to doubt his love, she never questions it.

She makes a loving and sympathetic mother. She knows all the sports news and probably has the latest board game to play with her children. Her cheerful manner makes her an invaluable playmate and encouraging guide.

Romance and the Sagittarius Man

The Sagittarius man is often an adventurer. He likes taking chances in love as well as in life. He may hop around quite a bit—from one romance to another—before really thinking about settling down. Many men born under this sign feel that marriage would mean the end of their freedom, so they avoid it as much as possible. Whenever a romance becomes too serious, they move on.

Many Sagittarius men are impulsive in love. Early marriages for some often end unpleasantly. A male Archer is not a very mature person, even at an age when most others are. He takes a bit more time. He may not always make a wise choice in a love partner.

He is affectionate and loving but not at all possessive. Because he is rather lighthearted in love, he sometimes gets into trouble.

Most Sagittarius men find romance an exciting adventure. They make attentive lovers and are never cool or indifferent. Love should also have a bit of fun in it for him too. He likes to keep things light and gay. Romance without humor can at times be difficult for him to accept. The woman he loves should also be a good sport. She should have as open and fun-loving a disposition as he has if she is to understand him properly.

He wants his mate to share his interest in the outdoor life and animals. If she is good at sports, she is likely to win his heart. The average Sagittarius generally has an interest in athletics of various sorts—from bicycling to baseball.

His mate must also be a good intellectual companion, someone who can easily discuss those matters which interest him. Physical love is important to him—but so is spiritual love. A good romance will contain these in balance.

His sense of humor may sometimes seem a little unkind to someone who is not used to being laughed at. He enjoys playing jokes now and again. It is the child in his nature that remains a part of his character even when he grows old and gray.

He is not a homebody. He is responsible, however, and will do what is necessary to keep a home together. Still and all, the best wife for him is one who can manage household matters single-handedly if need be.

He loves the children, especially as they grow older and begin to take on definite personalities.

Woman—Man
SAGITTARIUS WOMAN
ARIES MAN

In some ways, the Aries man resembles a wandering mountain sheep seeking high land. He has an insatiable thirst for knowledge. He's ambitious and is apt to have his finger in many pies. He can do with a woman like you—someone attractive, quick-witted, and smart.

He is not interested in a clinging vine for a mate. He wants someone who is there when he needs her, someone who listens and understands what he says, someone who can give advice if he should ever need it, which is not likely to be often.

The Aries man wants a woman who will look good on his arm without hanging on it too heavily. He is looking for a woman who has both feet on the ground and yet is mysterious and enticing, a kind of domestic Helen of Troy whose face or fine dinner can launch a thousand business deals if need be. That woman he's in search of sounds a little like you, doesn't she? If the shoe fits, put it on. You won't regret it.

The Aries man makes a good husband. He is faithful and attentive. He is an affectionate man. He'll make you feel needed and loved. Love is a serious matter for the Aries man. He does not believe in flirting or playing the field—especially after he's found the woman of his dreams. He'll expect you to be as constant in your affection as he is in his. He'll expect you to be one hundred percent his. He won't put up with any nonsense while romancing you.

The Aries man may be pretty progressive and modern about many things. However, when it comes to pants wearing, he's downright conventional: it's strictly male attire. The best role you can take in the relationship is a supporting one. He's the boss and that's that. Once you have learned to accept that, you'll find the going easy.

The Aries man, with his endless energy and drive, likes to relax in the comfort of his home at the end of the day. The good homemaker can be sure of holding his love. He'll watch a sports match with you from his favorite armchair. If you see to it that everything in the house is where he expects to find it, you'll have no difficulty keeping the relationship on an even keel.

Life and love with an Aries man may be just the medicine you need. He'll be a good provider. He'll spoil you if he's financially able.

The Aries father is young at heart and will spoil children every chance he gets. So naturally the kids will take to him like ducks to water. His quick mind and energetic behavior appeal to the young. His ability to jump from one thing to another will delight the kids and keep them active. You will have to introduce some rules of the game so that the children learn how to start things properly and finish them before running off elsewhere.

SAGITTARIUS WOMAN
TAURUS MAN

If you've got your heart set on a man born under the sign of Taurus, you'll have to learn the art of being patient. Taurus take their time about everything—even love.

The steady and deliberate Taurus man is a little slow on the draw. It may take him quite a while before he gets around to popping that question. For the woman who doesn't mind twiddling her thumbs, the waiting and anticipating almost always pays off in the end. Taurus men want to make sure that every step they take is a good one, particularly if they feel that the path they're on is one that leads to the altar.

If you are in the mood for a whirlwind romance, you had better cast your net in shallower waters. Moreover, most Taurus prefer to do the angling themselves. They are not keen on a woman taking the lead. Once she does, they might drop her like a dead fish. If you let yourself get caught in his net, you'll find that he's fallen for you—hook, line, and sinker.

The Taurus man is fond of a comfortable home life. It is very important to him. If you keep those home fires burning you will have no trouble keeping that flame in your Taurus mate's heart aglow. You have a talent for homemaking; use it. Your taste in furnishings is excellent. You know how to make a house come to life with colors and decorations.

Taurus, the strong, steady, and protective Bull, may not be your idea of a man on the move. Still he's reliable. Perhaps he could be the anchor for your dreams and plans. He could help you to acquire a more balanced outlook and approach to your life. If you're given to impulsiveness, he could help you to curb it. He's the man who is always there when you need him.

When you tie the knot with a man born under Taurus, you can put away fears about creditors pounding on the front door. Taurus are practical about everything including bill paying. When he carries you over that threshold, you can be certain that the entire house is paid for, not only the doorsill.

As a wife, you won't have to worry about putting aside your many interests for the sake of back-breaking house chores. Your Taurus husband will see to it that you have all the latest time-saving appliances and comforts.

The Taurus father has much love and affection for the children, and he has no trouble demonstrating his warmth. Yet he does not believe in spoiling the kids. The Taurus father believes that children have a place, and they should know their place at all times. He is an excellent disciplinarian and will see to it that the youngsters grow up to be polite, obedient, and respectful. You will provide mirth and fun to balance things out.

SAGITTARIUS WOMAN
GEMINI MAN

If opposites attract, as the notion goes, then Gemini and Sagittarius should be swell together. The fact that you two are astrologically related—being zodiacal partners as well as zodiacal opposites—does not automatically guarantee that you will understand each other, at least at first. Gemini is an air sign, you are a fire sign, so the initial contact between you should be warm and breezy.

The Gemini man is quite a catch. Many a woman has set her cap for him and failed to bag him. Generally, Gemini men are intelligent, witty, and outgoing. Many of them tend to be versatile.

On the other hand, some of them seem to lack that sort of common sense that you set so much store in. Their tendency to start a half-dozen projects, then toss them up in the air out of boredom may do nothing more than exasperate you.

One thing that causes a Twin's mind and affection to wander is a bore. But it is unlikely that the active Sagittarius woman would ever allow herself to be accused of dullness. The Gemini man who has caught your heart will admire you for your ideas and intellect—perhaps even more than for your athletic talents and good looks.

A strong-willed woman could easily fill the role of rudder for her Gemini's ship-without-a-sail. The intelligent Gemini is often aware of his shortcomings and doesn't mind if someone with better bearings gives him a shove in the right direction—when it's needed. The average Gemini doesn't have serious ego hang-ups and will even accept a well-deserved chewing out from his mate or girlfriend gracefully.

A successful and serious-minded Gemini could make you a very happy woman, perhaps, if you gave him half the chance. Although he may give you the impression that he has a hole in his head, the Gemini man generally has a good head on his shoulders and can make efficient use of it when he wants to. Some of them, who have learned the art of being steadfast, have risen to great heights in their professions.

Once you convince yourself that not all people born under the sign of the Twins are witless grasshoppers, you won't mind dating a few—to test your newborn conviction. If you do wind up walking down the aisle with one, accept the fact that married life with him will mean your taking the bitter with the sweet.

Life with a Gemini man can be more fun than a barrel of clowns. You'll never be allowed to experience a dull moment. But don't leave money matters to him, or you'll both wind up behind the eight ball.

Gemini men are always attractive to the opposite sex. You'll perhaps have to allow him an occasional harmless flirt. It will seldom amount to more than that if you're his ideal mate.

Gemini is your zodiacal mate, as well as your zodiacal opposite, so the Gemini-Sagittarius couple will make delightful parents together. Airy Gemini will create a very open, experimental environment for the kids. He loves them so much, he sometimes lets them do what they want. You will keep the kids in line and prevent them from running the household. But you and your Gemini mate's combined sense of humor is infectious, so the youngsters will naturally come to see the fun and funny sides of life.

SAGITTARIUS WOMAN
CANCER MAN

Chances are you won't hit it off too well with the man born under Cancer if your plans concern love. But then, Cupid has been known to do some pretty unlikely things. The Cancer man is very sensitive—thin-skinned and occasionally moody. You've got to keep on your toes—and not step on his—if you're determined to make a go of the relationship.

The Cancer man may be lacking in some of the qualities you seek in a man. But when it comes to being faithful and being a good provider, he's hard to beat.

The perceptive woman will not mistake the Crab's quietness for sullenness or his thriftiness for penny-pinching. In some respects, he is like that wise old owl out on a limb. He may look like he's dozing but actually he hasn't missed a thing.

Cancers possess a well of knowledge about human behavior. They can come across with some pretty helpful advice to those in trouble or in need. He can certainly guide you in making investments both in time and money. He may not say much, but he's always got his wits about him.

The Crab may not be the match or catch for a woman like you. At times, you are likely to find him downright dull. True to his sign, he can be fairly cranky and crabby when handled the wrong way. He is perhaps more sensitive than he should be.

If you're smarter than your Cancer friend, be smart enough not to let him know. Never give him the idea that you think he's a little short on brainpower. It would send him scurrying back into his shell. And all that ground lost in the relationship will perhaps never be recovered.

The Crab is most content at home. Once settled down for the night or the weekend, wild horses couldn't drag him any farther than the gatepost—that is, unless those wild horses were dispatched by his mother.

The Crab is sometimes a Momma's boy. If his mate does not put her foot down, he will see to it that his mother always comes first. No self-respecting wife would ever allow herself to play second fiddle, even if it's to her mother-in-law. With a little bit of tact, however, she'll find that slipping into that number-one position is as easy as pie (that legendary one his mother used to bake).

If you pamper your Cancer man, you'll find that mother turns up less and less, at the front door and in conversations.

Cancers make proud, patient, and protective fathers. But they can be a little too protective. Their sheltering instincts can interfere with a youngster's natural inclination to test the waters outside the home. Still, the Cancer father doesn't want to see his kids learning about life the hard way from the streets. Your qualities of optimism and encouragement and your knowledge of right and wrong will guide the youngsters along the way.

SAGITTARIUS WOMAN
LEO MAN

For the woman who enjoys being swept off her feet in a romantic whirlwind fashion, Leo is the sign of such love. When the Lion puts his mind to romancing, he doesn't stint. It's all wining and dining and dancing till the wee hours of the morning.

Leo is all heart and knows how to make his woman feel like a woman. The woman in constant search of a man she can look up to need go no farther: Leo is ten-feet tall—in spirit if not in stature. He's a man not only in full control of his faculties but in full control of just about any situation he finds himself in. Leo is a winner.

The Leo man may not look like Tarzan, but he knows how to roar and beat his chest if he has to. The woman who has had her fill of weak-kneed men finds in a Leo someone she can at last lean upon. He can support you not only physically but spiritually as well. He's good at giving advice that pays off.

Leos are direct people. They don't believe in wasting time or effort. They almost never make unwise investments.

Many Leos rise to the top of their professions. Through example, they often prove to be a source of great inspiration to others.

Although he's a ladies' man, Leo is very particular about his ladies. His standards are high when it comes to love interests. The idealistic and cultivated woman should have no trouble keeping her balance on the pedestal the Lion sets her on.

Leo believes that romance should be played on a fair give-and-take basis. He won't stand for any monkey business in a love relationship. It's all or nothing.

You'll find him a frank, off-the-shoulder person. He generally says what is on his mind.

If you decide upon a Leo man for a mate, you must be prepared to stand behind him full force. He expects it—and usually deserves it. He's the head of the house and can handle that position without a hitch. He knows how to go about breadwinning and, if he has his way (and most Leos do have their own way), he'll see to it that you'll have all the luxuries you crave and the comforts you need.

It's unlikely that the romance in your marriage will ever die out. Lions need love like flowers need sunshine. They're ever amorous and generally expect similar attention and affection from their mates. Leos are fond of going out on the town. They love to give parties, as well as to go to them. Because you, too, love to throw a party, you and your Leo mate will be the most popular host and hostess in town.

Leo fathers have a tendency to spoil the children—up to a point. That point is reached when the children become the center of attention, and Leo feels neglected. Then the Leo father becomes strict and insists that his rules be followed. You will have your hands full pampering both your Leo mate and the children. As long as he comes first in your affections, the family will be creative and joyful.

SAGITTARIUS WOMAN
VIRGO MAN

Although the Virgo man may be a bit of a fussbudget at times, his seriousness and dedication to common sense may help you to overlook his tendency to be too critical about minor things.

Virgo men are often quiet, respectable types who set great store in conservative behavior and levelheadedness. He'll admire you for your practicality and tenacity, perhaps even more than for your good looks. He's seldom bowled over by a glamour-puss. When he gets his courage up, he turns to a serious and reliable girl for romance.

The Virgo man will be far from a Valentino while dating. In fact, you may wind up making all the passes. Once he does get his motor running, however, he can be a warm and wonderful fellow—to the right lover.

He's gradual about love. Chances are your romance with him will start out looking like an ordinary friendship. Once he's sure you're no fly-by-night flirt and have no plans of taking him for a ride, he'll open up and rain sunshine all over your heart.

Virgo men tend to marry late in life. Virgo believes in holding out until he's met the right woman. He may not have many names in his little black book; in fact, he may not even have a black book. He's not interested in playing the field; leave that to men of the more flamboyant signs. The Virgo man is so particular that he may remain romantically inactive for a long period. His woman has to be perfect or it's no go.

If you find yourself feeling weak-kneed for a Virgo, do your best to convince him that perfect is not so important when it comes to love. Help him to realize that he's missing out on a great deal by not considering the near perfect or whatever it is you consider yourself to be. With your surefire perseverance, you will most likely be able to make him listen to reason and he'll wind up reciprocating your romantic interests.

The Virgo man is no block of ice. He'll respond to what he feels to be the right feminine flame. Once your love life with a Virgo man starts to bubble, don't give it a chance to fall flat. You may never have a second chance at winning his heart.

If you should ever break up with him, forget about patching it up. He'd prefer to let the pieces lie scattered. Once married, though, he'll stay that way—even if it hurts. He's too conscientious to try to back out of a legal deal of any sort.

The Virgo man is as neat as a pin. He's thumbs down on sloppy housekeeping. Keep everything bright, neat, and shiny. That goes for the children, too, at least by the time he gets home.

The Virgo father appreciates good manners, courtesy, and cleanliness from the children. He will instill a sense of order in the household, and he expects youngsters to respect his wishes. He can become very worried about scrapes, bruises, and all sorts of minor mishaps when the kids go out to play. Your easygoing faith in the children's safety will counteract Virgo's tendency to fuss and fret over them.

SAGITTARIUS WOMAN
LIBRA MAN

If there's a Libra in your life, you are most likely a very happy woman. Men born under this sign have a way with women. You'll always feel at ease in a Libra's company. You can be yourself when you're with him.

The Libra man can be moody at times. His moodiness is often puzzling. One moment he comes on hard and strong with declarations of his love, the next moment you find that he's left you like yesterday's mashed potatoes. He'll come back, though, don't worry. Libras are like that. Deep down inside he really knows what he wants even though he may not appear to.

You'll appreciate his admiration of beauty and harmony. If you're dressed to the teeth and never looked lovelier, you'll get a ready compliment—and one that's really deserved. Libras don't indulge in idle flattery. If they don't like something, they are tactful enough to remain silent.

Libras will go to great lengths to preserve peace and harmony— they will even tell a fat lie if necessary. They don't like showdowns or disagreeable confrontations. The frank woman is all for getting whatever is bothering her off her chest and out into the open, even if it comes out all wrong. To the Libra, making a clean breast of everything seems like sheer folly sometimes.

You may lose your patience while waiting for your Libra friend to make up his mind. It takes him ages sometimes to make a decision. He weighs both sides carefully before committing himself to anything. You seldom dillydally, at least about small things. So it's likely that you will find it difficult to see eye-to-eye with a hesitating Libra when it comes to decision-making methods.

All in all, though, he is kind, considerate, and fair. He is interested in the real truth. He'll try to balance everything out until he has all the correct answers. It's not difficult for him to see both sides of a story.

He's a peace-loving man. Even a rough-and-tumble sports event, and certainly a violent one, will make Libra shudder.

Libras are not show-offs. Generally, they are well-balanced, modest people. Honest, wholesome, and affectionate, they are serious about every love encounter they have. If Libra should find that the woman he's dating is not really suited to him, he will end the relationship in such a tactful manner that no hard feelings will come about.

The Libra father is patient and fair. He can be firm without exercising undue strictness or discipline. Although he can be a harsh judge at times, with the youngsters he will radiate sweetness and light in the hope that they will grow up to imitate his gentle manner. To balance the essential refinement the children will acquire from their Libra father, you will teach them a few rough-and-ready ways to enjoy recreation.

SAGITTARIUS WOMAN
SCORPIO MAN

Scorpio shares at least one trait in common with Sagittarius. You both are blunt. But Scorpio, who can be vengeful and vindictive, intends an insult as an insult, not just a thoughtless comment. Many find Scorpio's sting a fate worse than death. When his anger breaks loose, you better clear out of the vicinity.

The average Scorpio may strike you as a brute. He'll stick pins into the balloons of your plans and dreams if they don't line up with what he thinks is right. If you do anything to irritate him—just anything—you'll wish you hadn't. He'll give you a sounding out that would make you pack your bags and go back to Mother—if you were that kind of woman.

The Scorpio man hates being tied down to home life. He would rather be out on the battlefield of life, belting away at whatever he feels is a just and worthy cause, instead of staying home nestled in a comfortable armchair with the evening paper. If you have a strong homemaking streak, don't keep those home fires burning too brightly too long; you may just run out of firewood.

As passionate as he is in business affairs and politics, the Scorpio man still has plenty of fire and light stored away for the pursuit of romance and lovemaking.

Most women are easily attracted to him—perhaps you are no exception. Those who allow a man born under this sign to sweep them off their feet quickly find that they're dealing with a pepper pot of seething excitement. The Scorpio man is passionate with a capital P, you can be sure of that. When you two meet on the playing field of love, Scorpio will be much more intense and competitive than you.

If you can match his intensity and adapt to his mood swings, you are fair game. If you're the kind of woman who can keep a stiff upper lip, take it on the chin, turn a deaf ear, and all of that, because you feel you are still under his love spell in spite of everything—lots of luck.

If you have decided to take the bitter with the sweet, prepare yourself for a lot of ups and downs. Chances are you won't have as much time for your own affairs and interests as you'd like. The Scorpio's love of power may cause you to be at his constant beck and call.

Scorpios like fathering large families. He is proud of his children, but often he fails to live up to his responsibilities as a parent. In spite of the extremes in his personality, the Scorpio man is able to transform the conflicting characteristics within himself when he becomes a father. When he takes his fatherly duties seriously, he is a powerful teacher. He believes in preparing his children for the hard knocks life sometimes delivers. He is adept with difficult youngsters because he knows how to tap the best in each child.

SAGITTARIUS WOMAN
SAGITTARIUS MAN

The woman who has set her cap for a man born under the sign of Sagittarius may have to apply an awful amount of strategy before she can get him to drop down on bended knee. Although some Sagittarius may be marriage-shy, they're not ones to skitter away from romance. A high-spirited woman may find a relationship with a Sagittarius—whether a fling or the real thing—a very enjoyable experience.

As you know, Sagittarius are bright, happy, and healthy people. You all have a strong sense of fair play. You all are a source of inspiration to others. You're full of ideas and drive.

You'll be taken by the Sagittarius man's infectious grin and his lighthearted friendly nature. If you do wind up being the woman in his life, you'll find that he's apt to treat you more like a buddy than the love of his life. It's just his way. Sagittarius are often chummy instead of romantic.

You'll admire his broad-mindedness in most matters—including those of the heart. If, while dating you, he claims that he still wants to play the field, he'll expect you to enjoy the same liberty. Once he's promised to love, honor, and obey, however, he does just that. Marriage for him, once he's taken that big step, is very serious business.

A woman who has a keen imagination and a great love of freedom will not be disappointed if she does tie up with the Archer. The Sagittarius man is often quick-witted. Men of this sign have a genuine interest in equality. They hate prejudice and injustice.

If he does insist on a night out with the boys once a week, he won't scowl if you decide to let him shift for himself in the kitchen once a week while you pursue some of your own interests. He believes in fairness.

He's not much of a homebody. Quite often he's occupied with faraway places either in his dreams or in reality. He enjoys—just as you do—being on the go or on the move. He's got ants in his pants and refuses to sit still for long stretches at a time. Humdrum routine, especially at home, bores him. So the two of you will probably go out a lot or throw lots of parties at home.

He likes surprising people. He'll take great pride in showing you off to his friends. He'll always be a considerate mate; he will never embarrass or disappoint you intentionally.

He's very tolerant when it comes to friends, and you'll most likely spend a lot of time entertaining people—which suits you party animals royally.

The Sagittarius father, unlike you, may be bewildered and made utterly nervous by a newborn. He will dote on any infant son or daughter from a safe distance because he can be clumsy and frightened handling the tiny tot. The Sagittarius dad usually becomes comfortable with youngsters once they have passed through the baby stage. As soon as they are old enough to walk and talk, he will encourage each and every visible sign of talent and skill.

SAGITTARIUS WOMAN
CAPRICORN MAN

A with-it woman like you is likely to find the average Capricorn man a bit of a drag. The man born under this sign is often a closed up person and difficult to get to know. Even if you do get to know him, you may not find him very interesting.

In romance, Capricorn men are a little on the rusty side. You'll probably have to make all the passes.

You may find his plodding manner irritating and his conservative, traditional ways downright maddening. He's not one to take a chance on anything. If it was good enough for his father, it's good enough for him. Capricorn can be habit-bound. He follows a way that is tried and true.

Whenever adventure rears its tantalizing head, the Goat will turn the other way. Unlike you, he is not prone to taking risks.

He may be just as ambitious as you are, perhaps even more so. But his ways of accomplishing his aims are more subterranean than yours. He operates from the background a good deal of the time. At a gathering you may never even notice him. But he's there, taking everything in, sizing everyone up, planning his next careful move.

Although Capricorns may be intellectual to a degree, it is not generally the kind of intelligence you appreciate. He may not be as quick or as bright as you. It may take him ages to understand a joke, and you love jokes.

If you do decide to take up with a man born under the sign of the Goat, you ought to be pretty good in the cheering up department. The Capricorn man often acts as though he's constantly being followed by a cloud of gloom.

The Capricorn man is most himself when in the comfort and privacy of his own home. The security possible within four walls can make him a happy man. He'll spend as much time as he can at home. If he is loaded down with extra work, he'll bring it home instead of finishing it up at the office.

You'll most likely find yourself frequently confronted by his relatives. Family is very important to the Capricorn—his family that is. They had better take an important place in your life, too, if you want to keep your home a happy one.

Although his caution in most matters may all but drive you up the wall, you'll find that his concerned way with money is justified most of the time. He'll plan everything right down to the last penny.

The Capricorn father is a dutiful parent and takes a lifelong interest in seeing that his children make something of themselves. He may not understand their hopes and dreams because he often tries to put his head on their shoulders. The Capricorn father believes that there are certain goals to be achieved, and there is a traditional path to achieving them. He can be quite a scold if the youngsters break the rules. Your easygoing, joyful manner will moderate Capricorn's rigid approach and will make things fun again for the children.

SAGITTARIUS WOMAN
AQUARIUS MAN

Aquarius individuals love everybody—even their worst enemies sometimes. Through your love relationship with an Aquarius you'll find yourself running into all sorts of people, ranging from near genius to downright insane—and they're all friends of his.

As a rule, Aquarius are extremely friendly and open. Of all the signs, they are perhaps the most tolerant. In the thinking department, they are often miles ahead of others.

You'll most likely find your relationship with this man a challenging one. Your high respect for intelligence and imagination may be reason enough for you to set your heart on a Water Bearer. You'll find that you can learn a lot from him.

In the holding-hands phase of your romance, you may find that your Water Bearer friend has cold feet. Aquarius take quite a bit of warming up before they are ready to come across with that first goodnight kiss. More than likely, he'll just want to be your pal in the beginning. For him, that's an important first step in any relationship—love included.

The poetry and flowers stage—if it ever comes—will come later. Aquarius is all heart. Still, when it comes to tying himself down to one person and for keeps, he is almost always sure to hesitate. He may even try to get out of it if you breathe down his neck too heavily.

The Aquarius man is no Romeo, and he wouldn't want to be. The kind of love life he's looking for is one that's made up mainly of companionship. He may not be very romantic, but still the memory of his first romance will always hold an important position in his heart. So in a way he is like Romeo after all. Some Aquarius wind up marrying their childhood sweethearts.

You won't find it difficult to look up to a man born under the sign of the Water Bearer, but you may find the challenge of trying to keep up with him dizzying. He can pierce through the most complicated problem as if it were simple math. You may find him a little too lofty and high-minded. But don't judge him too harshly if that's the case. He's way ahead of his time.

If you marry this man, he'll stay true to you. Don't think that once the honeymoon is over, you'll be chained to the kitchen sink forever. Your Aquarius husband will encourage you to keep active in your own interests and affairs. You'll most likely have a minor tiff now and again but never anything serious.

The Aquarius father has an almost intuitive understanding of children. He sees them as individuals in their own right, not as extensions of himself or as beings who are supposed to take a certain place in the world. He can talk to the kids on a variety of subjects, and his knowledge can be awe-inspiring. Your dedication to learning and your desire to educate the children will be bolstered by your Aquarius mate. And your love of sports and games, the fun physical activities in life, will balance the airy Aquarius intellectualism.

SAGITTARIUS WOMAN
PISCES MAN

The man born under Pisces is quite a dreamer. Sometimes he's so wrapped up in his dreams that he's difficult to reach. To the average, active woman, he may seem a little passive.

He's easygoing most of the time. He seems to take things in his stride. He'll entertain all kinds of views and opinions from just about everyone, nodding or smiling vaguely, giving the impression that he's with them one hundred percent while that may not be the case at all. His attitude may be why bother when he's confronted with someone wrong who thinks he's right. The Pisces man will seldom speak his mind if he thinks he'll be rigidly opposed.

The Pisces man is oversensitive at times. He's afraid of getting his feelings hurt. He'll sometimes imagine a personal affront when none's been made. Chances are you'll find this complex of his maddening. At times you may feel like giving him a swift kick where it hurts the most. It wouldn't do any good, though. It would just add fuel to the fire of his complex.

One thing you'll admire about this man is his concern for people who are sickly or troubled. He'll make his shoulder available to anyone in the mood for a good cry. He can listen to one hard-luck story after another without seeming to tire. When his advice is asked, he is capable of coming across with some words of wisdom. He often knows what is bothering someone before that person is aware of it. It's almost intuitive with Pisces.

Still, at the end of the day, this man will want some peace and quiet. If you've got a problem when he comes home, don't unload it in his lap. If you do, you are apt to find him short-tempered. He's a good listener but he can only take so much.

Pisces are not aimless although they may seem so at times. The positive sort of Pisces man is quite often successful in his profession and is likely to wind up rich and influential. Material gain, however, is never a direct goal for a man born under this sign.

The weaker Pisces are usually content to stay on the level where they find themselves. They won't complain too much if the roof leaks or if the fence is in need of repair.

Because of their seemingly laissez-faire manner, people under the sign of the Fishes—needless to say—are immensely popular with children. For tots the Pisces father plays the double role of confidant and playmate. It will never enter the mind of a Pisces to discipline a child, no matter how spoiled or incorrigible that child becomes.

Man—Woman

SAGITTARIUS MAN
ARIES WOMAN

The Aries woman is quite a charmer. When she tugs at the strings of your heart, you'll know it. She's a woman who's in search of a knight in shining armor. She is a very particular person with very high ideals. She won't accept anyone but the man of her dreams.

The Aries woman never plays around with passion. She means business when it comes to love.

Don't get the idea that she's a dewy-eyed damsel. She isn't. In fact, she can be practical and to the point when she wants to be. She's a dame with plenty of drive and ambition.

With an Aries woman behind you, you can go far in life. She knows how to help her man get ahead. She's full of wise advice; you only have to ask. The Aries woman has a keen business sense. Many of them become successful career women. There is nothing passive or retiring about her. She is equipped with a good brain and she knows how to use it.

Your union with her could be something strong, secure, and

romantic. If both of you have your sights fixed in the same direction, there is almost nothing that you could not accomplish.

The Aries woman is proud and capable of being quite jealous. While you're with her, never cast your eye in another woman's direction. It could spell disaster for your relationship. The Aries woman won't put up with romantic nonsense when her heart is at stake.

If the Aries woman backs you up in your business affairs, you can be sure of succeeding. However, if she only is interested in advancing her own career and puts her interests before yours, she can be sure to rock the boat. It will put a strain on the relationship. The overambitious Aries woman can be a pain in the neck and make you forget you were in love with her once.

The cultivated Aries woman makes a wonderful wife and mother. She has a natural talent for homemaking. With a pot of paint and some wallpaper, she can transform the dreariest domicile into an abode of beauty and snug comfort. The perfect hostess—even when friends just happen by—she knows how to make guests feel at home.

You'll also admire your Aries because she knows how to stand on her own two feet. Hers is an independent nature. She won't break down and cry when things go wrong, but will pick herself up and try to patch up matters.

The Aries woman makes a fine, affectionate mother. Although she is not keen on burdensome responsibilities, like you she relishes the joy that children bring. The Aries woman is skilled at juggling both career and motherhood, so her kids will never feel that she is an absentee parent. In fact, as the youngsters grow older, they might want some of the liberation that is so important to her. One of your roles is to encourage the children's quest for independence.

SAGITTARIUS MAN
TAURUS WOMAN

The woman born under the sign of Taurus may lack a little of the sparkle and bubble you often like to find in a woman. The Taurus woman is generally down to earth and never flighty. It's important to her that she keep both feet flat on the ground. She is not fond of bounding all over the place, especially if she's under the impression that there's no profit in it.

On the other hand, if you hit it off with a Taurus woman, you won't be disappointed in the romance area. The Taurus woman is all woman and proud of it, too. She can be very devoted and loving once she decides that her relationship with you is no fly-by-night romance. Basically, she's a passionate person. In sex, she's direct and to the point. If she really loves you, she'll let you know she's yours—and without reservations.

Better not flirt with other women once you've committed yourself to her. She's capable of being very jealous and possessive.

She'll stick by you through thick and thin. It's almost certain that if the going ever gets rough, she won't go running home to her mother. She can adjust to the hard times just as graciously as she can to the good times.

Taurus are, on the whole, pretty even-tempered. They like to be treated with kindness. Beautiful things and aesthetic objects make them feel loved and treasured.

You may find her a little slow and deliberate. She likes to be safe and sure about everything. Let her plod along if she likes. Don't coax her, but just let her take her own sweet time. Everything she does is done thoroughly and, generally, without mistakes.

Don't deride her for being a slowpoke. It could lead to a tirade of insults that could put even your blunt manner to shame. The Taurus woman doesn't anger readily but when prodded often enough, she's capable of letting loose with a cyclone of ill will. If you treat her with kindness and consideration, you'll have no cause for complaint.

The Taurus woman loves doing things for her man. She's a whiz in the kitchen and can whip up feasts fit for a king if she thinks they'll be royally appreciated. She may not fully understand you, but she'll adore you and be faithful to you if she feels you're worthy of it.

The Taurus woman makes a wonderful mother. She knows how to keep her children loved, cuddled, and warm. She may have some difficult times with them when they reach adolescence, and start to rebel against her strictness. You can inject a sense of adventure even in the most mundane of household responsibilities, so you will moderate your Taurus mate's insistence on discipline.

SAGITTARIUS MAN
GEMINI WOMAN

You may find a romance with a woman born under the sign of the Twins a many-splendored thing. In her you can find the intellectual companionship you often look for in a friend or mate.

Gemini, your astrological mate, can appreciate your aims and desires because she travels pretty much the same road as you do intellectually. At least she will travel part of the way. She may share your interests, but she will lack your tenacity.

She suffers from itchy feet. She can be here, there, all over the place and at the same time, or so it would seem. Her eagerness to move around may make you dizzy. Still, you'll enjoy and appreciate her liveliness and mental agility.

Geminis have sparkling personalities. You'll be attracted by her warmth and grace. While she's on your arm, you'll probably notice that many male eyes are drawn to her. She may even return a gaze or two, but don't let that worry you. All women born under this sign have nothing against a harmless flirt once in a while. They enjoy this sort of attention. If Gemini feels she is already spoken for, however, she will never let such attention get out of hand.

Although she may not be as handy as you'd like in the kitchen, you'll never go hungry for a filling and tasty meal. The Gemini woman is always in a rush. She won't feel like she's cheating by breaking out the instant mashed potatoes or the frozen peas. She may not be much of a good cook but she is clever. With a dash of this and a suggestion of that, she can make an uninteresting TV dinner taste like a gourmet meal.

Then, again, maybe you've struck it rich and have a Gemini lover or mate who finds complicated recipes a challenge to her intellect. If so, you'll find every meal an experiment—a tantalizing and mouth-watering surprise.

When you're beating your brains out over the Sunday crossword puzzle and find yourself stuck, just ask your Gemini partner. She'll give you all the right answers without batting an eyelash.

Like you, she loves all kinds of people. You may even find that you're a bit more particular than she. Often all that a Gemini requires is that her friends be interesting—and stay interesting. One thing she's not able to abide is a dullard.

Leave the party organizing to your Gemini sweetheart or mate, and you'll never have a chance to know a dull moment. She'll bring out the swinger in you if you give her half the chance.

The Gemini mother has a youthful streak that guides her in bringing up children through the various stages. She enjoys her kids, which can be the most sincere form of love. Like you—and like them—the Gemini mother is often restless, adventurous, and easily bored. She will never complain about the children's fleeting interests because she understands how they will change as they mature. Gemini-Sagittarius parents, being true zodiacal mates as well as zodiacal opposites, can encourage variety and experience in life so the kids really get to know what the world is like.

SAGITTARIUS MAN
CANCER WOMAN

If you fall in love with a Cancer woman, be prepared for anything. Cancer is sometimes difficult to understand when it comes to love. In one hour, she can unravel a whole gamut of emotions that will leave you in a tizzy. She'll undoubtedly keep you guessing.

You may find her a little too uncertain and sensitive for your liking. You'll most likely spend a good deal of time encouraging her, helping her to erase her foolish fears. Tell her she's a living doll a dozen times a day, and you'll be well loved in return.

Be careful of the jokes you make when in her company. Don't let any of them revolve around her, her personal interests, or her family. If you do, you'll most likely reduce her to tears. She can't stand being made fun of. It will take bushels of roses and tons of chocolates—not to mention the apologies—to get her to come back out of her shell.

In matters of money managing, she may not easily come around to your way of thinking. Money will never burn a hole in her pocket. You may get the notion that your Cancer sweetheart or mate is a direct descendent of Scrooge. If she has her way, she'll hang onto that first dollar you earned. She's not only that way with money, but with everything right on up from bakery string to jelly jars. She's a saver. She never throws anything away, no matter how trivial.

Once she returns your love, you'll find you have an affectionate, self-sacrificing, and devoted woman for life. Her love for you will never alter unless you want it to. She'll put you high upon a pedestal and will do everything—even if it's against your will—to keep you up there.

Cancer women love home life. For them, marriage is an easy step. They're domestic with a capital D. The Cancer woman will do her best to make your home comfortable and cozy. She, herself, is more at ease at home than anywhere else. She makes an excellent hostess. The best in her comes out when she is in her own environment, one she has created to meet her own and her family's needs.

Cancer women make the best mothers. Each will consider every complaint of her child a major catastrophe. With her, children always come first. If you're lucky, you'll run a close second. You'll perhaps see her as too devoted to the children. You may have a hard time convincing her that her apron strings are a little too tight.

SAGITTARIUS MAN
LEO WOMAN

If you can manage a woman who likes to kick up her heels every now and again, then the Lioness was made for you. You'll have to learn to put away jealous fears when you take up with a woman born under the sign of Leo. She's often the kind that makes heads turn and tongues wag. You don't have to believe any of what you hear. It's most likely jealous gossip or wishful thinking.

The Leo woman has more than a fair share of grace and glamour. She knows it, and she knows how to put it to good use. Needless to say, other women in her vicinity turn green with envy and will try anything to put her out of the running.

If she's captured your heart and fancy, woo her full force—if your intention is eventually to win her. Shower her with expensive gifts and promise her the moon, if you're in a position to go that far. Then you'll find her resistance beginning to weaken. It's not that she's such a difficult cookie. She'll probably pamper you once she's decided you're the man for her. But she does enjoy a lot of attention. What's more, she feels she's entitled to it. Her mild arrogance, however, is becoming.

The Leo woman knows how to transform the crime of excessive pride into a very charming misdemeanor. It sweeps most men— or rather, all men—right off their feet. Those who do not succumb to her leonine charm are few and far between.

If you've got an important business deal to clinch and you have doubts as to whether you can bring it off as you should, take your Leo mate along to the business luncheon. It will be a cinch that you'll have that contract—lock, stock, and barrel—in your pocket before the meeting is over. She won't have to say or do anything, just be there at your side. The grouchiest oil magnate can be transformed into a gushing, obedient schoolboy if there's a Leo woman in the room.

If you're rich and want to see to it that you stay that way, don't give your Leo spouse a free hand with the charge accounts and credit cards. When it comes to spending, Leo tends to overdo. If you're poor, you have no worries because the luxury-loving Leo will most likely never recognize your existence—let alone consent to marry you.

A Leo mother can be so proud of her children that she is sometimes blind to their faults. Yet when she wants them to learn and take their rightful place in the social scheme of things, the Leo mother can be strict. She is a patient teacher, lovingly explaining the rules the youngsters are expected to follow. Easygoing and friendly, like you are, she loves to pal around with the kids and show them off on every occasion. Your family will be a bundle of joy.

SAGITTARIUS MAN
VIRGO WOMAN

The Virgo woman may be a little too difficult for you to understand at first. Her waters run deep. Even when you think you know her, don't take any bets on it. She's capable of keeping things hidden in the deep recesses of her womanly soul—things she'll only release when she's sure that you're the man she's been looking for.

It may take her some time to come around to this decision. Virgo women are finicky about almost everything. Everything has to be letter-perfect before they're satisfied. Many of them have the idea that the only people who can do things right are Virgos.

Nothing offends a Virgo woman more than slovenly dress, sloppy character, or a careless display of affection. Make sure your tie is not crooked and that your shoes sport a bright shine before you go calling on this lady. The typical Sagittarius male should keep the off-color jokes for the locker room. She'll have none of that. Take her arm when crossing the street. Don't rush the romance. Trying to corner her in the back of a cab may be one way of striking out. Never criticize the way she looks. In fact, the best policy would be to agree with her as much as possible.

Still, there's just so much a man can take. All those dos and don'ts you'll have to observe if you want to get to first base with a Virgo may be just a little too much to ask of you. After a few dates, you may come to the conclusion that she just isn't worth all that trouble.

However, the Virgo woman is mysterious enough, generally speaking, to keep her men running back for more. Chances are you'll be intrigued by her airs and graces.

If lovemaking means a lot to you, you'll be disappointed at first in the cool ways of your Virgo partner. However, under her glacial facade there lies a hot cauldron of seething excitement. If you're patient and artful in your romantic approach, you'll find that all that caution was well worth the trouble. When Virgos love, they don't stint. It's all or nothing as far as they're concerned. Once they're convinced that they love you, they go all the way, tossing all cares to the wind.

One thing a Virgo woman can't stand in love is hypocrisy. They don't give a hoot about what the neighbors say if their hearts tell them to go ahead. They're very concerned with human truths. So if their hearts stumble upon another fancy, they will be true to that new heartthrob and leave you standing in the rain.

The Virgo woman is honest to her heart and will be as true to you as you are with her, generally. Do her wrong once, however, and it's farewell.

The Virgo mother has high expectations for her children, and she will strive to bring out the very best in them. They usually turn out just as she hoped, despite her anxiety about health and hygiene, safety and good sense. You must step in and ease her fears when she tries to restrict the kids at play or at school. The Virgo mother is more tender than strict, though, and the children will sense her unconditional love for them.

SAGITTARIUS MAN
LIBRA WOMAN

You'll probably find that the woman born under the sign of Libra is worth more than her weight in gold. She's a woman after your own heart.

With her, you'll always come first—make no mistake about that. She'll always be behind you 100 percent, no matter what you do. When you ask her advice about almost anything, you are likely to get a very balanced and realistic opinion. She is good at thinking things out and never lets her emotions run away with her when clear logic is called for.

As a homemaker she is hard to beat. She is very concerned with harmony and balance. You can be sure she'll make your house a joy to live in. She'll see to it that the home is tastefully furnished and decorated. A Libra cannot stand filth or disarray or noise. Anything that does not radiate harmony, in fact, runs against her orderly grain.

She is chock-full of charm and womanly ways. She can sweep just about any man off his feet with one winning smile. When it comes to using her brains, she can outthink almost anyone and, sometimes, with half the effort. She is diplomatic enough, though, never to let this become glaringly apparent. She may even turn the conversation around so that you think you were the one who did all the brainwork. She couldn't care less, really, just as long as you wind up doing what is right.

The Libra woman will put you up on a pretty high pedestal. You are her man and her idol. She'll leave all the decision making, large or small, up to you. She's not interested in running things and will only offer her assistance if she feels you really need it.

Some find her approach to reason masculine. However, in the areas of love and affection the Libra woman is all woman. She'll literally shower you with love and kisses during your romance with her. She doesn't believe in holding out. You shouldn't, either, if you want to hang onto her.

She is the kind of lover who likes to snuggle up to you in front of the fire on chilly autumn nights, the kind who will bring you breakfast in bed on Sunday. She'll be very thoughtful about anything that concerns you. If anyone dares suggest you're not the grandest guy in the world, she'll give that person what-for. She'll defend you till her dying breath. The Libra woman will be everything you want her to be.

The Libra mother will create a harmonious household in which young family members can grow up as equals. She will foster an environment that is sensitive to their needs. The Libra mother understands that children need both guidance and encouragement. With your enthusiastic input, the youngsters will never lack for anything that could make their lives easier and richer.

SAGITTARIUS MAN
SCORPIO WOMAN

The Scorpio woman can be a whirlwind of passion, perhaps too much passion to suit you casual types. When her temper flies, you'd better lock up the family heirlooms and take cover. When she chooses to be sweet, you're overcome with joy. When she uses sarcasm, she can shock even a blunt Sagittarius.

The Scorpio woman can be as hot as a tamale or as cool as a cucumber, but whatever mood she's in, she's in it for real. She does not believe in posing or putting on airs.

The Scorpio woman is often sultry and seductive. Her femme fatale charme can pierce through the hardest of hearts like a laser ray. She may not look like Mata Hari (quite often Scorpios resemble the tomboy next door) but once she's fixed you with her tantalizing eyes, you're a goner.

Life with the Scorpio woman will not be all smiles and smooth sailing. When prompted, she can unleash a gale of venom. Generally, she'll have the good grace to keep family battles within the walls of your home. When company visits, she's apt to give the impression that married life with you is one great big joyride. It's just one of her ways of expressing her loyalty to you, at least in front of others. She may fight you tooth and nail in the confines of your living room, but at a party or during an evening out, she'll hang onto your arm and have stars in her eyes.

Scorpio women are good at keeping secrets. She may even keep a few buried from you if she feels like it.

Never cross her up on even the smallest thing. When it comes to revenge, she's an eye-for-an-eye woman. She's not one for forgiveness, especially if she feels she's been wronged unfairly. You'd be well-advised not to give her any cause to be jealous, either. When the Scorpio woman sees green, your life will be made far from rosy. Once she's put you in the doghouse, you can be sure that you're going to stay there awhile.

You may find life with a Scorpio woman too draining. Although she may be full of extreme moods, it's quite likely that she's not the kind of woman you'd like to spend the rest of your natural life with. You'd prefer someone gentler and not so hot-tempered, someone who can take the highs with the lows and not complain, someone who is flexible and understanding. A woman born under Scorpio can be heavenly, but she can also be the very devil when she chooses.

The Scorpio mother is protective yet encouraging. The opposites within her nature mirror the very contradictions of life itself. Under her skillful guidance, the children learn how to cope with extremes and grow up to become many-faceted individuals.

SAGITTARIUS MAN
SAGITTARIUS WOMAN

You are in sync with your zodiacal sister born under the sign of Sagittarius. This good-natured gal is full of bounce and good cheer. Her sunny disposition seems almost permanent and can be relied upon even on the rainiest of days.

Women born under the sign of the Archer are almost never malicious. If ever they seem to be, it is only seeming. Sagittarius are often a little short on tact and say literally anything that comes into their heads, no matter what the occasion is. Sometimes the words that tumble out of their mouths seem downright cutting and cruel.

Still, no matter what the Sagittarius woman says, she means well. Lover or spouse, she is quite capable of losing some of your friends through a careless slip of the lip.

On the other hand, you will appreciate her honesty and good intentions. To you, qualities of this sort play an important part in life. With a little patience and practice, you can probably help cure your Sagittarius partner of her loose tongue. In most cases, you both will have to use better judgment, and you both will have to practice what you preach.

Chances are, she'll be the outdoors type of woman who likes sports, recreation, and exercise. Long hikes, fishing trips, and white-water canoeing will most likely appeal to her. She's a busy person. No one could ever call her a slouch. She sets great store in mobility. She won't sit still for one minute if she doesn't have to.

The Sagittarius woman is great company most of the time and, generally, lots of fun. Even if your buddies drop by for poker and beer, she won't have any trouble fitting in.

On the whole, she is a very kind and sympathetic woman. If she feels she's made a mistake, she'll be the first to call your attention to it. She's not afraid to own up to her own faults and shortcomings.

You might lose your patience with her once or twice. After she's seen how upset her shortsightedness or carelessness with money has made you, she'll do her best to straighten up.

The Sagittarius woman is not the kind who will pry into your business affairs. But she'll always be there, ready to offer advice if you need it.

The Sagittarius woman is seldom suspicious. Your word will almost always be good enough for her.

The Sagittarius mother is a wonderful and loving friend to her children. She is not afraid if a youngster learns some street smarts along the way. In fact, both of you Sagittarius parents may compete playfully in teaching the children all about the world from your various and combined experiences. You both will see to it that the kids get the best education and recreation money can buy.

SAGITTARIUS MAN
CAPRICORN WOMAN

If you are not a successful businessman or, at least, on your way to success, it's quite possible that a Capricorn woman will have no interest in entering your life. Generally, she is a very security-minded female. She'll see to it that she invests her time only in sure things.

Men who whittle away their time with one unsuccessful scheme or another seldom attract a Capricorn. Men who are interested in getting somewhere in life and keep their noses close to the grindstone quite often have a Capricorn woman behind them, helping them to get ahead.

Although she can be an opportunist and a social climber, she is not what you could call cruel or hard-hearted. Beneath that cool, seemingly calculating exterior, there is a warm and desirable woman. She happens to think that it is just as easy to fall in love with a rich or ambitious man as it is with a poor or lazy one. She's practical.

The Capricorn woman may be interested in rising to the top, but she'll never be aggressive about it. She'll seldom step on someone's feet or nudge competitors away with her elbows. She's quiet about her desires. She sits, waits, and watches. When an opening or opportunity does appear, she'll latch onto it.

For an on-the-move man, an ambitious Capricorn wife or lover can be quite an asset. She can probably give you some very good advice about business matters. When you invite the boss and his wife for dinner, she'll charm them both and make you look good.

The Capricorn woman is thorough in whatever she does: cooking, cleaning, making a success out of life. Capricorns are excellent hostesses as well as guests. Generally, they are very well-mannered and gracious, no matter what their backgrounds are. They seem to have a built-in sense of what is right. Crude behavior or a careless faux pas can offend them no end.

If you should marry a woman born under Capricorn, you need never worry about her going on a wild shopping spree. Capricorns are careful with every cent that comes into their hands. They understand the value of money better than most women and have no room in their lives for careless spending.

The Capricorn woman is usually very fond of family—her own, that is. With her, family ties run very deep. Don't make jokes about her relatives; she won't stand for it. You'd better check her family out before you get down on bended knee. After your marriage, you'll undoubtedly be seeing a lot of her relatives.

The Capricorn mother is very ambitious for her children. She wants them to have every advantage and to benefit from things she perhaps lacked as a child. She will train her youngsters to be polite and kind and to honor traditional codes of conduct.

SAGITTARIUS MAN
AQUARIUS WOMAN

If you find that you've fallen head over heels for a woman born under the sign of the Water Bearer, you'd better fasten your safety belt. It may take you quite a while actually to discover what this woman is like. Even then, you may have nothing to go on but a string of vague hunches.

Aquarius is like a rainbow, full of bright and shining hues. She's like no other woman you've ever known. There is something elusive about her—something delightfully mysterious. You'll most likely never be able to put your finger on it. It's nothing calculated, either. Aquarius do not believe in phony charm.

There will never be a dull moment in your life with this Water Bearer woman. She seems to radiate adventure and magic. She'll most likely be the most open-minded and tolerant woman you've ever met. She has a strong dislike for injustice and prejudice. Narrow-mindedness runs against her grain.

She is very independent by nature and quite capable of shifting for herself if necessary. She may receive many proposals of marriage from all sorts of people without ever really taking them seriously. Marriage is a very big step for her; she wants to be sure she knows what she's getting into. If she thinks that it will seriously curb her independence and love of freedom, she might return the engagement ring—if indeed she's let the romance get that far.

The line between friendship and romance is a pretty fuzzy one for an Aquarius. It's not difficult for her to remain buddy-buddy with an ex-lover. She's tolerant, remember? So, if you should see her on the arm of an old love, don't jump to any hasty conclusions.

She's not a jealous person herself and doesn't expect you to be, either. You'll find her pretty much of a free spirit most of the time. Just when you think you know her inside out, you'll discover that you don't really know her at all, though.

She's a very sympathetic and warm person. She can be helpful to people in need of assistance and advice.

She'll seldom be suspicious even if she has every right to be. If she loves a man, she'll forgive him just about anything. If he allows himself a little fling, chances are she'll just turn her head the other way. Her tolerance does have its limits, however, and her man should never press his luck.

The Aquarius mother is bighearted and seldom refuses her children anything. Her open-minded attitude is easily transmitted to her youngsters. They have every chance of growing up as respectful and tolerant individuals who feel at ease anywhere. You will appreciate the lessons of justice and equality that your Aquarius mate teaches the children.

SAGITTARIUS MAN
PISCES WOMAN

Many a man dreams of an alluring Pisces woman. You're perhaps no exception. She's soft and cuddly and very domestic. She'll let you be the brains of the family; she's contented to play a behind-the-scenes role in order to help you achieve your goals. The illusion that you are the master of the household is the kind of magic that the Pisces woman is adept at creating.

She can be very ladylike and proper. Your business associates and friends will be dazzled by her warmth and femininity. Although she's a charmer, there is a lot more to her than just a pretty exterior. There is a brain ticking away behind that soft, womanly facade. You may never become aware of it—that is, until you're married to her. It's no cause for alarm, however; she'll most likely never use it against you, only to help you and possibly set you on a more successful path.

If she feels you're botching up your married life through careless behavior or if she feels you could be earning more money than you do, she'll tell you about it. But any wife would, really. She will never try to usurp your position as head and breadwinner of the family.

No one had better dare say one uncomplimentary word about you in her presence. It's likely to cause her to break into tears. Pisces women are usually very sensitive beings. Their reaction to adversity, frustration, or anger is just a plain, good, old-fashioned cry. They can weep buckets when inclined.

She can do wonders with a house. She is very fond of dramatic and beautiful things. There will always be plenty of fresh-cut flowers around the house. She will choose charming artwork and antiques, if they are affordable. She'll see to it that the house is decorated in a dazzling yet welcoming style.

She'll have an extra special dinner prepared for you when you come home from an important business meeting. Don't dwell on the boring details of the meeting, though. But if you need that grand vision, the big idea, to seal a contract or make a conquest, your Pisces woman is sure to confide a secret that will guarantee your success. She is canny and shrewd with money, and once you are on her wavelength you can manage the intricacies on your own.

Treat her with tenderness and generosity and your relationship will be an enjoyable one. She's most likely fond of chocolates. A bunch of beautiful flowers will never fail to make her eyes light up. See to it that you never forget her birthday or your anniversary. These things are very important to her. If you let them slip your mind, you'll send her into a crying fit that could last a considerable length of time.

If you are patient and kind, you can keep a Pisces woman happy for a lifetime. She, however, is not without her faults. Her sensitivity may get on your nerves after a while. You may find her lacking in practicality and good old-fashioned stoicism. You may even feel that she uses her tears as a method of getting her own way.

The Pisces mother has, as you do, great joy and utter faith in the children. She makes a strong, self-sacrificing mother through all the phases from infancy to young adulthood. She will teach her youngsters the value of service to the community while not letting them lose their individuality.

SAGITTARIUS
LUCKY NUMBERS 2000

Lucky numbers and astrology can be linked through the movements of the Moon. Each phase of the thirteen Moon cycles vibrates with a sequence of numbers for your Sign of the Zodiac over the course of the year. Using your lucky numbers is a fun system that connects you with tradition.

New Moon	First Quarter	Full Moon	Last Quarter
Jan. 6	Jan. 14	Jan. 20	Jan. 28
3 6 6 5	2 3 5 7	8 4 8 2	9 6 7 0
Feb. 5	Feb. 12	Feb. 19	Feb. 26
6 3 5 9	9 4 7 4	8 2 5 3	9 1 4 6
March 5	March 13	March 19	March 27
8 8 3 0	7 1 7 2	8 2 5 3	3 6 8 0
April 4	April 11	April 18	April 26
1 5 9 3	3 9 4 7	5 2 8 9	3 5 7 2
May 3	May 10	May 18	May 26
5 6 9 6	6 1 4 2	8 9 8 2	4 6 1 0
June 2	June 8	June 16	June 24
0 8 5 9	9 3 1 7	8 2 8 1	3 7 2 5
July 1	July 8	July 16	July 24
3 2 6 9	9 7 4 5	5 8 1 3	2 6 1 4
July 30	August 6	August 15	August 22
9 5 8 6	6 3 4 7	7 9 2 6	0 0 8 5
August 29	Sept. 5	Sept. 13	Sept. 20
4 3 1 0	7 8 2 4	4 6 1 0	8 5 6 0
Sept. 27	Oct. 5	Oct. 13	Oct. 20
7 2 8 9	9 3 5 7	7 2 6 9	6 1 4 7
Oct. 27	Nov. 4	Nov. 11	Nov. 18
5 2 3 6	6 8 1 5	5 9 3 9	4 7 1 8
Nov. 25	Dec. 3	Dec. 11	Dec. 17
2 6 9 2	2 4 8 0	3 6 3 7	1 8 4 1
Dec. 25	Jan. 2 ('01)	Jan. 9 ('01)	Jan. 17 ('01)
8 3 6 4	2 8 3 6	6 5 1 2	3 5 7 5

SAGITTARIUS
YEARLY FORECAST 2000

*Forecast for 2000 Concerning Business
and Financial Affairs, Job Prospects,
Travel, Health, Romance and Marriage
for Those Born with the Sun
in the Zodiacal Sign of Sagittarius.
November 23–December 20*

For those born under the influence of the Sun in the zodiacal sign of Sagittarius, ruled by Jupiter, the planet of faith and optimism, this is a year of industry and companionship. You are likely to be lighthearted and optimistic as the year 2000 begins. There should be considerable emphasis on your individual fulfillment, personal interests, and hobbies during the first six weeks of the year. Much of your time and energy in later months is likely to go into routine work activities and improving your job prospects. The combination of effort and enthusiasm should ensure your success. Where business matters are concerned, there is more scope this year to expand into foreign territories. Some of your most profitable links could be developed overseas. This can be a favorable year for trying to obtain funding, including venture capital, in order to begin or expand a business. The finance industry itself may hold new opportunities for business investment. It is important to budget carefully right from the start of the year. Otherwise you may be inclined to overspend in the first few months, making it difficult to remain on an even financial keel during the rest of the year. Taking on additional work, or working longer hours, may be necessary in order to enhance your income. With regard to routine occupational affairs, this may be one of your busiest years yet. More work and additional responsibilities are available for the taking. It is up to you to set limits regarding what you can realistically take on. Travel opportunities may be less abundant this year than last, partly due to your time being tied up with routine responsibilities. Nevertheless, you may be able to exploit off-season vacation bargains and your willingness to travel late at night. Your health demands extra attention off and on throughout the year. Excesses are likely to be your greatest enemy. If you can discipline yourself to a regimented routine where sleep, nutrition, and exercise are concerned, problems should be fewer. Your marriage or an ongoing romantic relationship is likely to be the source of much happiness and fulfillment. Both you and your mate or partner stand to benefit from taking a more adventurous approach. For single Sagittarius men and women, opportunities to make new connections with interesting individuals ready for romance and excitement are going to be abundant.

Professional Sagittarius people should focus on exploring in depth the possibilities of expanding into overseas territories this year. If your business has been successful locally or statewide, it may be equally prosperous in another region or country so long as you have the network available to support it. If you are looking to expand into a different business field, consider those relating to publicity, publishing, or travel. Some of these areas may not be as closed off to newcomers as they appear, provided that you have a new or unusual concept to offer. This is the year to look for gaps in markets and holes in the supply links. If you tap into what is missing and act on your hunches, you could start a whole new trend. It is also apt to be worthwhile to work on enhancing your current business reputation and image. A higher profile through advertising or the right public relations input could lead to vastly increasing your turnover, and within a fairly short time. If you need more capital to aid expansion this year, consider a partnership setup, with someone buying into the business. You need to look at all of the legal implications, but this may be a way of branching out in which everyone wins. If you are looking for ways to save money on overheads, investigate alternative employment opportunities. For example, you may be able to gain some financial benefit through hiring staff for more menial tasks through government enterprise initiatives. Changing circumstances which affect your existing network of contacts may at first seem daunting. Try to keep an open mind, however. If your situation obliges you to start looking for new connections, this may turn out to be very beneficial. Venturing into what at first seems alien territory could actually be a move in a far more friendly and profitable direction than you imagine. The most important period for expansion is between March 24 and June 30.

Where finances are concerned, you would be wise to begin the year as you mean to go on. You may think it reasonable to plan to catch up later in the year if you spend beyond your means in the first few months. However, unexpected costs or bills at a later time could disrupt such plans. It would be more prudent to begin on an even keel if you want to remain on one. For some reason this may not be possible; for example, if you have ongoing debts to pay off. You may be able to improve this situation by taking on extra work during the first half of the year. Opportunities to fully employ your talents, and to be paid accordingly, may mean that you are able to clear the deficit faster than you anticipate. It does not have to be a case of more work and more hours. Instead, it could be that you can increase your income by doing the same type of work but for a different company. A large corporation or government agency, for example, would be able to pay more. Another way of economizing this year is to reconsider your membership in certain groups, clubs, or societies. If you belong to a local gym, for example, you could consider off-peak membership if your schedule is flexible enough. Alternatively, you may be able to find a more reasonably priced equivalent to the service or tuition you are paying. Shop around and do not hesitate to accept a scholarship or other assistance. A change in perspective, in terms of what you want out of life, could mean that you start to alter your spending habits this year. You may begin to value a special hobby or other personal interest and want to invest more time and money in it. If the cost of the materials you require is quite high, it may be worthwhile to look at alternatives to purchasing a substantial amount of new equipment outright. Interest-free credit could be a boon in this respect, or you could consider buying certain items secondhand. Try to delay making extensive purchases and also to avoid nonessential expenditure during the period between February 13 and March 23, when you are prone to spend and splurge without advance planning.

In your routine occupational affairs you can anticipate a busy time ahead, particularly during the first six months of the year. Either choice or necessity may incline you to accept greater responsibilities. You may not be working longer hours, but the quality of your work is of paramount importance. Although as a Sagittarius you tend to prefer freedom and spontaneity to rigid plans, you could find it helpful to keep to a tight, set schedule in order to meet your commitments with ease. An erratic approach may cause you to fall behind all too often and have to drive yourself hard at times to keep to deadlines.

With regard to travel, there may be more need to make short, local trips this year. Long-distance and overseas travel is not such a priority. Although you could be eager to take off to other locales, the obligations on your home turf may make it difficult to find the time you need. However, you may be able to benefit from a work-pleasure combination trip even if your spare time comes during periods when it is unorthodox to visit certain destinations. It is possible that you can take advantage of lower fares, for example, in off-peak intervals. Your schedule may also allow for long weekend breaks. If these occasions are likely to arise often, track down literature which gives information on hotels and car rental companies which regularly offer discounts to those traveling for an extended period.

You should experience fewer health problems this year if you are strict about adhering to sensible habits. If you anticipate leading a more hectic lifestyle this year than last, you need to work a little harder to support good health. Erratic working hours, for example, may require compensation in restful and relaxing weekends. Burning the candle at both ends for too long is only asking for trouble. Sagittarius people who work from home would be wise to properly segregate break time from work time. Try to arrange to cook wholesome meals rather than eating junk food at home or making fast-food restaurants your home away from home.

Your romantic prospects for the year ahead are bright, whether you are well entrenched in an ongoing relationship or hoping to meet someone new. If you are single, take advantage of as many opportunities to socialize as you can. You have more chance of meeting someone if you push yourself to mingle in social circles. You do not necessarily have to look for love, but chance encounters are less likely if you closet yourself away. Where marriage or an ongoing relationship is concerned, your connection will tend to be more harmonious if you both take a relaxed attitude. It is important this year to allocate time to simple pleasures, so that you have a chance to truly appreciate one another's company and finer qualities.

SAGITTARIUS
DAILY FORECAST

January–December 2000

JANUARY

1. SATURDAY. Satisfactory. At the start of this new year, security is probably in the forefront of your mind. There is no need to think big or be too ambitious at this stage; take care of the pennies, and the dollars will take care of themselves. Because you have been paying more attention to your health recently, you should now be reaping the benefits. Other people may comment on your improved appearance, encouraging you to continue your efforts to diet and exercise. This fairly quiet day presents an ideal opportunity for doing odd jobs around the house. Your eye for detail is better than usual, so this is a good chance to get more small tasks out of the way.

2. SUNDAY. Excellent. As a Sagittarius you are not usually backward in coming forward, but when it comes to romance it is natural to be hesitant. However in this case you should not hesitate to make a move; it is likely that the other person is only too eager to respond. A social event in the neighborhood enables you to shine. If some guests are not perfectly at ease, it will be a pleasure for you to draw them into conversation and into the swing of things. Youngsters can be rather bored, and it can be a challenge to find an activity that engages them fully. Try to stimulate their imagination rather than using television as a babysitter.

3. MONDAY. Sensitive. Your colleagues are bound to have holiday tales to tell. Even if these interfere with your working time, it would be kind and enjoyable to listen. Good relationships at work ensure the best efficiency; if you are in a position of responsibility, do not be too eager to crack the whip. This is a good day for presenting written material. Sagittarius students can prepare essays without a qualm as long as research has been done thoroughly. Where romance is concerned, the least hint of criticism from you is apt to provoke an extreme reaction in your mate or partner. Be sure to think before you open your mouth. Words said in anger will be long remembered.

4. TUESDAY. Buoyant. You should be positively sparkling with ideas, but if they are not written down quickly they are almost bound to disappear. If your career involves selling, you should come across as more persuasive so long as you believe totally in what you are offering. For once there is no harm in letting your enthusiasm have full rein. Travel over a short distance can reveal surprises. A detour could take you through an area that you never knew existed, even though it may be close to home; make a resolution to come back and explore at leisure. Looking around your home, you are likely to notice changes and improvements that need to be made.

5. WEDNESDAY. Challenging. All creative work is favored. If you are working on personal projects, you should be able to push them ahead a stage or two. Try not to miss any opportunity to improve your talents and creative techniques. All advances made now will pay off later in the year. Romantically speaking, you should be walking on air. If a new affair seems almost too good to be true, there is no point worrying about the future; just enjoy it day by day. There is some extra money to be made from work that can be done at home. This would give your personal finances a timely boost, enabling you to buy a special item.

6. THURSDAY. Useful. If a colleague seems to be struggling, you can afford to lend a hand. Your light touch is just what is needed to enable them to finish off a tedious task. You are probably well aware that cutting down on rich foods is doing you a lot of good. Although you are bound to have lapses, these are not important if you stick to the overall plan of healthier eating. A greater sense of self-confidence can be gained from focusing on the small achievements of everyday life that are often overlooked. Not all brave or generous acts are obvious to other people. Give yourself full credit for moments of quiet courage.

7. FRIDAY. Disconcerting. Money is apt to be causing you a few headaches. Your naturally spontanous Sagittarius spirit sees no reason to hold back on spending when you feel like it. However, if you do not have sufficient income to support this habit, a day of reckoning is bound to come. Unfortunately a new romantic affair does not seem to be living up to its initial promise. Fools rush in where angels fear to tread, and it is likely that you jumped into this situation without considering how it was likely to develop. If you are playing a sport, try not to get too carried away. A sense of discipline is vital if you want to avoid a small injury and go on to victory.

8. SATURDAY. Mixed. It may be rather difficult to wake up this morning. Your dreams may seem vivid and haunting. Write them down if you can remember significant fragments; they are apt to have an important message. Loved ones are likely to get irritated when you just do not hear what they say. This is not the best time to be making plans because you keep drifting off into a world of private fantasy. Trips around the neighborhood can be curiously unproductive. If you go shopping locally, you will probably find you have spent a lot but have little to show for it. Revive the romance in a long-term partnership with a candlelit meal for two and a special night out on the town.

9. SUNDAY. Unsettling. Sometimes other people see you as rather manipulative, even though you are probably not aware of this yourself. However, turning on the charm to get your own way is really not satisfactory; allow each person to make a free decision. There is a chance of losing a favorite piece of jewelry when you are out socially. Check before you leave to home to be sure that fastenings are secure. Youngsters should be kept away from electrical equipment as much as possible. Their natural curiosity can lead them to be quite destructive, and there is also the danger of receiving a minor shock. A change of habit would probably do you a lot of good.

10. MONDAY. Variable. The workweek gets off to quite a promising start as a letter brings good news from a loved one. Do not put off replying; your good intentions are not enough. Neighbors can be helpful when it comes to getting a leisure project off the ground. Ask around and you will probably find someone with the necessary expertise who is more than happy to help out. Unfortunately there could be an argument brewing at home. Basically you and your mate or partner are not at odds, yet you seem determined to magnify small differences of opinion. Ask yourself just why you seem to enjoy fighting so much. Extra care is needed when working around the house.

11. TUESDAY. Manageable. Make the most of the early part of the day by concentrating on tasks you usually avoid. Routine maintenance of your home and health is never among your favorite occupation but is a necessity of life. The way a love affair is going could tempt you to cut your losses and end it. However, doing so will only leave you with a nagging sense of unfulfilled potential; have the courage to face the problems and solve them. Family relationships are not usually straightforward, and it is impossible not to get irritated from time to time. Try to be patient with parents and other older people, even if they are being intrusive into your affairs.

12. WEDNESDAY. Successful. After a long period of waiting, you finally have a chance to move ahead in your chosen career. No matter that the first step is only a small one; once you take it, the way ahead will be that much clearer. A long-term minor ailment can respond to treatment all the better if you stick to the recommended regime. This is one of those occasions where it would be foolish to claim that you know best. Love may strike like lightning, giving you no hesitation about declaring your feelings. Even if this relationship is short, it is going to be sweet and could open your eyes to a whole new way of looking at the world.

13. THURSDAY. Good. Although it may not be obvious to outsiders, there has been quite a change in your home life. The value of sensitivity to each other's needs is becoming obvious, leading to a better and more caring atmosphere. There is little to stand in your way if you are determined to embark on a course of self-development. All that is necessary is to find a method that is challenging enough to keep your interest through less exciting periods. Short-distance travel presents few problems, so there is no need to get upset or uptight. You will reach your destination all the quicker for not hurrying. Allow youngsters freedom of expression during a family discussion.

14. FRIDAY. Uncertain. It is not always easy to understand what other people mean if they are reluctant to explain themselves. Right now loved ones may be unwilling or unable to say what they mean, leaving you with the task of trying to interpret their wishes. Financially it is vital to trust your own judgment. Friends who appear to know what they are doing could give you a tip for making a lucrative investment, but they may not really be as knowledgeable as they claim. You can make a good impression on a new acquaintance by taking a bit of extra effort with your appearance. It might even be worthwhile buying a new outfit if you are going out with a group this weekend.

15. SATURDAY. Cautious. As a Sagittarius you usually find it quite hard to knuckle down to responsibility, but there are occasions when it is unavoidable. Family needs now require you to take control of a situation which must be handled with kid gloves. Slow down and do not feel you have to provide an instant solution. Household chores are likely to occupy more time than usual; this is what happens when they are allowed to pile up. Get to them with a will and do a thorough job; at least in that way you will be able to ignore them again for a while. Youngsters may give you little chance to have time to yourself, but try to enjoy a quiet hour or two with your mate or steady partner.

16. SUNDAY. Unpredictable. You may just not know where you stand as far as romance is concerned. Someone is drawing you closer on one hand while claiming they are unwilling to get into a relationship. All you can do is try to figure out based on your own feelings what is happening. Beware of making promises you do not intend to keep or will not be able to fulfill. They will be remembered when you have long forgotten them, and if you are not careful you could begin to get a reputation for unreliability. Some concentrated thought should show you a new way to improve your income. Failing this, there is nothing to do but cut down on your current spending.

17. MONDAY. Demanding. Be prepared to be thrown right into the thick of things this morning. There is an especially difficult task awaiting you, but it is tailor-made for your particular talents. Even though this is likely to be rough going for a while, there should be plenty of personal satisfaction to be gained. If you are shopping for a new home, you probably need to lower your sights a little. If you start looking for a more modest house, there will be more and better choice. Financially there could be a struggle going on between common sense and overoptimism. It is clear which side you favor, but right now you cannot afford to take a risk that could turn out badly.

18. TUESDAY. Changeable. There is a possibility of a real improvement in a long-term partnership as you finally realize the need to talk over a problem. Just getting to the position of facing the fact that all is not well is half the battle. Be brave and you will come out of this situation with a renewed sense of togetherness. A business proposal may appear quite revolutionary at first. However, it would be wise to check this out thoroughly before acting on it. Now more than ever it is important to realize that you can alienate potential partners or clients by being too frank.

The truth can hurt, so it is important to state it gently to people who are less resilient than yourself.

19. WEDNESDAY. Disconcerting. A vein of anger may be running through family matters at the moment. Once you become aware of it, it is up to you to find out just what is bothering a loved one. It is not like you to be nostalgic, but sometimes regret for the past threatens to overwhelm your more positive feelings. There is nothing to be done but brace up and put this sadness out of mind, since it will only blight your day if you succumb to it. Happily a relative is willing to help out if you need a lump sum of cash quickly. Just do not forget you are under an obligation to repay them. Make sure you lock up securely tonight if you are going out.

20. THURSDAY. Disquieting. There is apt to be a lot of emotion boiling under the surface where a love affair is concerned. You may be tempted to try to ignore it for the sake of peace, but until it is brought out into the open the relationship is unlikely to develop any further. Try not to use joint savings, even if you and your mate or partner both think it is necessary to do so. It will take a long time to restore your bank balance. Instead, put your heads together and see if you can come up with another solution to the problem. Youngsters' schooling is spotlighted. There may be a few questions you want to ask their teachers or principal. Keep in mind you know the children best.

21. FRIDAY. Deceptive. A brother or sister may be determined to protect you from an unpalatable truth. Although they are acting from the best motive, this secretiveness is bound to irritate you. Since it has become clear that there is something in the air, it might be necessary to point out that you have every right to be told what is going on. Be extra careful if driving; there is a strong possibility of a mechanical fault developing that could lead to delay. Sometimes you can be so preoccupied you risk running out of gas. This is not the best time to be planning a vacation with loved ones. More discussion is needed to settle on a really special destination.

22. SATURDAY. Happy. All seems to be going well romantically speaking. It is unlikely that you will be tempted to rock the boat since the positive aspects of the relationship far outweigh any minor drawbacks. Leisure activities are highlighted; postpone or ignore the household chores and concentrate on enjoying yourself. This might even be a good time to take up a new hobby that allows you more artistic expression. Trips are likely to be disrupted in some way. You may not even reach your planned destination, but as long as everyone is relaxed and happy together that might not bother you too much. Go with the flow, and make the most of what comes your way.

23. SUNDAY. Favorable. News from or about someone you met abroad could come via a friend. What they say is apt to please you, and it will be with good reason that you look forward to meeting again. An interest in more serious subjects need not mean you become bookish or dull. As a Sagittarius you thrive on broadening your outlook, so being drawn into exploring various beliefs and philosophical ideas can only enrich your life. Later in the day you may be inclined to concentrate on making plans to further your ambitions. It is not enough to have a grand aim; it is vital to work out the details of how you intend to take the first few steps.

24. MONDAY. Demanding. Starting the workweek in a rather vague mood is not of great help when it comes to impressing other people. However, for some reason you may just not be interested enough to pull out all the stops. If you miss an opportunity to win favor, you only have yourself to blame. If you are engaged in creative writing, this can be quite a useful day. Look within yourself for a storehouse of imagery that will appeal to a broad audience. Youngsters may not quite be hitting the mark at school. It might be a good idea to have a quiet word with them and find out if there is anything wrong, such as other children being troublesome or bullying.

25. TUESDAY. Changeable. It is not what you say but the way that you say it that often counts. Right now you may be letting negative emotions get in the way so that even a positive statement comes out as a discouraging comment. Buck up and do not impose your own feelings on undeserving other people. A marked reluctance to settle down to routine tasks could mean you are still struggling to complete phone calls at the end of the day. It is usually a sound plan to tackle the least appealing tasks first, so that you can spend more time later concentrating on work you enjoy. To brighten up the day, you need a good evening out with a compatible group of friends.

26. WEDNESDAY. Fortunate. This is an excellent day to make short journeys in regard to business matters. Try to schedule visits locally, where there is every chance of achieving your aims. Although you are not normally one for letter writing, now you have probably come to the conclusion that certain thoughts and feelings are best expressed on paper. This is not a bad idea, because in this way you give the recipient time to mull over what is on your mind and frame a reasonable reply. The continuing process of learning keeps most people young; remember that you are never too old to begin studying whatever engages your interest. A friend who needs support will be grateful for your help.

27. THURSDAY. Sensitive. You run the risk of losing a friendship due to arguing about a love interest. It is important to bear in mind that the love affair may not last long, whereas the friendship can be for life. Where future hopes and wishes are concerned, it is not possible to have your cake and eat it, too. One or another project will have to be put off if you really want to get results. Spread your energies too thin and nothing will be attained. It may be a waste of time to suggest that you have been spending too freely on leisure pursuits recently. However, try to bear this in mind if you receive invitations to expensive social events; you cannot attend all of them.

28. FRIDAY. Unsettling. Before you realize it, you could have said something that cuts right to the bone with a loved one. Once words have been uttered they cannot be recalled. The more accurate your observation the more it is bound to hurt, so try to hold your tongue. If you are in charge of youngsters, you will have your work cut out to keep them under supervision. They are like little balls of quicksilver, and mischief will be done if you turn your back for only a few seconds. No matter what you may think, there is still hope of a new romance getting off the ground. The other person may be playing hard to get, but probably they just intend to intrigue you.

29. SATURDAY. Mixed. Find some time to rummage through closets or drawers that you have been meaning to clear out for ages. Now is a good time to summon the energy for a really thorough purge of old and unwanted items. You will probably be happiest staying quietly with loved ones. Everyone needs a break from even close friends from time to time. In addition, there are loose ends to be tied up in personal and joint plans which you can now attend to. Much can be picked up from a tone of voice, quite apart from the words that are being said. Listen carefully if a relative seems to be upset; there are plenty of clues to be garnered as to the deeper reasons for their apparent disquiet.

30. SUNDAY. Satisfactory. There may seem to be little point yearning for perfection when it appears so difficult to achieve. However, the higher you aim the further you are likely to get, so do not listen to those who are trying to dissuade you from an ambitious personal plan. This is a good day for wandering quietly around the neighborhood to keep in touch with local people. As a Sagittarius you are enough of an idealist to believe that small groups of people can do a lot to help each other. If you dabble in writing or art you should find inspiration coming from quite mundane sources. Part of your skill lies in transforming reality into a much more magical vision.

31. MONDAY. Frustrating. A superior at work may certainly not seem to be impressed by a recent report you submitted. Now there may be a demand to put in more work, which you really cannot dispute. Expressing your opinion to loved ones is all very well, but there is a fine line between being articulate and being forceful. More arguments are won by proving a point through action; if you live up to your ideals, there is little other people can say to criticize. Changing even a few small details of your appearance can have quite a positive effect. Try combing your hair slightly differently or opting for a new hairstyle, then see how the compliments begin to flood in from friends and loved ones.

FEBRUARY

1. TUESDAY. Challenging. You can do yourself a lot of good if you just have the confidence to freely and openly express your ideas. You have something uniquely your own to contribute, and there should be no doubt in your mind that your ideas are just what is needed for an important project. This is one of those times when someone close to you seems to know just what you need to improve your lifestyle. The answer was probably staring you in the face; you just needed it to be pointed out. For once it is acceptable to be rather pushy when trying to get a point across. After all, your audience's understanding has its limits, and you may have to clarify your argument and restate your views in numerous ways.

2. WEDNESDAY. Rewarding. It is not always the most flamboyant acts that give the most satisfaction. Right now it seems that some work undertaken to help out a colleague is about to receive praise and recognition. A rather uncharacteristic mood of modesty may tempt you to play this down, but you should not hide your light under a bushel on this occasion. At last you are about to reap the benefits from being a little more careful in balancing your budget. The small sacrifices you have made now seem worthwhile, with money in the bank for an important occasion. A romantic affair can give you a sense of security even though it does not scale the heights of passion.

3. THURSDAY. Productive. Roll up your sleeves and vow to make a real dent in your domestic chores. There is much to be done in preparation for some intense work on your home, and you can make a good beginning today. Sagittarius people who are self-employed could probably earn more by putting in some extra hours. In fact, the work is likely to interest you so much that this is no problem at all. A family event can increase the sense of solidarity between relatives. For once there are no slackers, with everyone happy to contribute to make a gathering a really special occasion. Enjoy a quiet evening at home after this more hectic than usual day.

4. FRIDAY. Tricky. If you can pick your way through some minor problems, the day holds the promise of success. Beware, however, of hitches in communication. It is all too possible that there will be misunderstandings and that a vital appointment could be missed. There is no point playing the victim if a colleague appropriates a plan that you originated. You will not be able to live with yourself if you let them get away with it; face up to them and demand to be properly credited. It is up to you to say the right word in order to begin a new romance. Being sincere is most important; any hint of flattery will be picked up immediately and rejected.

5. SATURDAY. Variable. Take advantage of the chance to make a new start with a brother or sister. If you have had disagreements in the past, bury the hatchet and become friends once again. The focus this morning is on local trips. Get your shopping out of the way in the early part of the day. You could be surprised to find a new store that caters to a particular interest of yours. If you rush around too much you will just exhaust yourself. Stop for a while and consider whether you used to have more energy; if the answer is yes, it is a clear sign you must start taking better care of your health. An unusual night out with friends can give you a glimpse of new horizons.

6. SUNDAY. Unsettling. Someone within your family who has the power to upset you seems determined to do just that. If you rise to their provocation, there is no telling where this will end.

Try to keep your cool, difficult though it may be. A special trip with loved ones deserves to be recorded for posterity. It is all too easy to miss the subtle changes in youngsters when they grow up so quickly, so make sure you have a camera or camcorder to capture some precious moments. Romantically speaking, you may be in something of a quandary at the moment because while you value being independent, you may lose out on love by insisting on doing everything your way.

7. MONDAY. Mixed. A mood of quiet resolution helps you settle down to the new workweek. There is nothing like getting a challenging task out of the way to give you a sense of achievement. Pets can sometimes be more of a responsibility than you might want, but on the whole you probably would not choose to be without them. However, there is no reason you should be the only person in the family who looks after them. This is a good time to insist that others share the work. Moving can be very disruptive, and even the prospect of doing so is likely to bring up all kinds of reactions. It may help to realize that some nostalgia is inevitable.

8. TUESDAY. Uncertain. It is natural to feel protective toward loved ones, but sometimes they are not in the mood to be coddled. Recognize that they need some freedom to make their own mistakes, painful though it may be for you to watch them doing so. There is a danger of a small but annoying accident if you are using tools at home. Be extra cautious when performing intricate tasks; be sure to wear suggested protection. Financially this can be quite a good time as it becomes clear that you have made a sound investment and it is now beginning to pay off. If you are entertaining guests tonight, pamper them a little. They will appreciate small touches of luxury.

9. WEDNESDAY. Favorable. The stage is set for romance. Even if you do not go out looking for it, there is every likelihood that it will find you. Make sure you look your best; an attractive person could appear in your life at any moment. This is also a promising period for all types of creative work. It may be possible to find an outlet where you could show and even sell the products of your particular talent. Everyday tasks can take on an air of excitement if you put a little extra thought into them. Dare to be different; break the mold for once. You have nothing to lose and everything to gain by standing out from the crowd.

10. THURSDAY. Fair. This promises to be quite a sociable time. You should be raring to meet some unusual types of people, and a new acquaintance could give you the chance to do so. Just do not be shy and back out at the last minute. Youngsters are probably getting a lot of enjoyment out of learning at the moment. You would be foolish not to capitalize on this by augmenting their education at home or planning educational trips for when they are not in school. Sagittarius people who are romantically involved need to proceed cautiously with the affair. Although the affection between you and your significant other is a strong bond, your aims may be out of sync.

11. FRIDAY. Disconcerting. Small chores may be more of a challenge than bigger tasks. You forgetful mood can make it all but impossible for you to concentrate on details. If you are cooking something special during the day, it would be a good idea to double-check each stage of the recipe; otherwise there is a good chance that some vital ingredient will be left out. Journeys in the neighborhood could be plagued with delays, so allow ample time to get to appointments or to pick up children. Where romance is concerned, you cannot afford to take too much for granted. The other person in your life may not be feeling the same as you but choose not to talk about it.

12. SATURDAY. Useful. Just when you need it most, a friend or a family member is on hand to give you a few financial tips. You may now begin to appreciate that the older generation has been around and has had the chance to garner more life experience, even if their views are not always in complete harmony with yours. Give your body a treat by getting a relaxing massage or a health club workout. In this demanding world it's easy to get overstressed without even realizing it. There is no need to be a martyr and struggle to finish household chores alone; there are other family members around who just need a bit of prodding to get them to help out. Buy a loved one a gift they have been talking about for a long time.

13. SUNDAY. Stressful. It is said that a picture is worth a thousand words, but sometimes actions can be even more eloquent when it is hard to find the right thing to say. Make your point to a loved one by showing them what you mean; this will be far more effective than arguing. It is usually not wise to pry into the affairs of other people; you may be finding this out right now. Basically you simply do not have the right to invade another person's privacy, no matter what the excuse. Sagittarius singles who are on the lookout for romance do not need to look very far. There is an opportunity right in front of you; all you have to do is make a move before someone else does.

14. MONDAY. Uncertain. You are apt to be in something of a quandary when a business associate puts you on the spot for a decision. This is one of those tricky situations in which you probably cannot avoid upsetting one side or the other. It would be a sound plan to bargain for more time to mull over the pros and cons. You have the power to hurt loved ones if you continue to carry on the way you are doing. Everyone needs some freedom and autonomy, but the essence of a relationship is a good measure of give-and-take. This is not the best moment to buy any item for the house; your judgment is not as sound as usual and you could soon regret your purchase. Go to bed earlier than usual tonight.

15. TUESDAY. Successful. If you have a contract due to be wrapped up, hurry it along so that it can be signed and sealed as soon as possible. It should not be difficult to agree on terms that suit both parties, so be a bit pushy if necessary. Sagittarius people who are involved in legal matters could benefit from obtaining a second opinion. This could throw new light on the matter and give you a fresh sense of optimism. Financial matters may not entrance you at the moment. However, if you spend a little time sorting out details, it should be possible to arrange quite a satisfactory budget or pension plan. It is not too soon to start considering your future security and the retirement income you will need.

16. WEDNESDAY. Easygoing. You and your mate or partner should be in harmony when it comes to sharing responsibility. It can be quite comforting to slip into a routine where each of you knows exactly what is expected. The only important point is remembering that it is vital to make some changes from time to time. Bricks and mortar can be an excellent investment. Even if you have been dragging your feet over buying a property, it might pay to begin thinking a little more seriously about it. You do not have to be too ambitious; even a small home can increase in value over the years. A family member could tell you the details of an event which affected your childhood and still influences you.

17. THURSDAY. Disquieting. You may have to face up to the fact that a romantic affair just is not going to develop the way you would like. You cannot expect to enjoy close emotional bonding without an element of commitment; indeed, it is unfair to the other person to string them along in this way. Financially, things are not as secure as you would like. Every time you manage to build up some savings they seem to dissolve away. You need to be more severe with yourself to avoid unnecessary spending. Consider signing up for a new course of study; as a Sagittarius you are happiest when learning something new and exciting or when sharing your special knowledge and talents.

18. FRIDAY. Variable. No matter how much you try, it may seem impossible to do the right thing at work. It might be better to stop trying to please other people and just go your own way; that may be what they wanted all along. There is no doubt that extra money can be earned, but it is up to you to decide whether you are prepared to humble yourself to accomplish quite a demeaning task. This could lead you to do some serious thinking about your priorities, especially how important material possessions are when set against personal satisfaction. Romance should be delightful, even if it is little more than a light flirtation. An evening with friends may bring someone new into your life.

19. SATURDAY. Demanding. The weekend brings something of a challenge as your partner puts their cards on the table and demands that you make a decision. It is no use trying to procrastinate this time; there is a lot at stake and you have to sort out once and for all just how important this relationship is to you. A certain amount of tension is always generated when loved ones pull in the opposite direction from what you want to do for the day. Some compromise is necessary, but it may take a while to work this out. Try to get some exercise; good health demands that you improve your fitness level. Exercise does not have to be painful, just pleasurably tiring.

20. SUNDAY. Tricky. You have a choice to make: although you want to be out and about, there is a lot of work to be done at home. It would be possible to manage both, but if you attempt to cram too much into the day you will only wear yourself out and not enjoy any activity very much. As a Sagittarius you usually do not have much of a problem when it comes to asserting yourself. Occasionally, however, you meet someone who is able to overwhelm you. Bear in mind that you are just as good as the next person, and do not allow yourself to be bullied in any way. Arguments with loved ones are all but inevitable if you refuse to even listen to each other's point of view.

21. MONDAY. Quiet. The workweek is unlikely to get off to a flying start. If you have a new project in mind, it might be wise to put it off for a while. Begin now and you are almost bound to encounter resistance and misunderstandings that will complicate matters unnecessarily. If you are waiting for money in the mail, you might want to make a call just to check that it is actually on the way. There is a strong possibility that it has not been sent for some reason. This is a good period for taking time to get papers in order and to do little jobs that get put aside in busier times. You are unlikely to be interrupted, so make the most of this quietly productive period.

22. TUESDAY. Frustrating. When someone tries to tell you their feelings, it is not always easy to figure out exactly what they mean. Embarrassment can lead them to give quite the wrong impression, and you may end up having to use your intuition to come to an understanding. This is a good day for writing letters for pleasure rather than business. It can be all too easy to drift out of touch with friends and relatives who live at a distance. Social events are likely to be enjoyable, but make sure you do not overindulge. When drink flows free and you are having a good time, it is possible to take a glass too many without even realizing what you are doing.

23. WEDNESDAY. Challenging. You have no excuse not to speak up in a meeting if a subject that is close to your heart comes up and needs a defender. Happily you should have facts and figures at your fingertips, so that it is possible to make an impressive case. Sagittarius people who have been thinking about getting involved in a political cause may be on the point of taking the plunge. It would certainly be satisfying to be active and to feel that you are working for something you believe in and can make the world a better place. Friends can be a great support through times of change. There is no reason to be shy about asking for their help when you need it.

24. THURSDAY. Disquieting. After a long effort to improve your fitness and general health, you may have to admit that not much progress has been made. However, if you stop to think about it, you will realize that only you are to blame because your attempts have only been sporadic and half-hearted, even though you are well aware that sustained effort is necessary. If a colleague has given you a great deal of help recently, it would be extremely ungrateful for you to take continued assistance for granted. It could be a nice gesture to take them out for a meal or show your appreciation with a small gift. A lost item is bound to show up around the house, but you may have to do without it for a while.

25. FRIDAY. Disconcerting. If you are trying to get finished up for the end of the week, disappointment is in store. It is almost certain that you will have to leave loose ends hanging because some of your work depends on other people who are not as conscientious as you. It is rather late to realize that you have misplaced trust in someone who is really only out for themselves. Possibly the best way to react is to face the situation squarely and not give them the satisfaction of seeing that you have been hurt in any way. A loved one can help you break a habit which you have not been able to overcome by your own efforts. They will keep you to the mark if you waver.

26. SATURDAY. Happy. A conspiracy may be afoot to keep a friend in the dark, but it is entirely for a good reason. When other friends ask you to take part in preparing a special surprise, get into the swing with gusto. This is a good time to pluck up courage and propose if you have been trying to bring yourself to this point for some time. A traditionally romantic setting would be ideal, so see what you can arrange. Sagittarius women may want to start cultivating a softer, more dreamy image. Long flowing skirts and pastel colors can be pleasant to wear on informal social occasions. Avoid wearing black.

27. SUNDAY. Enjoyable. There is nothing standing in your way if you are looking for a romantic fling. When you meet a new person at a party, the immediate attraction may leave neither of you in any doubt that you want to spend some time together. Sagittarius people who have a creative hobby should be able to work at it with enthusiasm. Put caution aside and let feeling win out over technique; the results could give you a whole new direction in your work. If you put your mind to it, there is very little you cannot achieve when it comes to personal ambition. It is just important to be wholehearted in pursuing your aim.

28. MONDAY. Exciting. Even those who believe that love has passed on by could be in for a dramatic and delightful surprise today. Someone has been admiring you from a distance for some time and now cannot contain their feelings any longer. A new mood of determination makes it possible for you to turn a favorite hobby into a moneymaker. It is likely to be a labor-intensive business, but as long as you continue to enjoy what you are doing that should not be a worry. There is no need to be hasty when on the roads. Travel conditions should be good, so ease up a little and let someone else be first away from the light for a change.

29. TUESDAY. Challenging. Your responsibilities at work may be increased for a short period, which will be a good test of your abilities. Take this seriously; your performance could stand you in good stead when there is a chance for promotion. Being impatient with loved ones only makes an explosive situation worse. You know so well just what to say in order to rile them, but you must resist the temptation to do so. Sometimes silence can be golden when it comes to protecting a friend from news they would rather not know. Of course it will be necessary to reveal it at some point, but wait for a suitable time and place. A trip can open new doors for you.

MARCH

1. WEDNESDAY. Fair. A vast majority of problems within a family can be cleared up if only those involved are willing to talk and to compromise. You can play your part in this by encouraging interaction, perhaps taking the initiative and beginning the discussion yourself. Sagittarius people who are moving should be able to make most of the arrangements. At last it seems that negotiations are proceeding fairly smoothly, so you should feel slightly more confident that all will go as planned. Keep a close eye on your personal finances for a while. Just monitoring your spending can be illuminating, and sometimes rather surprising. Challenge yourself to plan ahead.

2. THURSDAY. Useful. You can be of great assistance to a relative who is having difficulties. Your advantage is that you have been through a similar situation and come out all right; offering this encouragement and support is probably as valuable as practical advice. A small legacy for which you have been waiting so long you almost forgot about it is at last likely to come through. The time lag may actually have been useful, giving you the chance to think over carefully just how the money can be put to best use. Try to resist the temptation to rush through any job; hasty work will be noticed and you may only have to do it all over again. Consider adding extra security measures at home.

3. FRIDAY. Exacting. Sometimes it is inevitable that you argue with loved ones, but on this occasion you probably will recognize that your behavior has been unreasonable. It is all very well expecting other people to toe the line up to a certain point, but it shows a lack of respect to become dictatorial. Try to reduce your demands and lower your expectations. This is not the best time to contemplate a complete change of image. Although you might feel it is appropriate to cultivate an air of stern authority, it will sit rather uneasily with your natural good spirits and spontaneity. It does not pay to worry about negative criticism that is unjustified, even though it may be difficult to shrug off.

4. SATURDAY. Sensitive. As a Sagittarius you dislike being tied down in a relationship. Secretly, however, a part of you enjoys it when someone cares enough about you to want all of your attention. Do your best to acknowledge this, and do not continue to insist on your freedom as if that were the whole truth. There is no use thinking you can charm your way into the good graces of a neighbor who is genuinely upset about a thoughtless act. It would be more generous to admit that you were careless, and apologize. If youngsters seem a little upset, a few extra hugs are in order. They might be feeling insecure and just need to be reassured that your love and affection is there for them.

5. SUNDAY. Favorable. This is a good day for doing tasks around the home. A rare burst of enthusiasm will make light work of even mundane tasks. There is no reason to go on leading a sedentary life when sports and health centers are available in most localities. Buy some new fitness gear and make a resolution to spend part of every weekend exercising. If thoughts of a distant relative pop into your head, you could feel a sudden urge to get in touch with them. Do not put this off; call right away and see how delighted they are to hear from you. Entertaining guests should be effortless, since they will all be eager to converse and share stories.

6. MONDAY. Good. If you have been determined to break an old habit and institute new ways of working, begin today and you stand every chance of success. There is a feeling of spring and fresh beginnings in the air, giving you extra energy to tackle life and its challenges. A business deal that has been dragging on for some time could be brought to a satisfactory conclusion, which is likely to be a great relief for all concerned. You have earned a rest before embarking on the next project. Normally a collection does not appeal to Sagittarius people, but a recent gift of a fine antique could arouse your enthusiasm to start looking for more items from a similar era.

7. TUESDAY. Exciting. If romance is on your mind, you probably have a hunch that there is someone special just around the corner. This is one occasion when you should not be too shy to take a chance; there seems to be no doubt about the other person's attraction to you. Creatively this promises to be a very stimulating day. If you can work without delay on ideas as they come up, so much the better. One thought breeds another, and the more spontaneous you can be the further you will be able to develop the process. Going to lunch with friends can have a surprising result as gossip reveals useful information that could improve your long-term finances or reduce current expenses.

8. WEDNESDAY. Fair. Recently you may have been feeling a strong urge to make a basic change in your life. Being a Sagittarius, the first thing you probably think of is getting away from it all. Actually, however, the need for change is within yourself, and right now you could begin to realize that there are ways of living a more satisfying and creative life. Romance can be more important than usual. Someone may enter your life who can have a profound effect on the way you think. At first this might not be obvious, but little by little you will find you are being drawn closer together. Do not take out a moment of bad temper on youngsters or others who look up to you.

9. THURSDAY. Buoyant. At last you should be able to tackle the idea of making sweeping changes at home. Your mate or partner will be pleased that you are ready to go along with their wishes and start on redecoration. Just make sure you do not duck out of your share of the work once it has begun. Where love is concerned, a more gentle and sensitive approach will work wonders. Everyone is allowed to be sentimental from time to time, so if you feel like succumbing to the lure of hearts and flowers, do so without embarrassment. Be aware of a tendency to overdo on the health front. There is no need to go to extremes with a new diet or exercise regimen.

10. FRIDAY. Slow. As the week draws to a close, it may feel a little as though you are wading through mud. Simple tasks may be almost too much to cope with, a sign that you have probably been pushing yourself too hard once again. The health of a pet could be causing you a few worries. If the animal seems to be under the weather, a visit to the vet might be in order just in case something more serious develops. This is a good time to insist that youngsters take a more active interest in caring for pets; there is a lot they can learn in this way. Travel is not without problems; getting worked up will not help at all. If your car is due for servicing, do not put it off any longer.

11. SATURDAY. Sensitive. Your loved ones are apt to be particularly sensitive, making it rather difficult to get through the day's chores. Since you may not be able to hit the right note, it might be best just to go your own way and wait for them to calm down. There is not much point looking for help with a practical task from family members who are set on having a good time. Even if you insist, they will only give you assistance grudgingly, so that you might wish you had not bothered. If you are entertaining at home this evening, some extra effort is needed to make it all go smoothly. Friction between you and your mate or partner should not be allowed to surface in front of your guests.

12. SUNDAY. Fair. You should be feeling quite confident about the way a romantic affair is developing, and rightly so. What is magical about this particular relationship is the mental rapport, which gives you both an understanding of each other that you can build upon during the time ahead. This is one of those days when you might have to swallow your own wishes and let loved ones have their way. As long as you do not harbor any negative feelings of resentment, there is no reason an enjoyable time should not be had by all. Meeting some new people could bring back an element of excitement into a long-term partnership, giving you new subjects to discuss.

13. MONDAY. Pleasant. A business associate may be eager to propound a new idea for expanding your aims. This person could be on to something both practical and profitable, so keep an open mind. Some tension between you and a loved one could spoil the day if you let it prey on your mind. Instead of doing so, make a phone call to sort matters out and leave you free to concentrate on other concerns. Future security is on the agenda at the moment. It would not be a bad idea to look into ways of making the most from joint savings. Your financial adviser should be able to help you tally up your assets so that you know exactly where you stand and what you can afford to invest.

14. TUESDAY. Productive. At last it is possible to press ahead with an important personal plan. If you have worked hard to overcome initial obstacles, you deserve to be pleased with yourself. This is likely to be quite a busy day. The mail may be heavier than usual, and there could be a lot that needs to be dealt with immediately. There could even be one or two bills you have forgotten about. You can do some useful work researching new ways of organizing your time; there are studies available that can give you some creative ideas. Improve your emotional and physical health by learning not to scatter your energy in many directions all at once; focus on what is most important.

15. WEDNESDAY. Unsettling. It might be hard to fight off a feeling that you are making no progress in your life, but this is only a moment of self-doubt. Besides, it is not possible to move forward all the time; periods of rest are necessary for you to absorb all that you are learning along the way. Do not hold back from telling a special someone in your life your true feelings. Find an occasion when it is possible to be alone together, and make this a really romantic moment. Even if you are short of funds, that is no reason to take a risk on making more money. Your natural optimism could be leading you astray, so try to be more realistic. A new budget may be necessary.

16. THURSDAY. Misleading. Although your colleagues are not at all averse to giving you a helping hand, there may have been some failure in communication recently. Unless you act quickly, you could wind up getting into a worse muddle than if you had attempted the job alone. As a Sagittarius you are well known for the grand sweep of your ideas, which can sometimes make it rather frustrating to have to deal with everyday life. Right now you need a channel for your dreams and a plan for the future that can run alongside mundane reality. A business trip could end badly unless you do your homework thoroughly before setting off; do not be tempted to wing it.

17. FRIDAY. Variable. It could be a real tonic to sign up for a course of study and open fresh horizons of knowledge. However, developing new ways of looking at the world can disrupt ongoing relationships if loved ones begin to feel they no longer know you as well as they once did. This is a good opportunity to put forward a business plan, allowing your colleagues to think about it over the weekend. If you feel strongly that you are onto a winner, pull out all the stops and present your case as forcefully as possible. You and a loved one may not be able to settle on plans for a vacation. If you keep on changing your mind you may never go anywhere.

18. SATURDAY. Rewarding. This is not the time to get bogged down in the daily grind; life is for living, and right now you should make the most of it. Arrange a special social occasion and celebrate with your best friends. Romance has never looked more promising, but it could just be that you are interpreting the facts to suit yourself. However, there is no denying that a very pleasant relationship is now getting off the ground, so enjoy it while it lasts. A decision must be made about your home, but as usual you are apt to be unable to choose between several plans. Family members only have so much patience, so make a decision for their sake and then stick to it.

19. SUNDAY. Manageable. You will probably find it most satisfactory to focus on practical issues rather than more frivolous matters. It would not hurt to spend some time with your mate or partner reviewing your separate ambitions and figuring out the details of moving ahead with your plans. Getting some fresh air would do you good, especially if you are also getting some gentle indoor exercise. Sagittarius people with gardens can get useful work done, but otherwise a walk in the open air would blow away the cobwebs. You are not normally impressed by authority figures. However, when you meet someone who knows what they are talking about, you have to respect them; indeed, they might have a great deal to teach you.

20. MONDAY. Successful. It is probably clear by now that the demands of work and home are in conflict. If you have been putting off dealing with this problem for some time, the point has been reached when it is necessary to give one or the other the majority of your attention. If you have to speak in a seminar or meeting, there is no need to feel nervous. As a Sagittarius you are rarely at a loss for words. As long as you have prepared well, there is every possibility of making an excellent impression. Your social circle can be enlarged by joining a club or association of like-minded people. It would be good to put your enthusiasm to work for a cause that is important to you.

21. TUESDAY. Satisfactory. Bring a wish closer to fulfillment by taking action. Dreaming is all very well, but if this aim is important to you, do something about it. A big change can come in life just when you are least expecting it. The influence of a friend can work for a long time in subtle ways, then one day you wake up realizing that your lifestyle has altered considerably for the better. This is a very promising time for idealistic projects. You will work all the better for firmly believing in what you are doing. In addition, this volunteer work might give a clue as to how your career should be developing. Do not sit at home tonight. Enjoy a lively night out on the town in the company of good friends. Just do not stay out too late.

22. WEDNESDAY. Stressful. Friendship is important to you, but it is likely that you have alienated a close acquaintance. If you allow this situation to continue, it will be increasingly difficult to close the rift. Make amends by climbing down off your high horse and apologizing right away. Find time for finishing off bits and pieces of paperwork so that the way is clear to begin a new project. Keep in mind that putting off work is not the answer, since it has to be done sooner or later. Where romance is concerned, you and that special person in your life are probably pulling in different directions. A certain amount of friction can be stimulating, but too much is wearing. Try to find more common ground.

23. THURSDAY. Difficult. Family life may seem a bit frustrating, leaving you feeling that all your energies have to be directed at pleasing other people. To a certain extent this is true, but do not forget how much loved ones also go out of their way to accommodate your wishes. You could lose something of value if you do not take more care. It is all too easy to put something down in a moment of absentmindedness; once gone, it may take quite a while to show up again despite all your looking. Your energy level should be higher than usual, but do not fritter it away on daily chores. Take this opportunity to capitalize on feeling good by living a healthier lifestyle that includes daily exercise and eating better.

24. FRIDAY. Easygoing. It should be possible to bring the workweek to a satisfying conclusion, winding up affairs so that all is ready for a fresh start on Monday. If you are asked to help a colleague, there is nothing to stop you from doing so. Memories of the past can be sweet, especially when they are shared by loved ones. In fact, you could breathe new life into your partnership by recalling the early days together. A stronger sense of self-worth can be fostered by going over your achievements so far. Some of them may not be obvious to outsiders, but that is no reason not to feel pleased with yourself. Relax at home with a travel book this evening, or enjoy listening to music.

25. SATURDAY. Happy. This is a good day for making a large or at least an expensive purchase. It is a good idea to shop around and compare prices; you should be able to get a real bargain by being a bit more selective than usual. Increase a youngster's sense of security by giving some extra loving care. Children like to know that home is a secure and stable place and that affection is always theirs for the asking. Romance can creep up on you quietly, as a friendship matures into something deeper. Right now, just being together is probably enough for both of you. The accent is on fun later in the day; a social event should be thoroughly enjoyable and could lead to an important new contact.

26. SUNDAY. Uncertain. Although it is not entirely clear where you are as far as a love affair is concerned, that should not worry you unduly. What is important is that this person is bringing some magic into your life, which is more than enough to make you grateful. Devote some time to playing with youngsters during the day. You could find that the years drop off as you begin to recall how it felt to be a child with an active and unsullied imagination. It would not be wise to push your luck with loved ones. Do not rely on the fact that they are usually willing to indulge all of your whims. Just for a change it might be worthwhile to put them first and go along with their ideas.

27. MONDAY. Buoyant. Physically you should be feeling good right now. If compliments are paid, accept them gracefully and do not brush them off. Just make sure you do not slip back into the habit of tiring yourself out by taking on too much. You could go a long way toward making sense of your personal finances by getting down to details. Casting a hasty eye over bank statements is not enough; you need to spend more time going through statements thoroughly. It might be necessary to take over a colleague's job for a short period, which could work in your favor. Do your best to prove how versatile you can be; your accomplishments are bound to be remembered at the right time.

28. TUESDAY. Changeable. There is an old saying that you cannot buy love, which may be exactly what you are finding out. Spend all you like on that special someone, but that will not change their feelings for you one bit; in fact, it could become embarrassing. A more positive attitude toward your colleagues can make life at work that much easier. Inevitably some of them get on your nerves, but if everyone makes an effort to be friendly, cooperation will become a pleasure. Usually you are not eager to spend money on your home, but now you may suddenly find yourself in the mood to add little touches that spruce up your environment and increase your comfort.

29. WEDNESDAY. Quiet. Possessions are not usually as important to Sagittarius people as having money to socialize and travel. However, everyone tends to hang on to items that have sentimental value, so do not be tempted to throw these out. It should be possible to rein in your spending by eliminating nonessentials that you buy without even thinking. For example, you probably do not find time to read all the magazines that are lying around the house. It is good to talk with neighbors and keep up with what is happening locally. There may be some way in which you can help out someone in need who lives nearby. Take a loved one to a favorite restaurant tonight.

30. THURSDAY. Difficult. Sometimes it is better to say too little rather than too much but, on the other hand, you should not leave a loved one in the dark. Although there is an important matter on your mind, you might not feel ready to share it all. It is going to weigh heavily on you if you keep it entirely to yourself. Constant interruptions can make daily chores more tedious than usual. You may be tempted to give up altogether, but it would be better to find a way of working in short bursts of energy. Double-check your calendar; there may be an appointment you have forgotten. If you are not careful, you might find yourself showing up on the wrong date or at the completely wrong time.

31. FRIDAY. Disconcerting. You have every right to feel disheartened if it has become clear that a colleague attempted to sabotage some of your work. It is not the time right now to speculate on their motives; what matters is that you have discovered the action while there is still time to salvage most of your efforts. Where romance is concerned, everyone but you may be aware that you are being led on. If you are able to be a little more objective, you will see that the other person is hiding a significant part of their life from you. Although you probably long to relax, first there is an important task to be finished. Do not expect much cooperation.

APRIL

1. SATURDAY. Enjoyable. Make the most of your higher level of vitality to get on with jobs you have been putting off for a long time. You should be able to complete them quickly and almost effortlessly. You probably do not need any convincing to exercise rather than just lazing around in your leisure hours. In fact, as a Sagittarius you are naturally restless and usually enjoy getting thoroughly tired out. A fresh approach to your diet could give you a whole new lease on life. Look up some delicious and healthy recipes. Entertain guests modestly; they should be more than able to provide their own amusement through stimulating conversation and shared jokes.

2. SUNDAY. Happy. Find time to work on a favorite hobby. There is a good chance of making real progress. You might even be surprised to find how far you can push a particular pursuit. There is every reason to believe this could become more than just a way of passing an hour or two. Where romance is concerned, the way forward is clear. However, you may be harboring no doubts as to what you want. There is no harm in stating your views strongly, since that will make the other person totally aware of the depth of your feelings. A family gathering could be enjoyable even though somewhat boisterous, especially when you begin to share memories of long-ago days.

3. MONDAY. Pleasant. Your ability to get along with almost everyone you meet is highlighted today, just when it is sure to come in handy. Having to play a certain role for a special occasion at work should be a positive pleasure. If you are thinking of re-decorating, take advantage of this good day for buying supplies and materials. As you look around at what is available, ideas for what you want to do are almost bound to develop way past your first modest imaginings. Much can be done to improve relations within the family. Keep in mind that a more tolerant attitude will foster real caring. There is no need to think of this just as a passing phase; with extra attention, the feeling will endure.

4. TUESDAY. Useful. Just as you were beginning to wonder about the future of your love life, an opportunity presents itself to make an exciting new start. There's no question but that you'll jump at this chance, which gives you a way to learn from your past mistakes. Get a creative project off the ground with a little assistance from your friends. Even if all they can offer is advice and moral support, that will give you enough confidence to forge ahead with a will. Short journeys can be made more pleasant by taking company with you; why not offer an acquaintance a lift so that you can get to know them better? Take in a shamelessly romantic film tonight.

5. WEDNESDAY. Satisfactory. Youngsters could surprise you with their unexpectedly good results at school. It appears they are developing talents that might not have been expected, and you should be only too delighted and thrilled to encourage them as much as possible. A romantic affair with someone who doesn't socialize in your usual circle can come as a breath of fresh air. This could be something of a whirlwind affair, but while it lasts there is plenty to enjoy and learn. Most Sagittarius do hate the feeling of being in a rut, and right now it's imperative to find new creative and social outlets. See if there may be local classes that would open up new interests.

6. THURSDAY. Fortunate. Jumping in at the deep end is a speciality of Sagittarius people, as you are doubtless the first to admit. Today this trait stands you in good stead when a minor crisis at work is prevented from developing into a disaster by your quick action. It is all very well playing sports for your health, but overdoing exercise can be just as harmful as not getting enough. Try to practice a sense of moderation, pacing yourself more carefully. This is not the best time for making detailed plans. Although you may be inspired by a grand vision, impatience might stand in your way. Let other people work out all of the practicalities, problems, and probabilities.

7. FRIDAY. Variable. Assume an air of caution, even if you do not really feel it. There is danger of blowing your top unless you really play it cool, and it is likely to be a very minor irritation that sets you off. A bothersome neighbor may just not be responding to reason, even though it is clear that they are definitely acting in an antisocial manner. If you have already tried all the means you can think of for getting through to them, it might be time to threaten legal action. You can complete numerous small domestic jobs, probably while you are thinking of something far more interesting. Go along with the ideas of your friends tonight.

8. SATURDAY. Fair. If you feel ready for romance, you need have no fears or worries. A promising affair is just waiting to happen. The understanding you have gained over the past few years should enable you to treat that special person with a greater degree of true tolerance and affection. This is likely to be quite a sociable day. You and your mate or partner will probably get most pleasure by attending an event together. Private jokes and shared reminiscences can turn even the most ordinary occasion into a special and memorable outing. Do not make loved ones suffer if you are upset with yourself for not yet achieving an important goal; just keep plugging away.

9. SUNDAY. Buoyant. This is a promising day for a pleasure trip. Take loved ones away from it all to get some fresh air in the country. You will all feel better after having a real break from routine, even if it is brief. Neighbors could have surprising news that might help you with a creative project. Just the helpful people you need are close at hand. You and your mate or partner can have fun together if you shrug off a sense of responsibility for a while and act in a spontaneous manner. It does not matter if you behave like children just for this once. Youngsters may become easily bored indoors, so arrange plenty of outdoor activities to keep them busily amused.

10. MONDAY. Profitable. Finally some money you have been owed for extra work should arrive, allowing you to boost your savings balance significantly. Do not be tempted to spend it all at once; just allow yourself a little for a special indulgence, and put the rest in the bank. If you look a bit more deeply at an everyday chore, it may be more of interest than you might expect. Everything depends upon your attitude; an inquiring mind can ferret out information from even the most unpromising sources. A romantic affair is likely to be rather sensitive at the moment. Basically you are very fond of each other, but that may not really be enough to sustain an intimate relationship.

11. TUESDAY. Fortunate. If you nurture ambitions to be a writer, take heart. An idea you recently came up with is a potential winner, although it will take some working out if it is to have a chance of gaining a measure of success. A new love affair is apt to be all but idyllic at the moment. It may just be that you are not used to someone treating you in a totally romantic manner. As a result, you are bound to find it utterly enchanting. If you have time to look in local shops, head right for the more intriguing small specialty stores. There may be an unusual item that just seems to have been waiting for you to come along and find it. Do not hesitate to splurge for once.

12. WEDNESDAY. Tricky. If you are traveling a long distance, there may be delays due to rather unusual reasons. If you are going to a specific event, you could be disappointed. A course of study may not be fulfilling your hopes. You could be tempted to give it up, but that would be a waste of the work you have done so far. Try to stay until the end; all the knowledge you are gaining will probably begin to make sense before then. Plans for retraining could rouse your ambitions, but there is a long way to go before you can acquire all the necessary skills for your chosen career. Patience is a virtue, especially for Sagittarius people with big plans and high hopes.

13. THURSDAY. Mixed. You will come out of the day well if you have the confidence to be yourself. Now more than ever it is vital to stand up for your own beliefs, and if someone challenges them severely then this is to be welcomed since it forces you to think them through more thoroughly. Holiday plans proceed apace, and by now you are probably pleased that you have broken the mold. It will be like a tonic to try a more adventurous vacation! Try not to allow colleagues to dishearten you with tales of minor problems. They can see that you are set on achieving better things, and may well be rather jealous. Let your partner choose the venue this evening.

14. FRIDAY. Easygoing. Make sure you put the final details for a business trip in place, so that when the time comes you will have nothing else to think about. Actually the prospect of getting away should be rather refreshing, even though work is involved. This is a good time for wrapping up reports that will be seen by superiors. You've done all the hard labor and now can get some pleasure at putting together a really well-presented package. As the day wears on it's unlikely you'll feel inspired to do much more than keep things ticking over. This is an ideal time to turn within and take a long, reflective look at your ambitions and inner ideals.

15. SATURDAY. Manageable. Finally you are beginning to realize what everyone has been trying to point out to you for some time: that you have been driving yourself too hard. If you continue on this way, your health could suffer. A few warning symptoms are probably already giving you some concern. Do not be too harsh on youngsters and their admittedly messy habits. There are more important traits than tidiness, which is something that will develop in good time if you set an example. Talk over joint plans for the future with your mate or partner. You can do more than you may think to take a positive forward step together, encouraging and strengthening one another.

16. SUNDAY. Confusing. Friends may just not seem to be hearing you right. When you are trying to tell them that you are upset by a certain thoughtless act, they may simply shrug it off or laugh about it. It is difficult to see just why they are being so unconcerned, but for sure you are wasting your energy talking to them. As a love affair comes to a crisis point, you may not be clear just how you want it to develop. This is not a positive sign of your long-term commitment. It is vital for the sake of the other person not to keep them hanging on in vain hope. Youngsters can be rather disruptive at social events, but the more you include them the better they will behave.

17. MONDAY. Rewarding. This is an excellent day for creative thought and for ideas coming from out of the blue. Opening your mind and not cluttering it up with ordinary matters will allow the answer to a long-term problem to surface from your unconscious. A letter from a special person in your life could give you just the assurance you need about your feelings being fully reciprocated. You are to be excused for being rather absentminded while allowing yourself to wander off in dreams of future happiness. Put a plan for self-improvement into action without delay; this learning process promises to be both enjoyable and profound. A loved one would be delighted to receive a special gift as a surprise.

18. TUESDAY. Stressful. You may reach the crunch point when you no longer feel you can stay in a group that has served you well in the past. There seems to be no alternative but to break away, since your thoughts are no longer in sympathy with those of the other members. A business meeting could have a somewhat surprising outcome. New ideas are often discussed, but for once there is apt to be a plan of real and startling originality that could prove beneficial. Try not to argue with a loved one, even though you have opposing ideals in some important areas. As long as you basically respect each other, you should be able to accommodate your differences of opinion and outlook.

19. WEDNESDAY. Deceptive. Your honest, trusting Sagittarius nature sometimes leads you to believe in someone who is not really worthy of your faith. It may not yet be apparent, but when you receive work that a colleague was doing as a favor you might learn that it is often better to rely only on yourself. Your personal paperwork may be in a bit of a muddle, making it hard to lay your hands on a vital document. An hour spent getting more organized would be time well spent. If you have a relative in the hospital, you may be more than due to pay them a visit. It is not fair to shirk this task, which will not take you long and is sure to be much appreciated.

20. THURSDAY. Unsettling. A failure is never easy to accept, but you need to realize that your optimistic Sagittarius nature sometimes pushes you into biting off more than you can chew. There is actually a positive side to this disappointment, since even if you have not achieved your main aim there are smaller benefits to be gained along the way. When youngsters act up, a firm hand is needed. It is fine to indulge them to a certain point, but they will feel more secure if they know that they can only go so far. What you think of as an exciting new idea may not go over well at work. There might be flaws that you cannot yet see, so try to be objective about it rather than pushy.

21. FRIDAY. Useful. When you meet someone who has a better way of expressing themselves than you, there is much you can learn from them. Listen and you may find out that it is possible to make your points more clearly by using fewer but better-chosen words. If you are trying to choose a school for a youngster, it is a good idea to rely on your own judgment rather than be swayed by the opinions of other people. After all, you know your own child's needs best. Make the most of a more cooperative atmosphere at work to bring your colleagues together in a group to work on a communications problem. It should be solved in time for all of you to celebrate your accomplishment this afternoon.

22. SATURDAY. Fair. There is no doubt that you can improve the quality of your lifestyle simply by adopting a more positive attitude. As a Sagittarius you tend to exaggerate when things get rough. Now, however, you should look on the bright side and not forget to count your blessings. It is a good time to indulge in some new clothes, and perhaps a new hairstyle as well. Surprise your friends by adopting a new persona. Romance is in the air, and the last thing you should do is to raise doubts about your special relationship. Be glad that you are with someone who so obviously thinks you are special. Leisure pursuits need to be extra interesting to hold your attention, so try a new activity.

23. SUNDAY. Exciting. Love's arrows could strike just when you are least expecting it. You are likely to meet someone who is certainly not run-of-the-mill. At first sight you may seem to understand each other; this relationship can only get more interesting the better you come to know each other. All creative pursuits are highlighted; it would be a shame to spend the day on mundane tasks. You need to relax and play for a while. Even if you do not take your hobbies too seriously, they can be immensely beneficial as well as fun. The evening brings a chance to wind down in comfortable surroundings. Loved ones are apt to be more thoughtful and affectionate than usual.

24. MONDAY. Steady. Be glad to settle down to routine chores that occupy you without demanding too much of your attention. It can be quite comforting to busy yourself with work that can be done without thought, giving you time to sort through the more pressing concerns that are on your mind. Improving your health is never a short-term project; real benefits develop slowly, but the plus side is that they then last. If possible, exercise the patience to continue with a program that will doubtless have positive effects in time. If you are thinking of buying a pet, consider all of the responsibility involved. Animals can be demanding, but they also certainly give much pleasure.

25. TUESDAY. Challenging. If you are trying to improve your employment prospects, you need to get noticed. While it would not be advisable to use shock tactics or to appear eccentric, it is important to showcase what you as a creative individual can offer that no one else can. Communication from a close relative could bring an opportunity for a short trip that would make a refreshing break; you would be foolish not to jump at this chance. Squirreling away small amounts of money here and there can actually make quite a difference to your financial situation. It should now be possible to start spending on essential items that you have wanted and needed for some time.

26. WEDNESDAY. Misleading. Although it is unlikely you have been deliberately fed misinformation, a mix-up in communications with a colleague could result in you arriving late for an important meeting. This is bound to reflect badly on you, and it will be a challenge to make up for the first impression you have made. When you realize that some written work is due, you can be forgiven for panicking. Sit down calmly and go over what you have already done toward composing it; there is probably more than you think, and finishing it up should not be a major problem. Overindulgence in rich food and drink is bound to leave you feeling a little under the weather.

27. THURSDAY. Disquieting. Be prepared for trouble with your car, especially if it has not been serviced for some time. It would be a good idea to leave plenty of time to get to appointments; otherwise you may find yourself stuck at the last minute. Go through contracts with a fine-tooth comb; there could be hidden clauses that are not in your favor. It would be extremely unwise to sign anything you have not read thoroughly, no matter how tedious that might be. This is not the best day for cleaning and clearing up at home because you are bound to be interrupted. Turn your attention instead to more personal pursuits that you really enjoy, such as a creative hobby.

28. FRIDAY. Lucky. Sagittarius romantics should wake up feeling hopeful and confident. This is an excellent day for beginning a new relationship. Someone new is almost bound to sweep into your life, making a difference in the way you see the world. Social activities promise to be very enjoyable; networking has never been easier. You are not normally shy about introducing yourself to strangers, so go ahead and make some new friends. Youngsters can be a delight. This is one day when you can afford to take time out to play with them. Take pleasure in their amusing comments. Do not let your temper get frayed due to minor irritations during the day.

29. SATURDAY. Fair. Concentrate on shopping and getting chores done around the home, which is where you will find the greatest satisfaction this morning. There may be bargains to be found, particularly if you are stocking up on food for the week. It is not the best time to plan sweeping changes to your home. If you act on the ideas that seem attractive now, in time it could become obvious that they were only passing whims. Family members can be helpful when it comes to making arrangements for a joint celebration. Working together to plan a party or other get-together can be part of the pleasure, so do not try to take on all the responsibility.

30. SUNDAY. Happy. This is a good time to settle down with loved ones and sort out how you hope to develop your lives together. There is no point just drifting along letting life happen to you. Definite aims and goals can be inspiring, even if they are challenging to achieve. If you have a garden, you should find working in it quietly therapeutic. Be sure to make time to sit back at the end of the day and relax, while other people admire your efforts. Finally it is possible to put an end to a disagreement that has been rumbling on in the family for some time. This will be a relief for all involved, improving the atmosphere greatly and allowing new plans to be made.

MAY

1. MONDAY. Good. Even if you do not usually enter competitions, there is no harm in giving one a try at the moment. Inspiration and luck could come together in a winning formula, so why not take a chance. This could be a good time to review communications systems at work. It is easy to get left behind as technology develops, and you want to make the most of your potential. Today's more social mood makes you feel like getting out and painting the town red with a few special friends. It is fine to do so, although it would be a good idea to keep in mind a temptation to do too much or to say too much. Let love come to you; do not go out looking for it or you are apt to be disappointed.

2. TUESDAY. Pleasant. This is a promising day for getting around in the office or your neighborhood and meeting new people. If your job calls for networking, put on a smile and go out to mingle; you are almost bound to make some useful contacts. If you are looking to extend your social circle you do not have to go far. There are like-minded people meeting in your vicinity. You may want to join an amateur dramatic group or give some time to a worthwhile charity. If you have a test coming up, put in more time practicing. You should be able to make good progress. The more regularly you study, the better you will know the subject. Cramming for an exam may not be satisfactory.

3. WEDNESDAY. Deceptive. Everyone has had the experience of putting papers in a safe place, only to find they mysteriously disappear. This could throw you into a mild panic if they are needed urgently, but keep calm. Otherwise you will not think of all the possibilities, such as that a colleague could have borrowed them. Be sure to keep backup files when using a computer. There is every likelihood of an unexplained power failure that can play havoc with recent work. A healthy diet need not be boring, so do not be put off by thinking you will have to do without most of your favorite foods. Try cutting back, not cutting out.

4. THURSDAY. Variable. Job prospects seem to be looking up. If you have been searching for a new position apparently without success, take heart. It might be worthwhile contacting former colleagues to see if they have any news of openings that have not yet been advertised. Resolve to be more organized in your daily routine; you can actually save time in this way so that there is more opportunity to do the things you enjoy. There is no need to go to extremes when it comes to doing a good turn. Being overly generous can be something of an embarrassment and might even cause resentment as the recipient of your goodwill wonders how to ever repay you.

5. FRIDAY. Mixed. It is not always possible to enjoy perfect harmony in a long-term partnership, but that is no excuse for flying off the handle over an insignificant matter. You may regret losing your temper when it is too late; unkind words will not soon be forgotten. Sometimes you are able to sense children's needs without them saying anything. This enables you to act promptly when little worries and problems are on the horizon. Conditions are good for signing legal papers, although you may still have a few doubts. However, as long as you have obtained sound advice you can act confidently. Be extra careful and alert in the kitchen or you could suffer an annoying burn.

6. SATURDAY. Misleading. You may tend to be lost in dreams this morning, so that humdrum tasks just do not get done properly. Loved ones are apt to be rather baffled by your mood, and even you might find it hard to explain exactly what you are yearning for. It is probably just that everyday life is lacking in some way. Shopping can be more confusing than anything else. You are likely to be faced with such an array of desirable items that choice seems impossible, especially if you are trying to buy gifts for other people. Try not to get into a tug-of-war with your mate or partner over a matter of control. As a Sagittarius you know very well that give-and-take is the name of the game.

7. SUNDAY. Pleasant. Although you might not be in a very sociable mood, that should not be a problem since a quiet day around the home is foreseen. In fact, taking a couple of hours during which you can retreat into yourself would do you a world of good. As a romantic affair begins to take emotional hold, you may realize that this is what you have been longing for. It is all very well refusing commitment for a while, but in the end the comfort of being close to a special person is bound to become a more attractive option. A friend could come to you for advice about a problem which you have experienced firsthand. You can be very helpful just listening to what they have to say with understanding.

8. MONDAY. Buoyant. You should be bubbling over with exciting ideas this morning. Your enthusiasm might even be a bit much for other people, although they will nevertheless be pulled along in your wake. If you are about to move to new premises you should be able to see very positive potential in a larger workspace. In particular, this could improve the atmosphere among colleagues by allowing each person a fairly private area. Youngsters' inquisitiveness about everyday life can sometimes be wearisome, but today you should be in a mood to enjoy their deceptively simple questions. Make a note of some of their observations and comments to share with grandparents or other family members.

9. TUESDAY. Tricky. A colleague may not be forthcoming when it comes to giving you essential information. This is a problem they have to work out for themselves. From your point of view, it might be easier to seek elsewhere for the answers to your questions. All the hard work you have been doing recently may now be having an effect on your nerves. If you are more jumpy or irritable than usual, it is a clear signal that you need to take a relaxing break. A business partnership can be cemented with a lucrative deal that has an overseas connection. Act decisively, since this opportunity will probably not be presented again. Get to bed early tonight.

10. WEDNESDAY. Manageable. It does not pay to be too much of a stickler when you are trying to diet. Every action provokes an opposite reaction, so if you sternly deny yourself all goodies it is almost inevitable that one day you will succumb to temptation in a serious way. The illness of an older relative could cause you a few worries. Some responsibility for care must fall on your shoulders, which may you have to fit in a whole new routine into your already demanding job. Phone calls could be cut short or go unanswered, making a series of re-calls necessary. Patience is not usually a Sagittarius strong point, so you will really have to grit your teeth to accomplish what must be done.

11. THURSDAY. Confusing. Just when you thought you had settled into a comfortable regular job, changes may be announced that require an upheaval in your everyday activities. However, it can be stimulating to be forced to find new ways of coping. Go into this with a positive attitude and you could actually find yourself relishing the change. There is no doubt that moving even a short distance is usually disruptive. You need to resign yourself to not being able to find essential items in the chaos, otherwise you will just get annoyed and waste time looking. It may be difficult to accept criticism of recent written work, but you probably must admit that a valid point is being made.

12. FRIDAY. Fair. If you have been mulling over a decision for some time, you should now feel happy that you are sure of the right choice. Loved ones will be relieved that you have taken their point of view into consideration. A temporary position with increased responsibility could change your status at work and enhance your reputation, but only if you perform to the best of your ability. It is finally possible to tell friends about a romantic affair that has been going on for a while. The change of circumstances you have been hoping for has finally occurred, so that you can now announce your relationship with true pride and a clear conscience. Stay close to home this evening.

13. SATURDAY. Variable. There is no need to get worked up when it becomes clear that all household chores just are not going to get done. The day beckons with the prospect of freedom, which is just what Sagittarius people love most. It can be difficult to keep a sense of proportion when shopping; your impulse to buy is apt to be blocked by an uncharacteristic sense of caution. As a result, you may not quite know what to do. It might be best to accept your mate or partner's advice, since otherwise you may not be able to make a decision at all. Socializing with good friends can be very pleasurable; if you are playing a sport together, good team spirit could bring success.

14. SUNDAY. Good. Dreams can come true, but it helps to enlist the support of other people who have similar ideals. Take a step toward a special aim by turning to a friend who will be able to open a few doors for you. You and your mate or partner will get along all the better if you go out together more often. Naturally you both need to pursue separate interests, but the more activities you share the closer you will become. Friends see you as someone who has the power to jolt them out of a rut; with your natural enthusiasm and love of life, that role comes naturally. There is no danger of being bored in your company because as a Sagittarius you tend to be the life and soul of the party.

15. MONDAY. Challenging. Sometimes you come up with ideas that seem quite radical to other people. Even though your plans are sound, you need to be very persuasive in order to get cooperation. Not everyone is as willing as you to embrace what is new. This is a promising day for travel. If you are your usual chatty self, there is no reason not to make a new friend on the journey. Just be sure to exchange phone numbers in the excitement of finding all the points of similarity between you. You can do good work for a cause that is important to you if you are prepared to volunteer some time. This should be even more satisfying than making a financial donation.

16. TUESDAY. Tricky. When you get the feeling that someone is working against you, it can be rather difficult to know how to proceed. You need more evidence than just a hunch before making an accusation, which could otherwise misfire. If you continue refusing to see that a romantic partner is not being honest, you are courting future heartache. Friends may have been trying to alert you to the truth for some time. It will be less painful to face the facts sooner rather than later. Your immune system could do with a boost; otherwise there is the likelihood of succumbing to a virus or other illness. Also be sure you are getting plenty of vitamins.

17. WEDNESDAY. Happy. Colleagues at work may be preparing a surprise in thanks for the help you have given them. It is always good to know you are appreciated, and on this occasion that is not in any doubt. Sometimes romance does not hit you between the eyes, but enters your life in a more subtle way. Finally you may begin to realize you cannot do without that significant other, which is a sure sign you are hooked. A legal case appears promising although the final decision is still pending. However, you have good reason to feel optimistic. Do not forget an appointment this afternoon when other, more pleasant events could distract your attention.

18. THURSDAY. Demanding. Your usual Sagittarius charm may fail you at a critical juncture, leading to other people not being as helpful as usual. The best response may be to simply set a good example by buckling down and getting on with the task at hand. In a long-term relationship, minor irritations often cause the most bother. If you find yourself getting angry because your loved one has left the top off the toothpaste or has not taken out the garbage, take a deep breath and ask yourself if it really matters. A surprise encounter during a short journey could excite and inspire you. It is unlikely you will run into the person again, but the strong impression will remain for a long time in your heart.

19. FRIDAY. Unsettling. This is a day when you have to be extra careful of what you say and to whom. As a Sagittarius you tend to come out with rather blunt statements from time to time. Loved ones may not be as willing as you think to hear the whole truth. A business associate may be trying to hurry you into a quick decision even though it is clear that the matter requires longer, more careful consideration. Even at the risk of causing a temporary rift between you, it is essential not to allow yourself to be bullied into taking premature action. If a legal case is not be turning out the way you hoped, you probably must just accept the fact rather than seek to cast blame on other people.

20. SATURDAY. Stressful. It may be virtually impossible to reach the end of the day without having gone through an argument of some sort with your mate or partner. Neither of you may be willing to back down. This could escalate out of hand unless you are prepared to humble yourself a little. There is little point hopping from one health program to another without giving yourself the chance to benefit from any of them. Try to curb your impatience; positive results are not achieved instantly no matter what system you are using. Sagittarius singles who are looking for romance are likely to be emotionally vulnerable at the moment. Do not give away your heart too easily or too quickly.

21. SUNDAY. Easygoing. If you feel like being a bit selfish and just pleasing yourself, do so, unless loved ones have prior significant claims on your time. It would do you a world of good to settle down to a favorite pastime, or even do nothing at all. This is a starred opportunity to catch up with your financial affairs. Even if you do not have all that much cash, it still helps to check through bank statements and store receipts just so that you can get a clear picture of your overall position. If you are due to go on vacation, you may want to ask a neighbor to keep an eye on your property and perhaps care for your pet or plants as well.

22. MONDAY. Favorable. This solid start to the workweek should enable you to get some good work done. Even though you might spend more time than usual sorting out details, laying the groundwork now will speed up your progress later on. Pay more attention to the security of your home. Check the house to make sure all locks and bolts are in good shape. A colleague could have a helpful tip for keeping trim. Their enthusiasm is likely to be strong enough for you to give their method a try at least. Praise from a friend for the way you get things done without fuss can boost your self-confidence. A promise must be fulfilled.

23. TUESDAY. Enjoyable. Sometimes one of the best things about a love relationship is the sense of self-worth that comes from being appreciated and valued. There is nothing to compare with knowing that you are special to someone significant. Make sure that person gets the same level of support from you. This is a good time to think about additional insurance for your possessions. Total up their worth and you will probably be surprised at the final amount. A close relative may seek advice concerning their private life, which you are well qualified to give. Remember to be gentle and as tactful as possible; the object is to make them feel better as well as offering suggestions.

24. WEDNESDAY. Fortunate. A business associate with whom you have never really gotten along may now seem eager to mend matters. Their motives probably spring from respect for you, so accept the implied compliment and be willing to meet them halfway. It can be tricky introducing a prospective partner to your family. In this case, however, there should be no problems, since everyone is likely to take to this person right away. Youngsters can progress in their lessons by leaps and bounds if you are prepared to support their schoolwork with some extra help at home. Just be sure to consult their teachers first so that your methods are in agreement.

25. THURSDAY. Difficult. Work that you recently completed hastily may have to be redone from scratch. Be aware of a tendency to rush through tasks that require patience and close attention. Sagittarius people in a long-term relationship could be feeling rather restless. This is natural and almost inevitable. The cure is to work on bringing some excitement and romance back into your partnership rather than blaming each other. Computer problems may hold up important written work, making it hard for you to meet a deadline. Try to reschedule your day so that you can leave other tasks and spend as much time as you need to catch up with a priority assignment.

26. FRIDAY. Disquieting. All may not be well on the domestic front, and there is no point pretending otherwise. Affection is sometimes not enough to bind a relationship together; willpower must be exerted to get through challenging times side by side. You can be your own worst enemy when it comes to dealing with property matters. A tendency to take too much for granted is bound to get other people's backs up. You must learn that deals involving large sums of money need careful handling. A social event this evening may not be as enjoyable as usual because you find it hard to let go of the workweek and relax. Make a conscious effort to do so and soon it will come naturally.

27. SATURDAY. Satisfactory. Let a loved one take charge when it comes to arranging the day's entertainment. Their unusual idea for a local trip is sure to delight the whole family. Parents or in-laws can offer very positive assistance if you are willing to let them see a little more of your private life than usual. Keep in mind that they have your welfare at heart and only want you to be happy. Take this opportunity to hunt out a special gift for a special friend; your inspired mood should enable you to focus in on exactly the right item. Swimming is excellent exercise for Sagittarius people. If you want to get in trim for a forthcoming vacation, an hour a day at a local pool could be just what you need.

28. SUNDAY. Disconcerting. Two separate emotions come into conflict today as you become aware of the need to bring more order into your daily life at the same time you are yearning for greater freedom. This could lead to a quarrel with loved ones who are trying to get you to exhibit a deeper sense of responsibility; you may have to admit that they have a valid point. A diet that swings between extremes of indulgence and self-denial is not going to do anything much other than throw your system into confusion. Try to strike a balance; you will find it much easier to stick to such a diet. Relax into a new relationship. There should be a fine harmony between your ideals and your expectations.

29. MONDAY. Exciting. You can bring back the sparkle in a loved one's eyes by being a little more romantic than usual. Recent disagreements will soon be forgotten as you begin to rekindle all the old affection. Sagittarius people facing an interview should try to keep as calm and as focused as possible. Although there is competition, as long as you have relevant qualifications there is no reason not to make a good impression. You may be so strongly attracted to someone new on the scene that you are prepared to keep up the pressure even if they do not return your interest right away. Just the fact that you are willing to wait may intrigue them into eventually showing corresponding interest in you.

30. TUESDAY. Successful. This is a favorable day for business negotiations. You should be able to get your way almost without trying. You can effortlessly say exactly the right things. Although doing so is not achieved without some solid research, the other people involved are not likely to be aware of that. If you have been worrying about taking the plunge into a long-term commitment, at last your final fears can be dismissed. When you are with a potential partner there is no longer any doubt as to what you both want, so do not hang back. There may be an opportunity to make some extra money, which should cover savings depleted by a recent necessary expense.

31. WEDNESDAY. Confusing. Everyone at work is apt to be unsure and uncertain. Unless one person takes charge, it will be difficult to get any kind of cooperation at all. It is fine to concentrate on your own particular area of responsibility, but you need to interact with other people on the job or you will not see how your tasks fit into the bigger picture. Youngsters can be discontented and hard to amuse. They need activities that allow them to develop their own fantasy world; imagination is more important than being surrounded by elaborate toys or play equipment. If you are feeling guilty because of a thoughtless remark, do not just brood about it but apologize and make whatever amends are necessary.

JUNE

1. THURSDAY. Frustrating. The day does not get off to a promising start. An upset is apt to be brewing with a superior at work or with an important client. There is little point pitting yourself against them, since they have the power to make life very uncomfortable for you. Go out of your way to be accommodating. A legal matter you took up in a fairly light spirit has become a potentially unpleasant affair. However, it is not too late to reach a compromise, although this will be best negotiated by a neutral third party. You would really benefit from a change in routine, although it may be difficult to manage this without causing some chaos. Be moderate in all of your requests and demands.

2. FRIDAY. Buoyant. There is no stopping you as it becomes essential to finish work involving contractual arrangements before the weekend gets underway. The sight of a deadline does wonders to focus the Sagittarius mind. In fact, some extra adrenaline is bound to boost your performance so that you can do your very best. Surprise your mate or partner by organizing a romantic break. Even a single night away together will come as a welcome chance to recapture the early excitement of your relationship. There should be no need to ride roughshod over colleagues; do not be tempted to exert power just for the sake of it. Share and share alike should be the order of the day.

3. SATURDAY. Disconcerting. Your mate or partner is apt to be looking for a chance to argue, and sooner or later is bound to find some excuse no matter how careful you are. It is time to bring an end to a pattern that has one of you leading and the other following. Learn to pull together or you will eventually find yourselves drifting further and further apart. Money may be an issue at the moment, as you probably feel you just cannot earn enough to cover all of your expenses. A cursory glance over your recent purchases will reveal that you have a taste for quality that just cannot be indulged all the time, so the answer to your money woes is staring you in the face.

4. SUNDAY. Easygoing. Relax in a private space. The demands of socializing should ease off today. This is a good time to look within and examine your deeper emotional life. Ask yourself if your needs are being met. If not, consider how to change your life to be more satisfactory. A relative who finds out a piece of intriguing information about one of your ancestors will be naturally eager to share the news. Once you hear it, you will probably gain great insight into your parents' life, which should explain a lot about their attitudes. Youngsters may be rather secretive; do not leave them to their own devices since mischief may be their mission. Pets, too, need extra attention.

5. MONDAY. Useful. Fully research a new work project before getting going. If you feel unsure about where to start, consult a colleague who has more experience in these matters. Your bank or financial adviser may be able to make some positive suggestions regarding how to increase your future economic security. While Sagittarius people tend to trust a lot to luck, it is also wise to take precautions. Your health can be improved if you learn a more positive way to channel troublesome emotions. Many physical ailments are caused by emotional blocks, and there are numerous safe techniques for letting out your feelings and lowering your blood pressure.

6. TUESDAY. Fair. Turn your mind to important long-term matters. Consider whether it would be useful to get additional training in some subject that could broaden your work prospects. You need not embark on an arduous or uninteresting course of study. Pick a subject that appeals, and choose the level of learning that you think is suitable to your time and talents. If you have not yet planned a vacation, there is no reason not to do so now. A last-minute getaway can be extra exciting. As long as you can get time off at short notice, proceed confidently with your plans. Take more notice of your mate or partner when they try to explain their actions to you; it is all too easy to take for granted the people who are closest to you.

7. WEDNESDAY. Disquieting. No long journey is likely to be accomplished without some problems along the way. Sudden disruptions of public transportation could play havoc with your timetable. If someone is expecting you at a certain time, make sure you have a contact number for them in case you are unavoidably delayed. Sometimes it can be tempting to put a good relationship at risk just because you want a little excitement. Stop and think, however, of the possible consequences before taking a step that you could regret for a very long time. A retraining course may have turned out to be rather demanding, but if you stick with it you are bound to benefit from the discipline required.

8. THURSDAY. Variable. A strong hunch or friend in the know could enable you to make a career move before anyone else becomes aware of what is going on. For once you should not turn a deaf ear to gossip since it is probably worth hearing. You can do a great deal of good for a friend who has recently been through a traumatic experience. Your optimistic outlook can provide a good balance to the way they are feeling right now. However, do not try too hard to cheer them up; just be your normal optimistic self. A relationship problem may make you feel that you must force a decision to break the deadlock, but this is not the right time to make such a move.

9. FRIDAY. Changeable. Strive to consolidate your position at work by being seen to be responsible. Also make sure superiors know who you are; there are benefits to be gained later on as long as you make sure you stick in their memory. Your mate or partner may seem eager to put you in the driver's seat. Although as a Sagittarius you like having a measure of control over any relationship, this pleasure will wear off after a while. It would be better to make it clear that a partnership involves sharing or the balance of power becomes unequal. Try to keep your temper when a colleague makes what seems to you to be a silly decision. There may be a method in their madness.

10. SATURDAY. Favorable. Social events are apt to appeal more than usual, bringing you out of yourself and offering the opportunity to meet new people. In fact, friends made now could have quite an effect on the course of your life. You should be able to find new places of entertainment locally if you look around a bit. You and your mate or partner will enjoy trying an exotic restaurant for a change. When you get close to someone, it can be almost natural to know what they are feeling. A friend will be grateful for your support, especially if you are able to understand their emotions without having them explained to you. Take youngsters out for an extra special treat.

11. SUNDAY. Exciting. Sagittarius singles who are in search of romance may be lucky as a relative introduces you to a very attractive person. Either ask them out directly or make some excuse to get in touch again. You have nothing to lose by being aggressive, and their answer should leave you in no doubt that they are interested too. A meeting with like-minded people may be less than straightforward. There is a lot going on behind the scenes that may spoil shared idealism; you will not be popular if you point this out. Make the most of an improvement in the relationship between you and your mate or partner to build a solid foundation of understanding.

12. MONDAY. Mixed. If you have to attend a conference or a meeting, there is no need to worry about being bored. There should be plenty of ideas for you to digest, and your own contribution will be welcome. Confide in a loved one if you are planning to fulfill a dream. They are bound to want to help you achieve your desire, and their support will keep you on course. As the day goes on it will probably become more difficult to concentrate. Take an hour out if possible. During this time, find space to relax completely or even take a nap; you will be refreshed for the rest of the day. Use your good sense of discrimination if you want to donate your time or money.

13. TUESDAY. Variable. A lot of useful work can be done in small ways, particularly if you are left alone to do it. It might be worth telling colleagues and loved ones to keep their distance so that you can get tasks finished without being disturbed. Youngsters need to know the facts of life sooner or later; you cannot put off telling them forever. It certainly will not help if they get a garbled version from friends at school, which is all too likely unless you act quickly. If you are going out tonight, leave the car at home and let a designated driver provide the transportation or take a cab. A breakdown could bring an otherwise enjoyable evening to an irritating end.

14. WEDNESDAY. Disquieting. You may be lacking in energy and enthusiasm, especially if recent work has been received with less praise than you were expecting. However, as long as you have faith in your own ability, it should be possible to buck yourself up and become cheerful again. If you have recently ended a relationship, do not allow yourself to brood on the past. Look on this period as a quiet time during which you can begin to look forward to a brighter future and a more satisfying love life. It would not be smart to neglect your health right now. As a Sagittarius you need to learn to care for your body's needs.

15. THURSDAY. Sensitive. Normally other people consider you an open book, so when you really want to keep something to yourself it is often plain what you are doing. It might be better to come clean to loved ones, since they are bound to learn your secret sooner or later. There is no point coming down hard on other people just because you are trying to avoid your own responsibility. No matter how you point the finger, there are others who are well aware that you have made a mistake and should admit to it. Make sure you do not let the day pass without phoning a friend. Chatting mixed with some light gossip will do you both good and take you out of yourselves.

16. FRIDAY. Demanding. You may be heading for a showdown with a business colleague, which could end badly unless you agree to shelve your differences. Be honest with yourself in analyzing if this is simply a power struggle rather than an honest disagreement over policy. If you are preparing for a family celebration, you may be wishing you had not volunteered to do so much. However, it is not too late to ask relatives to chip in and help. This is a good time to start thinking about finding a more satisfying job. If your current position does not offer enough scope for individual contribution, look for a more creative outlet for your talents. Indulge your whims tonight.

17. SATURDAY. Confusing. Although it may seem as though you are doing your best to please loved ones, that may not be the way they see it. In fact, if you look more deeply into your own motives you may be shocked to find that they are selfish at heart. The more you spend on clothes and personal adornment, the better you expect to feel. However, that may not be happening. What is more important and more difficult to achieve is a sense of self-confidence that comes from within yourself. Beware of buying items for your home on impulse. It would be particularly unwise to purchase anything without prior approval from your mate or partner, since they are almost bound to take issue with your choice.

18. SUNDAY. Unsettling. You need to sit down with your mate or partner and have a serious talk about joint finances. This discussion is not likely to be without its problems. You must remember that accusing each other of spending more than a fair share is not going to provide any long-term answers. A quiet day at home will give you the chance to recoup your energy and sort out several issues that have been niggling away at the back of your mind. Social events may not be as appealing as usual, and you probably need to learn to value the benefits of solitude. Sometimes trying to tell loved ones the truth can be a waste of breath. If they are not ready to hear it, you will just have to be patient.

19. MONDAY. Happy. Your health should be especially good if you have experimented until you found a regime of diet and exercise that suits you. The challenge now is to keep it up. This fairly undemanding day should leave you free to fulfill several obligations you have made to other people. There is quiet satisfaction to be gained from helping out someone in need. Sagittarius people with pets probably appreciate the sense of security and affection they give. However, it is easy to become so accustomed to their presence that you fail to notice small signs of less than perfect health, so make sure you keep an extra vigilant eye on them.

20. TUESDAY. Uncertain. It has never been easier to lose your way, even on short trips. Absentmindedness could lead you to take a false turn; you could find yourself in an unfamiliar area, so try to keep your mind firmly on the road. Relations with a brother or sister may be rather unsure; they could be harboring guilt for an action that inconvenienced you in some way. Since this matter did not worry you as much as they fear, it would be kind to make the first move to calm the troubled waters. Even if you do not think of yourself as a good writer, it can be valuable to keep a diary so that you can clarify your thoughts and dreams. Let your mind float free.

21. WEDNESDAY. Stressful. If you are in charge of youngsters, you may really have your hands full. They can move like quicksilver, and there is a real possibility of them causing some damage unless you are extremely vigilant. It is likely to be quite an uphill struggle to get written work completed. Although you may know exactly what you want to say, constant interruptions can make it difficult to keep the thread. An instant fascination for a new acquaintance could threaten to sweep you off your feet and far from reason. Be aware that an involvement based on physical attraction is almost bound to cause more trouble than it is worth, and it probably will not last long either.

22. THURSDAY. Fair. Today's more buoyant mood could tempt you to take on too many small and tedious tasks, confident that you can complete them quickly. However, if you are involved in detailed work, you could soon regret biting off more than you can comfortably chew. Investing in a home is a big step to take, but right now it is well worth serious consideration. Consult your mate or partner to see how they feel about it. Keep in mind this would be a move toward future security apart from anything else. When you finish research that has been absorbing and useful, you may have a feeling of deflation. It is imperative to find a new and equally interesting activity to take its place.

23. FRIDAY. Variable. A project that seemed ready to move ahead could be brought to a sudden halt. The circumstances involved in this stoppage are probably out of your control. The best way to deal with this is to spend some time doing more groundwork, since there is no reason for the situation not to be reversed again. Parents may confide in you more than usual, letting you into their private thoughts. This is a mark of respect and trust that you are mature enough to be talked to as an equal, which should make you proud. A quiet party could end up in chaos unless you are very well organized. Plan for every eventuality, and keep the menu and decorations simple.

24. SATURDAY. Manageable. It would be a good idea to spend some time making a thorough list of tasks that need to be done around the house. You may be surprised at the number of items that need your attention once you focus your energies this way. Let generosity rule the day when a relative requires your assistance. There is no reason not to give them all the time and support at your disposal. This is an excellent day to stock up on essential foodstuffs and other goods. The cost of buying in quantity might not be as high as you think and, once done, will not have to be done again for a long time. Spend a peaceful evening at home just being with your loved ones.

25. SUNDAY. Satisfactory. The urge to get some physical exercise is likely to be stronger than usual, and there is no doubt that you should act on it. However, be careful not to get carried away when playing sports, since it is all too easy to forget your personal limitations and do more harm than good. A romantic affair may be confusing you considerably. Although it is probably enjoyably passionate, the downside comes out in arguments and quarrels that can be deeply upsetting. It is important to decide whether this price is really worth paying. Money may be a worry. It certainly would not hurt to tighten your belt a little and stick to a budget.

26. MONDAY. Changeable. It is said that the early bird catches the worm. Getting a head start this morning could really work in your favor. A show of enthusiasm can only make a favorable impression on superiors. For once you can afford to take a risk on a commercial enterprise. Your Sagittarius instinct for value is sound. Since a quick reaction is essential, you should not hold back. A romantic partner may not appear to be getting the message that you think you are making quite plain. You might have to come up with another way of stating your feelings and needs in order to get through to them. After all, this may not be news they really want to hear.

27. TUESDAY. Mixed. If you allow yourself to drift off into daydreams this morning, you are apt to spend the rest of the day trying to catch up. Make enough effort to at least get organized, and you will find it is possible to relax later on. A letter from a relative could bring news so surprising that you do not quite know how to react. On the surface it may be good, but a deeper instinct tells you that the whole truth is not being revealed. There may be a chance to financially help out a friend in some small way. This will really be a big favor, even though it is unlikely to inconvenience you very much. Just make sure you agree on terms of repayment that suit both of you.

28. WEDNESDAY. Cautious. Repetitive tasks are never the favorite occupation of restless Sagittarius people, since you are always eager to be doing something new. For this reason it can be a drag when you are given extra responsibility for chores that need to be done daily. The most positive way of coping is to accept this as a useful discipline. If colleagues seem cold toward you, the answer may not be hard to find. It is possible that you have offended them quite without meaning to do so. Now it will be necessary to eat humble pie and apologize no matter how innocent you think you are. It can pay to check up on long-term joint savings and to establish a firm spending plan.

29. THURSDAY. Rewarding. Just when you were beginning to feel worn down by the daily grind, there is light at the end of the tunnel. A change of routine that will allow you much more freedom and flexibility is on the way. This should feel like a burden being lifted off your shoulders. Do not be shy about telling a loved one how much you appreciate them. Even if they know in their heart how you feel, just hearing the words can be a real pat on the back. It is essential not to get into arguments with colleagues over a personal matter. There should be no place at work for private concerns, no matter what your relationship may be during leisure hours.

30. FRIDAY. Lucky. If you have been feeling rather dubious about the prospects for a long-term partnership, you should now be able to lay all your fears to rest. A new period of increasing goodwill toward each other is about to begin. Use this time to build a solid foundation for the future. Arrangements for a family celebration should be going well. Be aware that this chance to unite relatives who rarely see one another is really special. You will not regret pulling out all the stops and creating an event to be cherished. Bring the workweek to a satisfying close by spending the evening somewhere new with that special person in your life.

JULY

1. SATURDAY. Stressful. You are likely to be aware that loved ones are worked up about something even though they will not tell you what it is. A good amount of tact is necessary to find out why they are in such a mood. If you recently withdrew more savings than is comfortable, the money may just not be there as a big expense comes due. It may be necessary to borrow at this point, but try to limit your obligations to other people as far as possible; repaying a debt is rarely as easy as it first appears. Romance is in the cards. Quite a tempestuous affair could result from a chance meeting with the friend of a friend.

2. SUNDAY. Favorable. An item you thought you had lost could make a surprising reappearance, especially if you are moving furniture. The relief you feel will only be matched by that of the person you accused of losing it in the first place. The unpleasantness aroused by this accusation can now be put behind you. You need to discuss a close relationship in order to get everything absolutely clear. Although the situation is complicated, as long as you and the other person are willing to face the facts there is no reason you cannot sort it out to your mutual satisfaction. Never underestimate the power of thought to bring you closer to your desires; positive thinking can make a big difference.

3. MONDAY. Fair. At last you should be free to concentrate on a grand scheme that has been on your mind for ages. With all the preparation now complete, you can forge ahead with the visionary enthusiasm that is one of your exceptional strong points. If you can put off starting on a long journey today, it would be wise to do so. There are likely to be so many delays that even if you set out tomorrow you might still reach your destination more quickly. Sagittarius people studying through home correspondence courses may feel rather isolated without the company of fellow students. See if there is a way for you to get in touch with a local group who are also learning independently.

4. TUESDAY. Confusing. If you have been planning a special getaway, you could have to change the arrangements at short notice. This is bound to be a letdown, but summon your natural Sagittarius love of adventure and allow yourself to become excited about taking off for an unexpected destination. It can be very useful to broaden your skills even if you are not thinking of changing your job. However, finding just the right training might be a challenge;

the last thing you should do is jump at the first available opening. Be prepared for disruptions with electrical equipment. Take extra precautions, following all safety regulations to the letter.

5. WEDNESDAY. Disquieting. You are apt to be at a crossroads where the demands of your job are concerned. On the one hand there is every possibility of promotion. On the other hand, you may feel the need to express yourself more as an individual. One or the other desire is going to have to be sacrificed. It is time to reach a decision about a long-term relationship. There are issues that need airing with your mate or partner. Unless you do so soon, the situation will only deteriorate further. It is said that home is where the heart is, although as a Sagittarius you probably prefer to feel secure in the affections of loved ones rather than in a permanent location.

6. THURSDAY. Lucky. All financial matters should go smoothly, particularly if you are making plans for the future. Make the most of this opportunity to obtain the advice of an expert on how best to budget your money. With care, it is possible to make even a little go a long way. A relationship that has been based more on shared emotion than open communication now needs the extra ingredient of shared thoughts and planning. Fortunately you now have an intuitive understanding of each other that is sufficient to start mapping out common ground. Close questioning could reveal that a loved one will benefit from your help but have simply been too shy to ask for it.

7. FRIDAY. Mixed. Anger that boils up from the depths is never easy to deal with. You may have been keeping the lid on a great deal of negative feeling for some time. If you now let other people suffer for your own inability to cope with these emotions, you will only make the situation worse. Financially this is the time to take the bull by the horns. You can no longer afford to hope that things will improve without your taking decisive action. Start by preparing a new, realistic budget. You stand a good chance of improving your career prospects by knuckling down to some hard work. Do not refuse overtime if it is offered or a chance to apprentice yourself to an expert.

8. SATURDAY. Variable. The urge to get out and about is almost sure to sweep over you. Phone a few friends and see what can be organized. You do not need to make elaborate arrangements; go where fancy takes you. There is almost no hope of salvaging a relationship that has been spoiled by unpleasant gossip and backbiting. No matter how inaccurate the reports may have been, perfect trust is probably no longer possible between you and the other person. A friend who needs a strong shoulder to lean on will be grateful for your support. Put aside your own feelings and devote yourself to someone whose troubles are more real than your own.

9. SUNDAY. Frustrating. Although you may be all set for a light-hearted day, it is unlikely to work out quite that way. A social event could be less enjoyable than expected. Friends who had promised to attend the get-together may not show up for some reason, leaving you feeling rather foolish. You might be reluctant to face up to your financial situation, but there is no point avoiding the truth. Your natural Sagittarius generosity may be responsible for getting you into trouble; now it might be difficult to get the money that is owed to you repaid on time. Tread especially carefully where romance is concerned. Keep in mind that there is a fine line between friendship and love.

10. MONDAY. Fair. Settle down this morning to finish off some pressing tasks that other people should have done. It will be quicker and simpler to get the work out of the way to your satisfaction than to waste time chasing up those who have not fulfilled their duty. Consider making a regular donation to a favorite charity. Even small amounts can be useful when they are regularly given, and after a while you will hardly notice the difference in your finances. You might be reluctant at first to make use of a legacy, since the circumstances surrounding it are sad. However, making the most of it is actually the best way to prove how grateful you are for the gift.

11. TUESDAY. Useful. Strive to wrap up arrangements for a long-term investment. Even though the process may have been quite complicated, it will be worth the hassle in the long run. A romance that starts in the workplace might be slow to get off the ground if you both are rather shy about expressing your feelings. Do your best to forget that other colleagues are around, or arrange to meet somewhere private so that you can get to know each other better. Sometimes an older friend is just the person to give advice on the knottier problems of life because they have been around more than you and have racked up that much more useful experience.

12. WEDNESDAY. Sensitive. On occasion it is absolutely necessary to fight for your rights. When this becomes imperative, there is no choice. Whatever happens, other people must not be allowed to walk all over you when a point of personal freedom is at stake. Even if you are tempted to make a complete change of personal style, hold back from taking any rash steps. The effect you think you want might just not be the right one, and once money is spent it is too late for regret. For everyone, entering into a long-term partnership changes life profoundly. In your most important relationship, at first you may find the necessity for compromise rather a strain. However, you will soon get used to it.

13. THURSDAY. Productive. If you have been considering taking a course of study, do not hold back. It will enrich your understanding and broaden your horizons, and for a Sagittarius person there is surely nothing that you like more than that. Attraction to someone who is your superior might not be as straightforward as you think. Consider whether it is the real person or is it the power they wield that has a hold over you. If you have recently moved, you may hardly have had time to catch your breath. Some exploration of the neighborhood is now in order; you are apt to be delighted at the facilities available. Do not hold back where romance is concerned; speak up and let your feelings be known.

14. FRIDAY. Calm. This is a good chance to make a good impression, and you will not have to go out of your way to do so. A course of action that is quietly efficient should have a very positive effect on your employer. After a period of disruption between you and your mate or partner, all should be well again. You may now begin to realize that all you need do is take their point of view into consideration more often. Finish up all financial matters before the end of the day, leaving papers and your accounts in apple-pie order. This will enable you to relax totally this evening. Prepare for the weekend by cutting back a bit on food and drink and being less self-indulgent.

15. SATURDAY. Happy. This is an ideal time to get away with your loved ones from the everyday rat race. Even if you cannot afford to take much time off, a break will enable you to catch up on the pure pleasures of life that get shunted aside in the hurly-burly of making a living. When it comes to buying a gift for a special occasion, you can afford to be generous. The recipient will then associate you with this happy day for a long time to come. As a Sagittarius you usually appear confident and full of optimism in public, whereas privately you might harbor some self-doubt. There is really no reason to be worried, as friends will readily tell you if you ask for their opinion.

16. SUNDAY. Variable. Your enthusiasm is not always shared by other people. Sometimes even your loved ones get a little weary trying to keep up with you. Right now it would be wise to hold your horses until you are sure that other people are involved in your plans because they truly want to be, and not just to keep you happy. Money matters must be addressed before too long or you run the risk of losing track altogether. Carve out a quiet hour for yourself this evening to get to grips with your bills and bank balance. This is a good time for working around the house. It should be simple to get several practical tasks done to your satisfaction before dinnertime.

17. MONDAY. Sensitive. Close relatives may seem to be giving you the runaround, changing their mind from one moment to another so that it is hard for you to work out exactly what they want. You may feel inclined to wash your hands of the whole matter, but actually your help will be appreciated when you finally manage to get plans underway. If you have been looking for a new job, you could hear of a promising position. It may pay to keep this opening under your hat until you have made a phone call or gone on an initial interview, since your application might cause some controversy. Where love is concerned, a light touch will be more effective than being too brash and demanding.

18. TUESDAY. Tricky. It is not always easy to keep calm when you are driving, but today you must try. Just let other drivers lose their temper while you keep yours; you will have enough to do just coping with their unpredictable behavior and maneuvers. As a Sagittarius you need your freedom, but this must be set off against the need to have order and regularity in your life. There are times when eccentric actions are totally out of place and your sense of individuality must be stifled in favor of mundane reality. Youngsters could be rather unruly, which is a clue that they are beginning to come down with a virus or some other infection.

19. WEDNESDAY. Disconcerting. Because you pride yourself on your personal appearance, it can be a letdown to receive any criticism. However, if you look a bit deeper it might become plain that the negative comments spring from jealousy. You may feel the struggle to keep fit just is not worth it, but do not lose heart. You have undoubtedly made gains along the way that have become so much a part of your general well-being that they are now taken for granted. A family gathering that has been arranged in order to end a quarrel could have a rather surprising effect. Goodwill is sure to be present, but overcoming old grievances might prove harder than expected.

20. THURSDAY. Variable. As negotiations for a property sale are finally brought to a satisfactory conclusion, you can begin to relax and plan the future with confidence. This sale should lay the groundwork for greater security that will be welcome to both you and your mate or partner. Every family has a skeleton in the closet. Although it is a shock to be confronted with an unpalatable truth about your ancestors, in another way it could be something of a relief. In fact, on reflection you will probably be able to put it out of your mind entirely. Nostalgia for the past can undermine your pleasure in the present, so keep it within reasonable bounds. The future needs your attention, not the past.

21. FRIDAY. Excellent. At last a big romantic scene is about to come off. If you have been longing to meet someone with whom you have mental rapport, and a physical attraction, just such a person is preparing to make an entrance into your life. Work done for a course may come in for praise from your teacher, who could even suggest that you do some further research. Take this seriously, since it could be a passport to further learning and earnings. A minor ailment can be cleared up simply and painlessly if you just face up to your need for professional medical attention. Do not keep a stiff upper lip and suffer when there is no need for you to do so.

22. SATURDAY. Exciting. You should begin the weekend in a positive mood, ready to take on whatever is asked of you. This attitude will actually attract good fortune to you, with no shortage of offers of assistance from your loved ones. As a romantic relationship begins to mature, you may turn your thoughts to long-term commitment. Happily the other person seems to be thinking along the same lines, making this an excellent time to sit down together and discuss your expectations. You can obtain a great deal of pleasure pursuing a hobby to the highest level of achievement. Do not be modest; determine to excel and you are almost bound to do so.

23. SUNDAY. Mixed. The secret of success today is to expect the unexpected and not get upset by any change of plan. While it is unlikely that entertainment will go smoothly, there should be enough to keep you amused as long as you keep an open mind. Be sure to keep in touch with family members who may not be as serious as you about calling, writing, or visiting. A phone call is easily made, and brothers and sisters living at a distance probably have all kinds of news to tell you. If you are involved in a romantic affair, you may feel as if you are sitting on a volcano. You may not be able to prevent an explosion of emotion, but at least it will clear the air.

24. MONDAY. Deceptive. It is not always good to be too trusting, since colleagues are sometimes all too eager to take advantage. When it comes to the crunch today, you could be let down rather badly. What is worse, there may be no one but you to take the blame. Unfortunately it seems that romance is not the most successful area of your life at the moment. You can keep on making excuses for the other person, but it should be clear by now that they are simply not treating you as well as you deserve. A business deal could develop complications due to import or export regulations. Try not to get embroiled in this if you can avoid it.

25. TUESDAY. Demanding. There is no point getting worked up if a training course is more demanding than you ever expected. Instead of giving up because of self-doubt, determine to rise to the occasion and show the world just how well you can do. You can get special pleasure in appreciating the arts, although it might take another person to point out subtleties to you. Once you begin to develop an appreciation of culture, it will add a new dimension to your life. Sagittarius people working in the field of education may have to put up a fight for ideals. It is important to stick to your guns; if you give in a little now there may be no end to the pressure put on you.

26. WEDNESDAY. Manageable. Keeping daily tasks under control could thwart you from setting out on a more important venture. Although this is bound to be frustrating, it is vital to keep the wheels of ordinary life turning smoothly. You can handle money for other people with confidence, which is not normally the case. For once you know exactly what you are doing; as long as you keep good records of all stages of every transaction, there is little that can go wrong. There is every reason to look forward to the conclusion of a legal case. Even if it has been a long process, hopefully you will get a satisfactory result. Enjoy a special evening with your mate or partner and rekindle romance.

27. THURSDAY. Unsettling. You may be completely surprised after meeting someone on a journey who appears to know quite a bit about you. Probably this person is simply observant and intuitive, but you are sure to be fascinated by their slightly eerie knowledge. Hopes of a romance that started abroad may have to be abandoned as time goes by. It is one thing to have a relationship that is somewhat divorced from reality, another to try to fit it into the everyday world. When a business associate questions your decision, you may be tempted to launch a return attack. However, it would be wiser to consider whether they in fact have a valid point.

28. FRIDAY. Satisfactory. If you have been waiting for exam results, there should be no cause for worries. It is almost impossible not to feel some doubt at this stage, but as long as you did the work as well as possible you should be reasonably confident. Plans for a getaway with your mate or partner look good; you will both be glad if you decide to go all out for luxury. It will be worth spending a bit more than you had budgeted since you will benefit greatly from being able to relax and be waited on. This is not the best time to push a romantic relationship a stage further. Proceed gently, since the other person may need more time.

29. SATURDAY. Unpredictable. Just when you were feeling that life had no more surprises in store, news you receive today could turn your world upside down. After the first shock, you will probably be delighted to have a new challenge to face. This is just what you needed to get out of your current rut. Youngsters can ask awkward questions, which may be particularly embarrassing when you are out in company. The best thing to do is to deal frankly with them, since they are unlikely to be put off or distracted from what they want to know. An injection of cash could come at just the right time. However, do not take this as a sign that you can always rely on luck to help you out.

30. SUNDAY. Variable. Sports activities will help you keep fit, even though you usually prefer more private means of getting trim. Just be careful not to get carried away, or an old injury could flare up. There is no point being angry with parents when they only intend to do good. They will be hurt, and rightly so. It would be far better to explain how your ideas vary from theirs. You and your mate or partner can benefit from developing an interest in learning together. There may be an evening class you could take together, studying in tandem. This should be very enjoyable. There is probably little you can do to get a romance back on course, so perhaps you should just let it go.

31. MONDAY. Pleasant. It should be possible to make a fresh start in your attempts to better yourself. All self-development efforts will eventually bear fruit, but you need to have confidence in yourself. A business trip can open new doors, possibly giving you an idea for turning your career in another direction. The people you meet now could pinpoint talents that do not get fully used in your present position. As a Sagittarius you are apt to be constantly searching for meaning in life. Now might be a favorable time to consider a spiritual or religious approach. If someone whose opinion you respect encourages you in that direction, follow their lead.

AUGUST

1. TUESDAY. Slow. There is no point giving in to impatience, since work is not likely to move ahead quickly no matter how you tackle it. Resign yourself to some slow progress and you will get on much better. Attraction to an older person could take you by surprise; at least half the allure may be their greater knowledge of the world. You can certainly learn from them, but a romantic liaison would probably not be appropriate. Err on the side of generosity when it comes to lending a hand to a colleague. You can probably provide an overview of the situation which makes sense of the details, which is just what is required. Settle down tonight with a good travel book.

2. WEDNESDAY. Challenging. As a Sagittarius you are not usually caught up in trivial concerns and pursuits. Right now, however, it will be a big step in your life if you can rise above petty matters and concentrate on the underlying significance. In fact, if this becomes a habit it could really change your understanding of the way life works. Long-distance travel is favored; any trip you take now should make a deep impression. You have a natural pleasure in observing foreign cultures and adopting some of the positive points of a more exotic way of life. It should be possible to outline a business plan to a superior so persuasively that they are impressed and agree to all the details.

3. THURSDAY. Rewarding. There is every reason to celebrate if you achieve a test result to be proud of. This marks the culmination of a long-held dream, and you can really enjoy your success fully. A friend could open your eyes to new job opportunities which you would not have thought of for yourself. They may have useful contacts and connections that enable you to take a giant step forward in your career. If you are playing sports, go all out to win. Team games, in particular, are favored. Put your individuality aside and play in harmony with the others on your side. New information concerning a financial package could enable you to finally make a decision.

4. FRIDAY. Easygoing. The workweek should glide to a fairly peaceful close. Meetings which at first might not seem very productive could in fact sow seeds of ideas which later turn out to be extremely fruitful. Make sure you stay awake so that you do not miss an important hint. Try to socialize more with your mate or partner's friends. You may be surprised how different they can be when they are with another set of people. This is a good time to look forward and to plan your future. You are building up a more confident sense of your ability to get where you want to go. Be proud of this newfound willpower and determination to succeed.

5. SATURDAY. Fair. You can start looking forward to being with friends, even if it is some time in the future. Do not over-organize. Just be casual and allow the brief holiday to take its own form. If you have not yet explored local facilities for leisure, do not delay any longer. You might be surprised at what is offered, especially the water sports. This could turn out to be a regular routine, especially if you are trying to get fit. Money can be a thorny problem when it is obvious that friends are on a tight budget. Naturally you want to help out, but if they do not ask it can be rather difficult to find a tactful way of broaching the subject. Treat local gossip with skepticism and caution.

6. SUNDAY. Frustrating. There is a romantic problem looming on the horizon. You and the other person in your life may not be able to agree on the most basic principles. If this is causing you trouble now, just imagine the long-term effects. If you do not sort out financial practicalities, there is no hope of freeing up money for more indulgent treats. The necessities of everyday life cannot be ignored. Bills must be paid before you can start thinking about a vacation trip. The temptation to dwell in the past can be strong when things are not going so well, but brooding over old photos of happy times will not help you view the present in a positive light.

7. MONDAY. Variable. You should not feel out of your depth for long when asked to tackle a new job. This is apt to offer something to sink your teeth into, so the workweek should get off to quite a satisfying and productive start. Do not worry too much if a pet is missing; it is bound to turn up before too long and is unlikely to be far away. In fact, it may even be hiding somewhere around the house. A colleague may be eager to give you a financial tip that could be extremely useful. Be a little cautious, although they know what they are talking about so take their advice seriously. Boost your health with some extra vitamins and outdoor exercise.

8. TUESDAY. Tricky. A long trip could turn out to be an ordeal as rerouting adds to the traveling time. Make sure you have a good book with you. If you are traveling with youngsters, take along plenty of entertainment for them. It is all very well having a lot of enthusiasm, but as a Sagittarius you tend to scatter your energy rather than concentrating on one piece of work. If you focus on a particular goal, you will do better; the problem is that your low boredom threshold tends to trip you up. A romantic affair that seems glamorous at first could turn out to be a disappointment when you come back to earth. Do not let your hopes soar too high.

9. WEDNESDAY. Misleading. A business matter concerning overseas investments is probably not as straightforward as it once appeared. There may be some dirty dealing going on, so you would be wise to step back from this affair. Otherwise you could find yourself being used by other people for their own ends. Youngsters could be underachieving at school, making you suspect that all is not well. It could be that they are a little under the weather, or maybe there is a good reason for them to be unhappy in the classroom. Try to find the reason before too long. Be sure to listen carefully when getting instructions. You could make a bad mistake if you allow your mind to wander during on-the-job training.

10. THURSDAY. Unsettling. Getting into a long-term relationship usually includes an element of hard work, although not many people want to accept that this is so. There is no need to turn your back on romance, but dealing with the nitty-gritty of everyday life can come as a bit of a shock at first. A legal case may be dragging on with no sign of a conclusion. You may already be regretting getting involved, but there is no hurrying the law; you will just have to be patient for a while longer. You could get slapped down quite harshly for speaking out of turn in a learning situation. Try not to be a know-it-all. Be as willing to learn as you are anxious to teach.

11. FRIDAY. Fortunate. There is a very promising opportunity to develop your knowledge in a way that can be of great use. There is never any harm adding another string to your bow. The more talents you can draw on, the better your chances of maintaining a truly satisfying career. Sagittarius people who work in the publishing business may be able to put ideals into action for once. Commercial pressures are now less important than acting on your principles. A last-minute hitch could mean you have no time to wind down toward the weekend, but actually this can be a blessing in disguise as you make a new contact who will be able to pull strings on your behalf.

12. SATURDAY. Good. This is a day to enjoy all forms of beauty. Take in an art gallery or whatever appeals to your aesthetic sense; it will nourish your soul. Practical matters should go smoothly as you get a lot done with only a little extra effort. Check around the house to see if any small jobs need to be completed, and do not turn down offers of assistance. You can build up a network of friends overseas during the course of a vacation abroad, who will be pleased to exchange visits. Keep in touch by letter, and offer your hospitality to those who may want to stay with you while sightseeing in your area.

13. SUNDAY. Mixed. Try to get out and about. You have energy to burn, and it would be a pity to hang around indoors all day. Take loved ones somewhere special, or organize games that everyone can join in. There is not much point trying to concentrate on mental pursuits, particularly if you are required to do some detailed research. Your rather absentminded mood makes it difficult to focus on any one subject for very long; you probably prefer to drift off into irrelevant dreams. A brother or sister can perform a truly selfless act to help you out of a tight spot. That is certain proof of their affection, if you have been in any doubt of it.

14. MONDAY. Sensitive. There is probably no denying that someone at work has really upset you, and they are certainly well aware of it. However, you will not gain anything except a bad reputation if you continue to make them suffer for it. Instead, let go of the past and be friends again. You may feel like forcing a confrontation with a romantic partner just for the sake of clearing the air. However, to do so now could do more harm than good. Secretly you might even have a negative urge to bring the relationship to an end, and this must be recognized and controlled. Do not be hasty about making travel plans or you could miss out on an important price break for transportation or lodging.

15. TUESDAY. Difficult. The last thing you should do today is focus on the past. Even though you might be tempted to review your prior goals and bemoan achievements not yet reached, that will not help you arouse confidence for the future. Once you have faith that you can reach your goals, you are already on the way.

A quarrel with a neighbor may have reached the point of no return. Always one for the drastic measure, you may even have considered moving. However, the situation could be solved when a mutual acquaintance intervenes. Even though the responsibilities of family life sometimes are rather wearing, loved ones provide a sound basis of security for your life.

16. WEDNESDAY. Changeable. Anyone foolish enough to stand in your way is bound to have regrets as you steamroller on to broaden the horizons of your life. Be determined to have your own way when it comes to furthering your ambitions; there is little anyone can do to stop you. Despite indications to the contrary, it should be possible to set off on a trip earlier than expected. This might not go over well with loved ones who feel your timing is less than ideal, but it is important to grasp the moment. Sagittarius students could have a breakthrough in understanding. This may come just as you were beginning to feel you would struggle forever.

17. THURSDAY. Calm. A project can be finished, leaving you with some free time on your hands. Although as a Sagittarius you dislike being idle, right now it could come as a blessed relief to be able to relax for a while. Family gatherings should be pleasant, with everyone ready to take a positive approach. Old disagreements can be forgotten in this atmosphere of warm affection. You could look at your home with fresh eyes and realize just how much work needs to be done in order to make it really comfortable as well as beautiful. This is a good time to make tentative plans, although you should not rush into an ambitious redecoration scheme without thinking it over carefully.

18. FRIDAY. Useful. If you collect antiques or bric-a-brac, you could pick up a special item quite cheaply. The trick is to find it in a place where its true worth is not recognized. You can improve your fitness by exercising at home if you are reluctant to go to a gym or outdoors to jog. There are plenty of enjoyable regimens that can be followed in your spare time, with the advantage that you do not have to get dressed to go out. Romance is smiling on you at the moment. At first you might not think of the other person as a possible partner, since they are not the type you usually seek. However, that difference in itself can be a source of fascination.

19. SATURDAY. Favorable. If your hobbies are beginning to bore you, it could be time to take up something new. Consider joining a club that would enlarge your social circle at the same time it stretches your talents. As youngsters grow up they require more freedom. Parents naturally want to protect them, but try to remember how you felt at their age, then act accordingly. If you are embarking on a new romance you may have quite an effect on the other person. You should not have to do much of the running, since the attraction is apt to be mutually powerful right from the first. A local trip could be full of pleasant surprises for you and a family member.

20. SUNDAY. Fair. Although for some time you may have been feeling that it is difficult to see the way ahead, finally the mists are beginning to clear and you can take the next step with confidence. It is important not to give up on the process of self-development. Keep on your chosen path through life, even if you have to slow up from time to time. A trip to visit a friend who lives quite a distance away could lead to a romantic encounter. At first you are likely to be drawn to the other person's charm and wit, but once you have the chance to spend some time together, the relationship is bound to appear increasingly promising. A prospective lover is sure to add joy to your life.

21. MONDAY. Disquieting. You are apt to trip yourself up if you try to hurry this morning. Rush out of the house because you are a few minutes late and you are bound to leave behind an essential item that could make the day difficult. Communications systems may seem to have a life of their own; messages could get misdirected or lost. Do not be surprised if appointments have to be rescheduled. If there is urgent business to discuss, do what you can now and then leave the rest for a more favorable time. Youngsters may need more attention than you are prepared to give them, but keep in mind that their wants are more important than your personal work.

22. TUESDAY. Unsettling. If you have come to a decision that is going to affect loved ones, it is only fair to tell them so. There is no point putting this off, even if the news is not to their liking. A business colleague may be determined to put the damper on a new idea that you feel has promise. If you are convinced that it is really worth fighting for, do not give up without trying your best to convince them of its value. Sagittarius people who are waiting for a divorce decree to come through will naturally be feeling the strain, but eventually all will be well. You will then be able to look toward the future with a renewed sense of hope. Focus on small attainments for best success.

23. WEDNESDAY. Difficult. Sometimes you have to admit that you are in a no-win situation. Right now someone in authority seems to be calling all the shots. As a Sagittarius you do not usually relish head-on clashes of temperament, so let this person have their way even if your pride gets wounded in the process. Loved ones may criticize you for not being more ambitious, but you know your own limitations best. Point out to them that a supportive attitude on their part would be more conducive to urging you on to greater achievements. Financially it is time to get better organized. There should be plenty of money for your needs if you budget carefully and then stick to it.

24. THURSDAY. Variable. This is not the moment to hang back from making a greater commitment to the one you love. In fact, you might be inspired to speak on the spur of the moment, asking whether your long-term plans are the same. Written work could come in for some rather harsh comments, which will naturally be disheartening. However, if you make the suggested changes, you are apt to see that there is a big improvement. Do not let a superior flatter you into taking on more responsibility than you are comfortable handling. When the going gets rough, they may not be there to offer you promised support. A short trip could give you a welcome break from everyday routine.

25. FRIDAY. Favorable. Although Sagittarius people normally thrive on quite a dramatic sort of existence, there are times when the quiet life does appeal. Right now you will probably be quite happy to stay out of the limelight and concentrate on domestic tasks. Thorough research could pay off if you are looking for a better job. Do not go for an interview before you have checked out every aspect of the employment being offered; at the very least this will enable you to ask some intelligent questions and prove your interest. There is much to be said for getting expert help when the problems of life get the better of you; there is no need to struggle on alone.

26. SATURDAY. Pleasant. Settle down to a fairly quiet day. You do not have to rush around; just proceed at your own pace and do not allow other people to hassle you. It should be relatively straightforward to come to a decision about joint finances with your mate or partner. Common sense is all you need to agree on the best policy for saving for the future. A rumor that you hear via a friend could have a grain of truth, which might point you in a new career direction. At least you have been alerted to the possibility of changes, so that you can do something about the situation in good time. Treat yourself to a relaxing bath and an early bedtime.

27. SUNDAY. Frustrating. It can be difficult to avoid arguments about what everyone wants to do. Some compromise is necessary, but it will just not be possible to please all the family. There is no point having a family outing when loved ones are disgruntled. It might be simpler to just do your own thing for a change. Youngsters may give you a fright by hiding out during the course of the day. They are apt to be deliberately trying to upset you, and there may be further repercussions before the day is over. A loved one could introduce you to some interesting new acquaintances who have become a part of their life through a course of study they have been pursuing.

28. MONDAY. Productive. You have every reason to be annoyed when your work is not properly appreciated. However, this could be a sign that it is time to move on and find a job where your special Sagittarius talents can be put to better use. A romantic affair from the past could be rekindled when a certain person turns up in your locale after having lived at a distance for some time. This is hardly calculated to fit in with the way you are living your life now. You will probably have to make it quite clear that you are no longer interested, no matter how temptation tugs at your heartstrings. For peace of mind, make sure you have adequate insurance to cover all your possessions.

29. TUESDAY. Deceptive. There is nothing a Sagittarius person generally likes so much as the chance to trust fate. In this case, however, you would be unwise to plunge into a foreign business deal without first sounding it out very carefully. This is one occasion when you just cannot rely on being able to wing it. Practical tasks should be avoided if possible, or taken on with a sense of extra caution. Patience is not your strong suit right now, and you could simply end up spoiling work so that it has to be done again. The urge to win might lead you to overreach when playing sports; start slowly and increase your pace as you go.

30. WEDNESDAY. Quiet. Take this opportunity to finish up jobs that are outstanding. Try to leave no loose ends, so that when things get busy again you can go right ahead. If you have to speak before an audience, practice until you are word perfect; there is little more you can do to prepare ahead of time. You have nothing to fear if you know your subject well and can speak with authority. If you are looking for a new job, consider whether you are aiming high enough. There is not much point exchanging one position for a similar one, especially since you could do with more money. Set your sights somewhat higher and settle for nothing less.

31. THURSDAY. Satisfactory. A more social period is beginning. The phone will probably ring so often that you might even get tired of it. Set aside a reasonable sum so that you can go out and enjoy yourself without worrying about the cost. If you have an interview this morning, you should be able to carry the day with your Sagittarius charm and persuasiveness. Quick thinking allows you to adapt your qualifications to suit whatever is needed. Someone has been harboring tender feelings for you for some time, and finally they are ready to come out into the open. At first you might be too overwhelmed to respond, but they are willing to be patient.

SEPTEMBER

1. FRIDAY. Successful. You should have no problem speaking up in a meeting, and indeed can inspire other people through your ideas. Do not be afraid to put forward fairly radical suggestions, since the prevailing mood is openly receptive. If you have to travel on behalf of a group of like-minded people, the journey is likely to be swift and pleasurable. Keep your ears open and you may hear something to your advantage along the way. It is not too soon to begin considering long-term aims for youngsters' education. Talents can be fostered from an early age. As long as you do not become too ambitious, there is no harm pushing them to develop.

2. SATURDAY. Manageable. Your mate or partner may have your need to balance work with spending time in their company all out of proportion. Although they are probably not in a mood to be swayed by reason, it might be worth pointing out that you need both kinds of satisfaction in order to live a rich and fulfilling life. This is not the best moment to fall under the influence of any person, even someone you respect, because you are a bit too eager to take their word as gospel. In fact, their opinion is worth no more and no less than your own. It would be disastrous to make big changes in your life based solely on their say-so. Unwind by watching a good movie this evening.

3. SUNDAY. Exciting. A friend may be about to make romantic overtures to you and be busy setting up a suitable situation in which to do so. At last you will be sure that they truly are harboring affection for you and have your best interests at heart. This is a good day to go swimming, whether in a local pool or in a lake or the ocean if it is within reach. Make a day of it by inviting a bunch of friends for a daylong get-together. As the day goes on, you will probably need to withdraw for a while to recharge your emotional batteries. Find time to have a private hour or so reminiscing happily with loved ones about shared occasions you enjoyed together.

4. MONDAY. Difficult. Brace yourself for a bumpy ride. You may really have got a superior's back up, and now they are out gunning for you. Unfortunately your tendency to fight back will only make matters worse. It would be far wiser to state your reasoning in a carefully worded letter that can be digested when the atmosphere is less stressful. Money issues are apt to come between you and your mate or partner. There is no point struggling to gain control; the real answer is that you both need to trust each other and to plan together. Drastic action could be necessary when it becomes plain that an acquaintance has not been dealing fairly with you.

5. TUESDAY. Disquieting. As a Sagittarius you do not usually have a suspicious nature. However, once your doubts have been aroused, you are likely to worry away at them until you have worked yourself into a stressed-out state. Stop and consider the consequences before starting to snoop into the affairs of other people, since you could do a great deal of damage. It should be possible to manipulate a business partner sufficiently to get your way, but there will be a price to be paid at a later date. They undoubtedly resent being pushed around, and probably will not be very forthcoming with you in the future. Happily the day should come to a pleasant conclusion with an invitation to a friend's house.

6. WEDNESDAY. Fair. Get ahead of the opposition this morning. It will not hurt at all to get to appointments a little ahead of schedule. This may give you time to chat and to pick up some very useful information that is not generally available. Academic matters are favored. Even if you have not thought of yourself as the sort of person who could benefit from more education, it is worth looking into regular college courses or evening classes. The process of learning is stimulating in itself, and joining a class is also a great way to meet new people. A job interview could be tricky, with some subtle questions really putting you to the test, but you can rise to the occasion.

7. THURSDAY. Tricky. It is good to do what friends want to a certain extent. However, if you find yourself being drawn into activities that go against your principles, then it is time to stop. This is one of those occasions when you have to be firm, letting other people know how you feel even if doing so is slightly hurtful to them. There is no point splurging on expensive dating schemes to get you in touch with possible romantic partners because all that will probably happen is that you end up out of pocket. Do not let anyone take advantage of your vulnerability. Use your good Sagittarius instinct to judge whether you are likely to get anything positive out of meeting people through commercial means.

8. FRIDAY. Pleasant. When you settle down with a partner, it can be easy to let former friends drop as you adjust to a new way of life. Sooner or later, however, you are going to want to integrate them into your lifestyle once again, so it might be nice to start planning a big party to bring them all together. You can make a very strong and positive impression on someone who is able to help you bring a dream to fulfillment. As long as you are enthusiastic about your goal, people should be willing to pull strings to keep you on course. A conference being held away from your usual base of operations gives you the opportunity to shine with greater confidence and authority.

9. SATURDAY. Deceptive. Do not be fooled by appearances; a new neighbor is probably not quite what they seem. You might think you have sized them up very astutely, but before long they may begin to reveal a different side of their character that comes as a complete surprise to you. Shopping can be problematic since you are not in the most practical of moods. If you allow yourself to be sidetracked, there is no telling what you might bring home. This is a good day for buying tickets for a special theatrical or ballet performance. From time to time it helps to escape into a fantasy world; you and your loved one certainly deserve to allow yourselves a treat.

10. SUNDAY. Favorable. Conditions are ideal for a social day. Do not stick to convention, but arrange an informal gathering that can go on as long as participants want. Youngsters have their own dreams and hopes, which it is your duty to encourage as far as is reasonable. They want support and approval, which should be a positive pleasure to give. A brother or sister would be pleased to hear from you; some mutual assistance may result. If you are able to draw on better resources of education and contacts, there is no reason your relatives should not take advantage of these benefits. It is better to speak few words rather than too many.

11. MONDAY. Unsettling. There could be trouble with computer equipment. If you are trying to get used to a new system, you need considerable patience in order to accustom yourself to its quirks. It is simply not possible to cut corners while learning: if you do, you will soon find yourself in trouble with the programming. Journeys are likely to be disrupted, but it will not help to lose your temper with officials who really are not to blame. The calmer you remain, the more pleasantly will you be treated; smile and the world smiles with you is a good motto to live by. If youngsters do not get on well with their teachers, this can negatively affect their education, so the problem must be dealt with immediately.

12. TUESDAY. Frustrating. Just as you begin to feel that a long-term relationship is settling down comfortably, your mate or partner may start to find fault with your living arrangements. They may actually have been discontented for some time without letting on. It looks as if you will have to build up your life together again almost from scratch. A legal decision could be overturned on appeal, this time going against you. This is bound to be a shock, but it has to be dealt with reasonably. As a Sagittarius you are not usually prone to thoughts of revenge, but the behavior of a family member could tempt you to come up with some negative and even harmful ideas.

13. WEDNESDAY. Disconcerting. Family matters have rarely got you as emotionally wound up as you are today. You may be suffering divided loyalties, but if you are honest with yourself there is no doubt where your duty lies. If you work from home, you could be facing a crisis as the demand for your skills increases. Expansion of your business would undeniably complicate your life, but it may be the only way to capitalize on all of your success to date. If you are contemplating buying a home, a firm decision may be necessary right now. Delay could mean losing a potentially good buy, so consult with your mate or partner and make a firm choice.

14. THURSDAY. Satisfactory. It is not always the case that idealistic work is voluntary. There are ways of making the world a better place that can help you make a living at the same time. Just think how enjoyable it would be to do such work. A declaration of affection coming out of the blue may take you by surprise. It may be that you simply had not dared hope that the other person was interested, but now there is no doubt of it. You can dare to feel happy and excited. Express yourself in words, even if you only scribble down notes for a diary. Writing can be an excellent way of defining your feelings and getting a grip on the events of the day.

15. FRIDAY. Variable. You may get a chance to contribute creative ideas to a work project. There is apt to be research to be done, and you should not skimp on it if you want to impress higher-ups with the caliber of your work. Take a chance on romance; this could be your lucky day. There is nothing to be lost by asking out someone you have had your eye on for some time. A potentially lucrative business venture may be roughed out, but then mull over the details during the course of the weekend. It might not seem so simple once you begin considering all of the implications. Do not allow yourself to argue with friends over a trifling matter.

16. SATURDAY. Enjoyable. It is not likely that you will have much interest in getting household chores done. What you want is to feel the wind in your hair and see the horizon rolling away in front of you. Even if it is not possible to indulge in total freedom literally, there is nothing to stop you from letting your imagination soar. Sports are favored; Sagittarius spectators should get just as much pleasure out of the day as those who are actually playing. Set your sights on winning, and do not be satisfied with second place. Youngsters may be a handful, but their high energy levels are healthy; at least they will give you some good exercise.

17. SUNDAY. Uncertain. No one may be able to make up their mind about what to do. If you are in an impatient mood, this can be extremely frustrating. However, forcing your plans on loved ones will only produce resentment and annoyance. Keep youngsters away from water. Your dreams may carry a message, but you will have to do a lot of decoding. Write down as much as you can remember. If you dreamed about a friend or a loved one, let them know; the dreamscape may mean something to them. Practical tasks can be more of a nuisance than usual because your mind just is not on what you are doing. Phone a friend and pour out your feelings to a sympathetic ear.

18. MONDAY. Stressful. You have definitely been working hard lately. When you begin the workweek already feeling a bit under the weather, it is not a good sign. Look for some way to delegate responsibility so that you are able to relax from worry. The emotional demands of your mate or partner may be getting on your nerves, but you will not solve anything by trying to ignore the fact that there is a problem. Instead, face it squarely and at least discuss what is going on. More fresh air would do you a world of good. It is all too easy to move from car to four walls, rarely glimpsing the world outside. Give a pet a treat; indulge yourself, too.

19. TUESDAY. Mixed. The way to get the best out of the day is to communicate your wishes directly to other people. You can get across ideas more clearly than usual, and you should find that your friends and colleagues are sufficiently intrigued to follow your lead. This is a good time for planning a party. Invite neighbors as well as friends so that you can get to know them better and perhaps form the basis of a closer relationship. If a business partnership is tough going at the moment, the only thing to do is to soldier on. When work becomes a bit of a burden you naturally lose some enthusiasm, but the effort you put in now will be well rewarded in good time.

20. WEDNESDAY. Good. One way of meeting a romantic partner is to look through the personals column in your local newspaper. At the very least you will get an idea of the sort of person who is out there looking, and you could just strike it lucky with someone suitable. If you have to buy or upgrade electrical equipment for your home, this is the day to do so. Do not be tempted into buying the cheapest; pay a little more and assure yourself of quality. Business meetings and seminars can be very instructive. Even if you do not feel you have much to contribute, there are plenty of ideas that you could pick up and put to use in your own work environment.

21. THURSDAY. Variable. During the early part of the day you are likely to feel that it is virtually impossible to forge ahead. No matter how simple the task, other people may seem determined to make it more difficult than need be. It will take patience and tolerance on your part to keep a cool head. You and your mate or partner may be at loggerheads when it comes to future plans. One of the hardest challenges of life together is getting your ambitions in balance. Often one partner has to sacrifice their aims in favor of the other person, but this must not be allowed to happen. Chatting with someone who is an expert in their field could be highly profitable, but use tact.

22. FRIDAY. Misleading. There are times when friends go behind your back, perhaps without realizing how deeply their actions are going to affect your relationship. When it comes out that personal information you revealed in confidence has been passed on, you will have to come to terms with the fact that not all of your friends have proper respect for you. Financially you may be looking to the future, but with no great sense of confidence. There is no point investing in a madcap scheme that promises high returns; play it safe and you will reap the long-term benefit of a more solid investment. Youngsters need a bit of extra protection from bullying at school or in the neighborhood.

23. SATURDAY. Stressful. Just when you need emotional support, there is someone offering a shoulder for you to cry on. You need not feel ashamed of a moment's weakness. In fact, you will feel all the better for letting go, and the situation will suddenly appear in a much more positive light. There is no denying that when one door shuts, another one opens. As you achieve a long-held dream, new peaks to conquer will open up for you. The older generation can have pertinent advice to offer about the practicalities of everyday life. Do not discount their ideas just because they may seem a little old-fashioned. A sociable night out should round off the day nicely.

24. SUNDAY. Fair. You may feel like withdrawing quietly for an hour or so. Going through old papers and photos could take you back into the past, with memories of former friends and lovers returning to enchant you. This is a good opportunity to lay the ghost of an old relationship to rest. Just try to be realistic, and remember the downside of the affair as well as the romance. A surge of energy makes you eager to get out and about, and you are likely to want to explore new places. Either take loved ones with you or go alone; the important thing is to absorb some fresh impressions. If you are studying you can usefully put in time on a new area that seems promising and intriguing.

25. MONDAY. Changeable. The workweek may start with news of developments concerning a project you have entered into with friends. It should be possible to push it a stage further slightly earlier than you had hoped, so take advantage of whatever opportunity arises. Your ideals can sometimes be a little wearisome to other people, but right now they are able to appreciate that you can only act when you feel it is morally right to do so. If you go against your conscience you will only come to regret it. It would be wise to check out the credentials of anyone you are thinking about becoming financially involved with. They may not be quite as authoritative as they claim or not as rich.

26. TUESDAY. Rewarding. A new acquaintance who is outside your usual social circle may have you in something of a spin. Their ideas could seem so strange in comparison with yours that you feel like rejecting them out of hand. However, that may not satisfy a nagging feeling that they are actually worth looking into more deeply. Local trips can be delightful if you are intent only on pleasure, but be sure not to forget the practical purpose for which you set out. It is all too easy to get sidetracked, especially when you are in congenial company. A relationship crisis could tempt you to cut your losses and leave, but this will only result in feelings of bitterness and disappointment.

27. WEDNESDAY. Sensitive. It can be hard for other people to know how to deal with you. It may seem as if you are missing some form of protection, so the slightest misplaced word can hurt. The question is why you should be feeling this way. You may have allowed yourself to sink into an uncharacteristic mood of self-pity that must be conquered. You are apt to be attracted strongly to a close acquaintance, but this requires some careful handling. It certainly would not be appropriate to come straight out and reveal your feelings. Instead, bide your time and consider a more indirect approach. As a legal case draws to a close, you can look forward to making a new beginning.

28. THURSDAY. Favorable. Do not hide your light under a bushel. Speak up in a meeting and you will find your ideas are treated with respect. This should give you the confidence you need to be more outspoken in standing up for your beliefs. Compliments about your appearance should be accepted gracefully; if you receive them bashfully you will only spoil the effect. Just take pleasure in knowing that you are attractive to other people. A business relationship may be developing into a friendship after hours. This can actually be to your advantage in many ways, not least that you are beginning to get a better sense of each other's quirks and eccentricities.

29. FRIDAY. Variable. Bring the workweek to a satisfactory conclusion by making sure you have made all the calls you need to and have put paperwork in good order. It should be possible to finish up a project, leaving you with a pleasant sensation of achievement. Youngsters may play hide-and-seek with you, making it hard to keep an eye on them. There is no harm in letting them have their way for once, just as long as you do not lose track of their whereabouts. One-to-one relationships require extra tolerance if you are to weather the current bumpy patch. There is no doubting the affection you hold for each other, so do not succumb to irritation or pettiness.

30. SATURDAY. Mixed. If you have the opportunity to do someone a good turn, be as generous as you can. Their situation is likely to appeal to your sympathy, and it should be a real pleasure to help out. Sagittarius singles mourning the end of a love affair need time to go through this very natural process. Before long you will be able to put away the happy memories and begin looking to the future with a renewed sense of hope. This is a good day for finishing off chores outdoors. Leaving work undone is never very satisfactory, so put some effort into it and you will feel much better. Do not snap at youngsters; be patient even if they are getting on your nerves.

OCTOBER

1. SUNDAY. Confusing. This is a day when nothing is likely to go as planned. Even short trips are subject to delays and diversions. The only successful way to cope is to just follow along wherever events take you. There is no point harboring a sense of guilt for something you said; what is necessary is to make amends as soon as possible. Otherwise your words will rankle, and there could be real damage done to a relationship that is important to you. It can be difficult to get time to yourself when the needs of youngsters must be put first. Even if you have to sacrifice time that you set aside for a personal project, they are your first and most pressing responsibility.

2. MONDAY. Mixed. You may be very tempted to put your foot down when a superior orders you to act against your better judgment. Make sure, however, that your motives are straightforward; if there is a tinge of resentment in your mind, it will be recognized and trouble could ensue. A relationship that has been on-again, off-again for some time is finally going ahead in a more definite fashion. You have probably been kept waiting for so long that it is a great relief to be able to tell friends that all is well. In a situation where it is necessary to consider all points of view, be sure to take your time before coming to a binding decision or making any type of commitment.

3. TUESDAY. Variable. Friends value you for your ability to come through all kinds of crises and go on as if nothing had happened. Do not be surprised if they turn to you for advice and assistance during their own tough times, then do your best to give support. If you are not careful you could become the butt of a colleague's bad temper. Try to steer clear of any potential trouble spots or you might get drawn in out of your depth. Although ambition is all to the good, there are times when even you must realize your limits. Aim high by all means, but if you overreach there is going to be a price to pay. A quiet night at home should be unusually appealing to you and to your mate or partner.

4. WEDNESDAY. Changeable. You need to keep a good sense of balance. On one hand there is a sense of cooperation, while on the other people seem to be working against you. This can be a case of two steps forward and one step back, so resign yourself to taking more time than expected to complete a project. Your mate or partner may be developing an interest in a group activity that could be beneficial for you as well. Go along and give it a try, then decide how you feel about it. Everyone needs role models, but it can come as a bit of a shock to find that your idol has feet of clay. Bear in mind that everyone is only human after all.

5. THURSDAY. Fair. Financial planning should be comparatively easy. Once you get your papers in order, you might be surprised to find that your situation is not so bad after all. In fact, there could even be a small sum of money squirreled away that you have completely forgotten about. If you are too shy to tell someone your true feelings, then write a letter. This will give the person time to absorb your revelation and frame a well-considered reply. It would not be wise to rely too much on a peer group to give you a sense of purpose. In the end your aims are your own, no matter how much you may be tempted to identify with the ideals and long-term goals of other people.

6. FRIDAY. Fortunate. Sometimes it can be a welcome relief to turn to someone in authority when you are in doubt. Right now a difficult decision can be illuminated by an older person who has the right qualifications to help you out of a tricky situation. Trips around the neighborhood can bring you back into contact with people you have drifted out of touch with. Just visiting old haunts may give you a better sense of belonging. On occasion you may find that youngsters seem wise beyond their years. Their perceptive comments should not be dismissed as humorous just because you are a little taken aback; they may actually have penetrated to the truth.

7. SATURDAY. Uncertain. It probably will not be easy to get off to a prompt start this morning because no one is very well organized, including yourself. This is actually a good time to just relax and let the day unfold at its own pace; otherwise you will only be frustrated. A romantic proposal could put you on cloud nine, and nothing else will seem important by comparison. Try to be aware that you could be getting this out of proportion. If you do not do so, there is every possibility of coming down to earth with a bump. Sometimes looks can be more eloquent than words, and loved ones can be hurt by a cold or critical stare. Since you probably do not really mean it, be verbally kind instead.

8. SUNDAY. Difficult. It is apt to be rather difficult to finish off tasks without being interrupted. Loved ones may just not seem to appreciate that sometimes you need time alone, as they keep on breaking in and expecting you to join in their plans. You could greatly upset a love affair by saying the wrong thing. It is not always as wise as you might think to tell the truth directly. If what you have to say is not palatable, lead up to it slowly. Do not expect friends to be punctual, since they are almost bound to be unavoidably delayed. You might want to call to check that they have not forgotten the date altogether. Try to wind down this evening from the stressful events of the day.

9. MONDAY. Disquieting. If you are hoping to close a property deal, you may have to wait a while before you get your heart's desire. Such matters are never simple. It is better to make sure that every detail is in order rather than rush into a contract you could regret at a later date. Relatives may be causing you a few headaches. Your sense of responsibility for what is happening in the family could lead you to exaggerate a minor problem. Youngsters would certainly benefit from some sober advice in an effort to get them back on the straight and narrow. Colleagues begin the workweek in an uncooperative mood, so you must rely on yourself rather than count on team effort.

10. TUESDAY. Surprising. It should be a real delight when an old friend reappears out of the blue. Even if you have not seen each other in years, the rapport between you will still be strong. You will probably start talking again as if you had never stopped. Help for a personal project could come from someone who can put you in contact with resources that would otherwise be unavailable. Make sure you show just how grateful you are for this unexpected and valuable boost. If you lay down the law at home, certain family members may respond by rebelling. Sometimes it is necessary to just live and let live. Keep in mind that loved ones are reasonably tolerant of your faults and failings.

11. WEDNESDAY. Good. You may be amazed at the difference small touches around the house can make to the general cheerfulness of your surroundings. This is not the best time to begin ambitious redecoration. However, just throwing out or giving away shabby possessions is a positive start. Find time to visit a relative who cannot get out and about. They are bound to be very appreciative, and this could even become a regular date that you begin to enjoy. If you are short of cash, try looking in the pockets of your clothes and down the back of the sofa. There is bound to be a small amount that has been mislaid without you even noticing. A small wager could pay off.

12. THURSDAY. Favorable. A romantic affair may be developing even better than you hoped when you first got involved. You may now feel it is time to take steps toward a long-term commitment. Introduce this possibility with tact rather than as a definite decision on your part. Luck is with you, so there is no harm in taking a small gamble. However, do not risk more money than you can afford to lose. All writing projects are highlighted; get down to creative work without further planning. Do not try to work out your ideas in extreme detail. Just letting the words flow can sow the seeds of an exciting work. Do not expect anyone to read your mind.

13. FRIDAY. Challenging. As a Sagittarius you can usually afford to follow your own desires with a sense of confidence, and this attitude creates its own good fortune. This is especially true now, so embark upon the day with a positive outlook and you will make the most of it. As a love affair reaches a turning point, you might wonder whether you should just be friends. However, it is impossible to go back to a state of affairs that was left behind some time ago, so this is make-or-break time. Now more than ever it pays to be cautious with your money. Do not listen to what friends have to say, no matter how much they may urge you to take a chance on a risky investment.

14. SATURDAY. Deceptive. The true nature of a close acquaintance may begin to emerge when you attempt to get a favor returned. They are willing to accept help from you, but less eager or even available when it comes to repaying your kindness. This is not the best day for clearing out bathrooms and kitchens; tackle cupboards and drawers and you are likely to end up with a worse muddle than what you started with. For some reason you find it more difficult than usual to actually throw anything out, so wait until a more ruthless mood descends upon you. Keep a close eye on youngsters' health, particularly if they seem a bit lackluster. Make sure they are getting a balanced diet and a daily dose of exercise.

15. SUNDAY. Tricky. Relations with a brother or sister that have been deteriorating for some time should take a sudden turn for the better. All that was needed was a little more sympathy and imagination to understand each other's feelings. No matter what your head is telling you, your heart may be sure that a loved one just is not reciprocating your feelings. You can put a positive interpretation on all their actions and words, but the truth is staring you in the face. A recent change in accommodations still may be causing disruptions as you find it hard to get back into a familiar routine. This proves how deeply you had sunk into a rut and offers an escape route.

16. MONDAY. Variable. A task you thought you had finished may come back to haunt you. In your heart of hearts you may be aware that it was not done properly the first time around. Make sure it is completed faultlessly this time. Pay more attention to your health. If you recently let an exercise program slip or went off your diet, you may begin to feel the difference. Get back in shape without further delay; all that is needed is a renewed sense of discipline. Sometimes you can intuit what your mate or partner needs, then fulfill their desires before they even ask. Do not allow an obstinate mood to hold you back from an act of selfless generosity and thoughtfulness.

17. TUESDAY. Mixed. In legal matters you may have played a hunch and come out the winner. That is fine, but it would be unwise to take this as a general rule since you may not have the same luck again. A potentially lucrative business deal needs some additional consideration. The temptation is to say yes without going in to all the ramifications, but there might be a catch. You have no excuse for keeping an important decision from your mate or partner. Even if you are unsure of what their reaction will be, they still have a right to know. Taking a more cooperative attitude toward neighbors can greatly improve the atmosphere in your environment. When everyone gives a little, congeniality can be maintained.

18. WEDNESDAY. Fair. There is no doubt that where negotiations are concerned you hold a winning hand. Now it is up to you how you play it; this could make a vital difference. You may be getting involved in a relationship which is based on friendship rather than passion. This might take some getting used to, but mental rapport is important to you; in fact, this could be just what you need at this time in your life. Social events should be enjoyable. You could meet someone who might be able to give you a helping hand up the career ladder. This is no time to be shy; if you miss a golden opportunity, another may be a long time in coming.

19. THURSDAY. Difficult. If you continue to put your trust in someone who is treating you coldly, you are probably riding for a fall. Other people are well aware that you are beating your head against a brick wall, but their advice may not seem to affect you at all. However, the truth cannot be avoided forever. A generous loan to someone in need could have left you short of money for your own essentials. You can hardly ask for an early repayment, but at least consider whether you have done more overall harm than good by being so liberal. There is no point going from one extreme to another in diet. In fact, indulging to excess and then fasting can be quite harmful to your health.

20. FRIDAY. Mixed. The last thing you should do right now is poke around in a friend's private affairs. Even if you are genuinely concerned, there are more positive ways of doing some good than using stealth. There may be extra money to be made by taking on more responsibilities at work. At first you might not be eager to do so, but think of the boost this would give to your savings. Self-development courses can be highly illuminating, teaching you more about yourself and giving insight into your relationships with other people. Always curious, as a Sagittarius you are in fact the ideal person to benefit since you are not afraid to know and to face the truth.

21. SATURDAY. Variable. If you are going out with your mate or partner, no expense should be spared. Splurge and give yourselves a really good time; it will be a weekend to remember and to cherish. Other people may accuse you from time to time of trying to run before you can walk, but even they have to admit that you score some spectacular successes. Right now it does not pay to think small; be ambitious and you will achieve a lot more. It is important to listen closely to loved ones and not drift off into a daydream while they are talking. They are trying to tell you something that means a lot to them, so be as glad to support their dreams as they are to help you with yours.

22. SUNDAY. Buoyant. The way to woo a lover is by being fascinating and elusive. If you fling yourself at them, you run the risk of being too obvious. But act a little distant and you are bound to intrigue them. You may want to take loved ones out locally without revealing your destination until you arrive. The only drawback with this is that youngsters might get overly excited as they try to guess what treat lies in store. It is not always easy to plan for the future, but as long as you follow your heart you will keep on course. There is no point pushing yourself to follow a career that does not satisfy you. Nor should you aim for achievements that have been chosen for you by other people.

23. MONDAY. Disquieting. Do not be tempted to think you can walk into an interview without thorough preparation. If you do so, you could be in for a nasty surprise. It is probably best to err on the side of caution. An overconfident manner will not go over well in any situation. For some reason you may be determined to undermine your own efforts to achieve an important ambition. Perhaps success would mean you have to take a more positive view of your capabilities, and this in turn means no longer being satisfied with less. If you are spending the day at home, switch off as you go about your tasks. As you work your subconscious will be mulling over solutions to problems.

24. TUESDAY. Slow. Although as a Sagittarius you usually have a rather low boredom threshold, you might be glad of a chance to enjoy this fairly peaceful, slow day. It will give you time to think thoroughly about what you are doing and to complete a really good job. If friends are pressing you to get involved in a project that does not seem absolutely aboveboard, do not let them prevail. Right now it is vital to associate only with people in whom you have absolute trust. All practical tasks are favored, but as usual you must be careful when using sharp tools, especially in the open air. Do not hesitate to speak up in your own defense to a superior or a bureaucrat.

25. WEDNESDAY. Lucky. Everyone needs something to believe in. You might have the opportunity today to get involved with an event that is designed to spread a message you know to be important. Even if the work is voluntary, there is a lot you can both contribute and gain from joining in and doing your best. It should be possible to charm a friend into agreeing to do things your way. As long as you are acting from the right motives, there is nothing wrong with turning on the flattery. Where romance is concerned, all you have to do is wait patiently. A long-standing friendship could soon begin to develop into a deeper and more intense personal relationship.

26. THURSDAY. Deceptive. It is never pleasant to realize that you have put your trust in someone who is betraying you. Right now, however, it seems that is exactly what you have to face. The primary lesson to be learned is not to be so open with people before getting to know them well. Short journeys could be somewhat troublesome; road repairs may confuse the route so that you have to spend some time reorienting yourself. Be sure to keep a local map handy. There is nothing to be gained by trying to pull a fast one on an acquaintance. They are bound to catch you at it, and then there will be a shouting match or worse. Honesty truly is the best policy.

27. FRIDAY. Disquieting. You may have been going out of your way recently to please a romantic partner in every respect, so that they have had things entirely their own way. Unfortunately, the only result is that they are beginning to take your compliance for granted. If you are honest, you will realize they may never give you the relationship you want. There is no point throwing away money on legal fees when it is not at all clear that you have a sound case. If it is still possible to settle out of court, that might be the wiser course. Where your health is concerned, you need to make fresh efforts to get in better physical shape. Consider joining a gym or health club.

28. SATURDAY. Sensitive. There is something to be said for trying to attract what you want by the power of positive thinking, but beware of the danger of becoming obsessive. In the end you cannot really enchant someone from a distance. If they are truly not interested in you, there is little you can do to persuade them otherwise. A complete change of image may be in order, especially if you have been wearing the same style for a considerable length of time. Take a critical look at yourself. Try to view your personal style as others do; you might be in for a shock. A spending spree can be good therapy, but keep in mind that money cannot buy everything.

29. SUNDAY. Fair. You may be eager to get on with some personal work in privacy. Stress to loved ones that they must not disturb you. This is a good chance to get paperwork in order and clear out old correspondence and files. You can also benefit from some exercise. A discipline such as yoga may be more suitable for you than more boisterous sports. Quiet, rhythmical movements give you the opportunity to calm your nerves and enter a meditational state. There is little that needs to be done in a practical sense that cannot be put off for a day or two. Devote the day to gentler pursuits such as writing and talking. Get to bed early tonight.

30. MONDAY. Manageable. If you have been chewing over a problem for some time, you may have finally come to a reasonable conclusion about what to do. Do not delay putting your plan into action, because if you miss the first impetus you might lose the mood. You may have to keep youngsters at home due to a minor ailment, throwing the day into some confusion. They will need attention and entertainment; if you devote yourself to this, you can make the togetherness really special for them. It can be something of a shock to come across receipts for purchases your mate or partner has made without telling you. Actually, it may be that you were simply not listening at the time.

31. TUESDAY. Disquieting. Sagittarius people who have been waiting for the result of a job interview are unlikely to receive good news. It might be worth getting in touch with the interviewers and asking them where you failed to come up to the required standard. Your impetuous nature does not usually respond well to discipline, but right now there is danger of rebelling in the wrong situation. Try hard to accept that sometimes you have to knuckle down to another person's orders; one day you will get your turn to be in charge. Do not upset loved ones just because you are not in the best of moods. They are not to blame for your upset and should not have to bear the brunt of your anger.

NOVEMBER

1. WEDNESDAY. Tricky. It is not always easy to know how to handle a situation when you come into possession of knowledge that is not commonly available. Right now you could have a moral obligation to confront a colleague who has been misbehaving, but it will be difficult to do this without setting yourself up as judge and jury. If you are in charge of youngsters you are likely to find yourself soothing the inexplicable fears that all children have from time to time. It is essential to take them seriously; do not be tempted to laugh them off or you may damage the child's trust in you. A cash windfall could come from an unexpected but most welcome source.

2. THURSDAY. Excellent. Romance could take you unawares as you come face-to-face with a new acquaintance and feel an electrical spark of attraction jump between you. There is no need to put on airs in order to make a favorable and lasting impression. This is one of those occasions when you have an immediate intuition of each other's true nature. Workwise this should be a very productive day. Your concentration and attention to detail ensures the success of an important project, and the results will enhance your reputation. Health matters must not be neglected just because you are feeling good. Regular exercise will increase your energy level and give you extra sparkle.

3. FRIDAY. Variable. Recently you have been fairly cautious with money, and the savings are now beginning to show. When you need to buy essential goods there should be enough cash to go for the best quality. There is no reason to stint on yourself. Small achievements can boost your self-confidence. As a Sagittarius you like to think big, but at the same time do not overlook the minor triumphs of everyday life. You need to watch your tongue, especially if you are not speaking from your heart. Errors of speech are then likely to reveal your true thoughts. Your listeners will be quick to pick up such slips, leaving you feeling somewhat embarrassed. Be alert for careless driving if you go out this evening.

4. SATURDAY. Fair. This is an ideal day to take a loved one out for a special treat, and maybe buy a gift that has a particular meaning. It is all too easy to begin taking each other for granted. Making an effort to show your appreciation can rekindle buried romantic feelings. Make sure you are up-to-date with personal correspondence. There could even be a letter you wrote ages ago languishing in some coat pocket still waiting to be mailed. If you have been thinking of buying computer equipment for yourself or the kids, this is a good time to look into it further. Computers can be an excellent educational tool as well as fun for you and for youngsters. Just be sure to shop for good quality.

5. SUNDAY. Mixed. Sometimes household chores can seem a real burden, but all the same they do have to be done. Your natural reaction is to do a rush job, but this is not going to be satisfactory. If you are feeling a little under the weather, it could be a sign that you need to pay more attention to your diet. When you are living a busy life it is natural to rely on convenience food. However, it is important to get plenty of fresh fruit and vegetables as well. Family affairs are likely to occupy quite a lot of time. You should be able to help a relative who has problems by using your experience and compassion. Do not wait to be asked; offer your assistance.

6. MONDAY. Productive. Home redecorating or remodeling is always apt to cause some irritation. The disruption may now be getting to you, but do not allow the noise and dirt to spoil the process. If you keep the end result firmly in mind, even the chaos can become less worrisome. Parents or in-laws may be too eager to take a hand in your life, when what you really want is independence. Try to understand that they are attempting to be helpful. Tell them gently that you have to make your own mistakes; they must realize that that is the only way anyone ever learns. This is not the best time to make any sweeping changes to your appearance or work routine.

7. TUESDAY. Changeable. As a Sagittarius you do not usually take a back seat, but today is likely to be an exception. In fact, you might want to keep certain work under wraps until you have perfected it and are ready to show it off to other people. If you work for a charity you could have the opportunity to bring a project to a happy conclusion. Your organizational powers may have been taxed to the fullest, but your particular talent for generating goodwill should prove invaluable. A mood of impatience with a loved one could tempt you to bring the relationship to an end. However, you will surely regret doing so; hang in there and it is bound to take a turn for the better.

8. WEDNESDAY. Fair. Problems with electrical equipment should finally be resolved. This will undoubtedly be a relief since you can now get on with work that has been hanging fire for some time. Communications with a close relative are about to ease up after a rather tense period. Once you can bring yourself to see each other's point of view, the reason for your disagreement should simply vanish. This is a good time to send off written work, whether for class work or in hopes of publication. You will probably be cheered and encouraged by the positive reception. A quiet evening at home may seem so appealing that you even cancel another engagement by making up an excuse.

9. THURSDAY. Disquieting. If you have been indulging in gossip recently, you may now be confronted with the results. There is really no good reason for passing on rumors that could damage someone when you know very well they are likely to be inaccurate. And you can hardly blame the person involved when they become angry. Be extra careful on the roads. A minor lapse of attention could mean you miss a turn or even have a small but upsetting fender-bender accident. As a brother or sister brings a personal problem out into the open, your first reaction is apt to be to rush in and sort it out for them. Help by all means, but do not try to completely control the situation.

10. FRIDAY. Rewarding. If you have been hoping for sponsorship in order to get an important project under way, this could be the day you hear good news. Especially satisfying is your own enthusiasm, which is capable of firing up the imagination of other people. This gives you great potential for spreading the word. Romance could come your way through the friend of a close relative. At first the relationship might not seem very exciting or promising. Although it will probably take time to develop, there is plenty of positive potential. You should be enjoying leisure pursuits at a higher level, and this can be an excellent means of self-development and even of part-time income.

11. SATURDAY. Stressful. There is no point continuing to spread yourself thin; all that will happen is that you will perform badly and eventually could harm your health. Listen to loved ones when they warn you that it is vital to slow down and not take on so much responsibility. Keeping your temper with youngsters may be more of a challenge than usual, since they seem determined to test your will. It is probably not possible to make them toe the line on this occasion. The best that you can hope for is that they will calm down of their own accord. A trip with friends may not turn out quite as planned, but do not let this spoil the occasion; just enjoy the company and whatever comes along.

12. SUNDAY. Unsettling. This is probably not the best morning for organizing pleasurable activities. Chores left undone will only prey on your mind, so it would be preferable to get them out of the way first and then have the rest of the day clear for enjoyment. Do not be hard on yourself if you have lapsed from a diet. There is probably little damage done, and everyone succumbs to temptation from time to time. Family festivities can go a long way to improve relations. Both you and your mate or partner should reach the end of the day in a better mood. Take steps to bring about a dream. Life is not worth living for you unless you are busy realizing some ideal and contributing to the overall good.

13. MONDAY. Fair. There is hope for a business partnership that has been through some rocky times recently. Now you need to rise to the challenge and work together in order to make the most of an opportunity that has come your way. Your choice of a long-term partner is a wise one, even though there may be some difference in your social status. However, that simply will not be important once you are seen as a couple with identity of your own. It is not always easy to judge whether you should stand up to adverse criticism or accept it without argument. On this occasion you would probably be unwise to defend yourself too vociferously.

14. TUESDAY. Variable. Financial issues are crying out for attention, even though you may be unwilling to face them. It is impossible to ignore the fact that your plans for future security are rather thin and could benefit from some serious thought. A romantic affair that has been kept fairly quiet may no longer be giving you what you need. If you are beginning to suffer more than you enjoy, it is time to make a big change. You will do yourself or the other person no good by carrying on as you are. Some private research could give you a head start when looking to challenge others on their home ground. There is nothing to beat sound knowledge of your subject.

15. WEDNESDAY. Confusing. This is one of those days when you may be caught doing something wrong even though it is not usual for you. The trouble is that as a Sagittarius you have such a frank and open manner that you have little idea how to conceal unworthy actions. Loved ones may not be particularly communicative. All the same, they will not have much difficulty conveying an impression that you have upset them in some way. If they continue to keep up this sort of silent protest, you might feel justified in ignoring them until they are ready to openly reveal and discuss the problem. Friends are likely to cancel a date at the last possible minute.

16. THURSDAY. Excellent. You should be able to mobilize friends and loved ones to give some financial support for a cause that is close to your heart. If you are seeking sponsorship for a charitable event, you can raise a very useful sum of money. It does not pay to always go along with what your peer group says and does. A better sense of individuality arises from thinking for yourself. It can also help to work out ideas by discussing them with your mate or partner. Normally you are not very interested in formal social occasions, but when it is necessary to attend one you could be surprised how enjoyable it is. Keep a secret under your hat for a few more days.

17. FRIDAY. Mixed. Confusion is all too likely for Sagittarius travelers. You may find your flight or train schedule being altered at short notice. However, getting into a stew will not hurry things along, so try to keep calm. Use the waiting time to read and plan. The reappearance of an old flame could put you in a quandary, especially if you have never mentioned this person to your current mate or partner. Now it may be necessary to make light of a relationship that was actually very important to you, unless you are prepared to deal with some jealousy. Where business is concerned, your flair for seeing the big picture will eliminate a lot of unnecessary worry over details that can be handled by other people.

18. SATURDAY. Disquieting. It can be disappointing when your studies are not going as well as hoped. You may have to redo work that you thought would be acceptable. When you start looking it over, you will begin to see the flaws. Do not let past failure undermine your confidence in completing a creative project. No one ever gets it right first time. When you are drawing on the wellsprings of your imagination, there is no telling what will come up. A health problem, possibly one contracted abroad, could flare up again; this time you really must get it professionally treated. It can probably be cured simply and effectively with antibiotics or other drug therapy.

19. SUNDAY. Uncertain. Getting back on your feet again after ending a relationship can be a trying time. This is where friends and family members should be able to help. The more you are able to express your feelings rather than repressing them, the sooner you will be ready to start looking for romance once again. If you have been feeling physically under par for some time, you may not even realize that your health is not as good as it could be. Now there is no excuse for not taking a long, hard look at your lifestyle and making adjustments where necessary. Be especially kind to loved ones who have their own private worries to contend with.

20. MONDAY. Productive. The workweek should get off to quite a productive beginning. If you are starting a new job you need have no fears. You will probably feel at home right away, and very quickly begin to see where it is possible to make a valuable contribution. Do not be afraid to make a hard decision where health matters are concerned. If it seems that a more severe treatment would be beneficial, go for it with your customary Sagittarius enthusiasm and firm sense of discipline. You may realize that someone is acting as a benefactor for you but without wishing to draw any attention to themselves. Until you find out more, all you can do is be duly grateful.

21. TUESDAY. Variable. Make the most of a chance to network with colleagues and make contacts that do not usually come your way. Reaching out to other people can only be beneficial at this time. Although the results might not show in a material sense, they are real all the same. Helping a loved one achieve an ambition can draw you closer together. You might have access to assistance that would not otherwise be easily available to them, so that you become an integral part of their project. Recently you may have been spending quite freely on social events, and now begin to feel the pinch. The only thing to do now is to find less expensive forms of entertainment.

22. WEDNESDAY. Tricky. Although it might not seem very comforting at the moment, it is true that in romance you often get what you need rather than what you want. If you are beginning to feel that a loved one is practically impossible to deal with, think again. Go over the positive points of the relationship; there may be more than you expect. Borrowing money from a friend can change the nature of your friendship unless you are absolutely honorable about paying them back. Tardiness in repaying is sure to rankle with even the most generous of companions. Involvement in local politics might not always be to your taste, but it is certain that you can do some good.

23. THURSDAY. Satisfactory. When loved ones know you so well, it is almost impossible to keep a secret from them no matter how virtuous your motives. If you are planning a special surprise, it could be more effective just to leak a little of your idea so that they can at least anticipate the event with pleasure. Romance may not be fulfilling your dreams at the moment. When the other person is elusive, it is natural to feel distrust. You might even wonder whether you actually want to become more involved with them. Written work that requires close attention, especially an important letter, cannot be done when your mind is on other matters. Pull yourself together this evening and concentrate.

24. FRIDAY. Fair. There may be a possibility to end work early and spend some time socializing with colleagues and superiors you do not usually get to chat with. This could be a surprisingly intense experience, deepening your understanding of each other considerably. A tough physical workout would do you a world of good, but be sure to take along a friend to monitor your activity and ensure that you do not get carried away and overdo. Money should not be a problem since it seems possible to find an ingenious way of making some extra cash. Even if your idea is a little off the wall, you have nothing to lose by trying it out; even take a bet on your success.

25. SATURDAY. Demanding. You may not know how to react when a close relative attacks you verbally for no reason that you can fathom. Perhaps they are really worried about something else and you just got in the way. Whatever their motive, it would be unwise to snap back without thinking. Youngsters are likely to have more energy than usual and will really keep you on the go. Their boredom threshold is low, but they may be entranced and entertained by electronic games. Where romance is concerned, you have the opportunity to make a fresh start. Wipe the slate clean and forget the past; you and your significant other can look confidently toward the future.

26. SUNDAY. Useful. It should be possible to do a lot of good by getting involved with a neighborhood project. A sense of community is always worth fostering. In addition, you could find yourself meeting neighbors you never knew. This period marks a new phase in your personal self-improvement. You should be feeling more self-confident since your talents have recently been accorded well-deserved recognition. No matter how you try, it does not seem likely that you and your mate or partner will see eye-to-eye regarding an issue of personal beliefs. This is one occasion when you just have to agree to differ, although it would do no harm to give each other's viewpoint some serious thought.

27. MONDAY. Good. You are apt to wake up feeling bright and breezy, and this mood can carry other people along with you. It may be easier than usual to get your ideas across at work, so make the most of this opportunity to enhance your reputation for original thought. Do not be surprised if the phone rings more or less nonstop. Even if you are trying to do other things, it would be unwise to ignore it. There may be news coming your way that could open up exciting possibilities for a change in your work environment, and you do not want to miss out. Local social events should give you a chance to shine. Enjoy yourself, and be the life and soul of the party.

28. TUESDAY. Tricky. Most long-term relationships go through periods when both parties feel rather bored. However, that is no excuse to look elsewhere for companionship. If you succumb to this temptation, you could lose far more than you gain. Think long and hard before taking such a chance. A legal case has reached a turning point, and you may no longer be confident of success. At this point it will not do any good to count your chickens before they are hatched. Spending on personal needs and wants is fine as long as you also take into consideration your other responsibilities. Other people should not have to suffer because you have rushed to gratify your own desires.

29. WEDNESDAY. Mixed. One of the great things about a close relationship is the boost to your confidence that is a byproduct of the appreciation of a loved one. Right now you are lucky enough to enjoy the support of someone who has total belief in your talents and abilities, and this should by no means be taken for granted. A welcome addition to your income could be made by juggling finances and planning some extra work. There may be a friend who would welcome your assistance on a freelance project, and this could be a learning experience as well as lucrative. Be extra patient with friends and relatives who are not as decisive as you are. Give them more time.

30. THURSDAY. Uncertain. Unfortunately it is all too possible to mislay some vital paperwork just when it is needed. In addition, your usually faultless memory may desert you, so that it becomes a real challenge to fill in the gaps at short notice. Travel has its problems. Your car could probably benefit from an oil change. In fact, you might do better to rely on public transportation and resign yourself to a slower journey. Grasp an unusual opportunity to consolidate a dream project; a moment's hesitation could mean you lose out. Some sacrifice may be required, but if you believe in your aim that will not seem important or too much to pay.

DECEMBER

1. FRIDAY. Variable. You can get the best out of the day by simply putting on a smile and agreeing with those with whom you have any dealings. A positive approach will work wonders, encouraging other people to cooperate with your desires. Although routine work can be a bore at the moment, there is no available shortcut. You cannot attempt to avoid it in hopes that it will just go away or be done by someone else. Your nerves could do with a tonic; a good rest might be a sound place to start. It may not go over too well if you insist on solitude, but family members will just have to do without you for a while. On occasion it is necessary to consider yourself ahead of others.

2. SATURDAY. Enjoyable. This promises to be an enjoyable day. Friends can lift a lot of the burden of organizing events from your shoulders. Just allow this to happen; after all, you have taken your turn many times. A new neighbor could become quite a close friend if you take the trouble to help them move in. Do your best to welcome them, reminding yourself what it feels like to settle in a strange area. Sports can be exciting. Although the outcome is not guaranteed to please you, there should be enough thrilling moments along the way to make attendance well worthwhile. Make sure youngsters are not left out of your activities.

3. SUNDAY. Disquieting. There is little so disturbing as finding out that you have been the subject of gossip. You are well within your rights to be angry if this is the case. Unfortunately even if the rumors are not true, they tend to stick. This makes it hard to restore the balance to truth. As youngsters play in the neighborhood, you may feel they are safer than they actually are. As a Sagittarius you prize freedom very highly, but that does not mean that kids should be left unsupervised. A sick friend or relative might not be as appreciative as expected when you pay them a visit, but take into account the fact that they are not feeling well. At least they know you care.

4. MONDAY. Difficult. It is all very well having confidence in yourself, but this does not give you any excuse for lording it over other people. You are riding for a fall if you become too assertive, so tone down your behavior and keep a sense of proportion. Big changes are on the horizon regarding the course of your self-development. You may soon meet someone who will become a guide and mentor. Just make sure you are in a receptive mood to profound new ideas. There could be a tussle for supremacy going on within the family. Do not allow other people to manipulate you through emotional blackmail. Stand up for yourself.

5. TUESDAY. Excellent. Your personal financial situation seems sound, thanks to your recent efforts to cut expenditure. Before congratulating yourself, however, renew your resolve to continue along this course. Then you can celebrate by buying yourself something very special. Romance is promising, although you are unlikely to be transported to the heights of passion. Past experience has probably taught you that a solid sense of companionship is more valuable in the long run, and this is exactly what you should now find. Your creative ventures are in line for sincere compliments. You may be surprised to find how enthusiastically the public responds to your work.

6. WEDNESDAY. Successful. This is an encouraging day for presenting a written or verbal report. You should be able to express yourself concisely and also come up with new ideas of real value. A journey could turn into a little voyage of discovery; look around and view your surroundings with fresh eyes. It is all too easy to become so jaded that remarkable features are hardly noticed, but it is a pity to lose your sense of wonder at the world. Where romance is concerned, you may not really have much choice in the matter. Someone new on the scene is determined to sweep you off your feet, and you will probably be only too happy to go along with their wishes.

7. THURSDAY. Confusing. Even though you have the best of intentions, other people may just not be reading you right. For some reason you are coming across as being opinionated and even overbearing, probably because you are so enthusiastic about a new idea. Trouble is looming in a romantic affair. You and the other person are unlikely to agree on your joint future prospects. If you have been going along with their ideas, vaguely hoping that the differences will somehow sort themselves out, take a hard look at the situation. If you are going to stay together, some conscious effort is needed. Be careful when exercising; keep well within your physical limits or you will suffer tomorrow.

8. FRIDAY. Frustrating. Although a recent purchase may not have lived up to your expectations, it might be difficult to exchange the item for something more satisfactory. You may just have to make the best of a bad job, while reminding yourself not to indulge in impulse buying too often. Mental work can be surprisingly tiring. Do not be too hard on yourself if you become emotionally worn out from working on a knotty problem. In this situation it can actually be invigorating to have a change and give your body a workout instead of your mind. It might not be wise to drive if you are going out tonight; leave the chauffeuring to friends, who should be quite happy to offer you a lift.

9. SATURDAY. Happy. A romantic affair has never looked more hopeful. Right now, much depends on how you handle a delicate situation. As long as you are able to respond with sensitivity to the needs of your loved one, there is every reason to think the future is rosy. Someone whose opinion you respect could offer praise, which is bound to go to your head. However, it does not hurt to be given a little extra self-confidence from time to time, especially if it encourages you to continue with a personal project. As winter closes in, it is time to pay more careful attention to your health. Be sure you are getting a soundly nutritional diet and sufficient daily exercise.

10. SUNDAY. Mixed. You can improve the tone of a long-term partnership by revisiting haunts of your early days together. If this is not possible, an hour or so spent looking at photographs and reminiscing together should awaken tender emotions. There is little doubt that you like having your way in most things, but of course that is not always fair to other people. In particular, do not allow yourself to wield power over youngsters just because it can be done. They will be well aware that you are taking advantage of them. When a relative is in trouble, your instincts of generosity are bound to be aroused. Do the best you can, since they are relying on you to offer a helping hand.

11. MONDAY. Fair. Get an early start this morning and impress your associates. An informal meeting with them could prove very productive. It should be much easier to get the ball rolling when you are all in a relaxed situation and open to new ideas. There is likely to be a breakthrough in a legal case that could take matters a welcome stage further. Make sure this advantage is pressed home, otherwise it could be lost again. Even if you are used to your mate or partner reacting emotionally to what seem to you to be rational decisions, their response could still come as a shock. You may just not realize how powerfully a change in your lifestyle would affect them.

12. TUESDAY. Disconcerting. A secret may be weighing heavily upon you. You probably wish there was a way of sharing it with someone. This is what close friends are for, but make sure you choose one whose discretion is totally assured. If local shops are expensive, it can be worthwhile going further afield to make regular purchases. Of course this entails getting a little more organized, but that should not be beyond your powers. Where romance is concerned, you may simply not be clear about what you want. While it would be disastrous to rush into a decision just for the sake of it, you should not keep your mate or steady date in continuing suspense.

13. WEDNESDAY. Variable. For once you should not mind very much having your time taken up with small chores and financial tasks. There is a certain satisfaction from tidying up details and seeing that all is in order, reluctant though you may be to admit it. Dealing with friends' problems can become an everyday activity if you get a reputation for being helpful. Other people will turn to you as a matter of course, so you had better decide whether this is a role that you are happy to play. Joint funds should not be taken out of the bank unless it is absolutely necessary. It would be unforgivable to do so just to gratify a personal whim or fulfill a passing fancy.

14. THURSDAY. Deceptive. A close relative may not be as reliable as you expect when it comes to helping you organize a family celebration. It is naturally upsetting to be let down, but in this case there is nothing to do but proceed the best you can without their help. Long-distance travel can be problematic as inclement weather causes delays. Try to make your arrangements as flexible as possible in order to cut down on the stress factor. You could come across an exciting new book that opens your eyes to a fresh area of learning. Other people may wonder at your absorption in it, but there is apt to be an important life-changing message that makes great sense to you.

15. FRIDAY. Changeable. Quick-fire verbal exchanges are perhaps appropriate when you are with loved ones but not when you are dealing with superiors. Among your peers you can joke and fool around as long as you do not get carried away. Youngsters are apt to be particularly keen to learn at the moment, so take advantage of this phase; it may not last long. It might be a good idea to get in touch with their teachers to see if they can suggest ways of supplementing school lessons at home. You could regret not being better equipped for a lengthy journey; it is usually a good idea to take more than you think you will need rather than less.

16. SATURDAY. Confusing. Although a clear decision is required in regard to a long-term partnership, this is not the moment to make it. While you are pondering, it could be necessary to find some kind of compromise until you are ready in your own mind to make a choice. Financially this is not the best time to commit funds to an investment that carries potential risk. Your hopes may not be fulfilled, and you may soon regret your loss. A friend's personal beliefs are no business of yours until and unless they affect the way in which you relate to each other. Then it very definitely is up to you to challenge them, although this must not be done in a manner that could cause offense.

17. SUNDAY. Slow. You will probably be quite happy this morning puttering around doing little tasks at your own speed. This gives you the chance to mull over a problem and come to a reasoned conclusion. It is best to stay close to home; there is plenty to occupy you, and there is value in conserving your energy for once. If you begin to get restless, a good book can transport you to a thrilling realm of romance without you moving out of your chair. When youngsters insist on having their own way, let them do so but point out that they must bear the consequences. This hands-off approach could be a useful lesson in responsibility and decision-making for them.

18. MONDAY. Pleasant. It can be flattering when someone you respect shows signs of wanting to be more friendly with you. They may be ready and willing to assist you in realizing a personal dream. Do not pass up this offer of friendship, which could be both pleasant and useful. Although travel to a conference could take you away from loved ones, there is much to be learned at your destination. Once you are there you will not have time to be lonely, and the separation can make your reunion all the more delightful. A friend's children may brighten up the day with their amusing comments and observations. It is usually easier to appreciate other people's youngsters than your own.

19. TUESDAY. Favorable. You should have no difficulty charming your way into a social circle you have been eager to enter for some time, even though you might have to bend the truth a little. Once you have made friends, they will excuse any exaggerating on your part. You can earn some extra money by exploiting a personal talent that would come in handy during the holiday season. Do not be shy about promoting and marketing your skill locally; there may be an ideal niche for it. This is not the time to hang back if you want to get involved in a new romance. Make your feelings known and the other person is almost sure to be flattered by your interest.

20. WEDNESDAY. Variable. Success can be achieved through making friendly overtures to those whose ideas you want to use. They will appreciate your understanding of their concepts, and you will learn something along the way. There is a danger of having an upsetting argument with a close friend. You may have been getting on each other's nerves for some time, which is a sign that you are beginning to grow apart and perhaps should go your separate ways. Even if you are dragged against your will to a political meeting, you might be surprised how stimulating it is. In fact, you could be inspired to become actively involved in a campaign for election.

21. THURSDAY. Sensitive. Romance is on a razor edge as the other person seems to almost deliberately be finding fault with you. It could be that they want an excuse to end the relationship, but it wouldn't be fair to do so without some discussion and an attempt to explain. Money is a ticklish issue right now because recently you have been spending it like water. If your reserves are low, the last thing you want to do is get further into debt by borrowing or using your credit line. Do not let youngsters get away with rudeness; it is never too early for them to learn courtesy. Their bad manners can be especially distressing to older family members who have stricter morals.

22. FRIDAY. Fair. As you begin to look back over the past year, it should be clear that a special wish is close to fulfillment. This is a good reason to celebrate. It would be a good gesture to bring together all those who have helped you draw nearer to this goal. Speak up in a meeting; your opinion could be valuable in building a consensus. You may be the only person present who has the courage to voice a positive criticism that needs to be pointed out. You may have to scramble in order to finish off work, especially if this is your last day before the holiday break. Try not to leave any loose ends, since you will not relish coming back to them. End the day with a sociable drink with friends and colleagues.

23. SATURDAY. Cautious. If you are busy with last-minute preparations for the days ahead, it can be all too easy to let irritation get the better of you. Be aware of this, and do your best not to snap at loved ones. Doing so will spoil the atmosphere of what should be an enjoyable day. You may have to go off by yourself to buy an extra special gift for your mate or partner. It is important to remember that it is the thought that counts, not the cost. As a Sagittarius you are naturally generous, but a gift that is merely expensive rather than appropriate will not be well received. Make the most of the afternoon by finishing up final details of practical tasks that could otherwise prey on your mind.

24. SUNDAY. Disconcerting. You could be taken by surprise when a relative drops in out of the blue. All you can do is offer them a welcome and be the best possible host. After a while, you will probably be glad they have come. A neighbor could have a slightly startling piece of news they are just longing to tell someone. Even if you are not all that interested, pay attention for their sake. Though you have been hanging back from making a declaration of love, go ahead now. This can even be done over the phone if you are too shy to meet face-to-face. What is important is that you get your feelings out in the open. Then it is up to the other person to respond.

25. MONDAY. Merry Christmas! This day offers a great sense of security because it is very apparent that you have loved ones who support you. You are likely to opt for a fairly private celebration, surrounded by your nearest and dearest. Nevertheless, there will be no shortage of noise and chatter, particularly if youngsters are the focal point of the day. As a Sagittarius you do not always express your affection in material ways, but right now a few well-chosen gifts and a lovingly prepared meal should say it all. If you have been going through a rough period recently, there is now a chance to make a whole new start. Your renewed sense of understanding and sympathy will probably be intuitive and unspoken.

26. TUESDAY. Easygoing. There is certainly no need to rush around clearing up and initiating new entertainment to keep family members occupied. Everyone is probably quite content to spend a quiet time mulling over yesterday and enjoying their gifts. Take it easy, and allow yourself proper rest and relaxation. This is a good time for private reflection on your recent achievements. You should be feeling a deeper sense of self-worth than was the case at this time last year. Pat yourself on the back and give yourself credit for what you have managed to accomplish over the past few months. If you get a chance, talk with your mate or partner about your plans for future security as you size up your current situation.

27. WEDNESDAY. Tranquil. Today's uncharacteristic mood of patience allows you to get to chores you usually avoid like the plague. Now it should seem positively pleasant to do little tasks around the house. You might even be inspired to take on the larger jobs of cleaning and clearing out that have needed to be done for some time. The rich foods you have been indulging in recently may be having a negative effect on your digestion, and your waistline is not immune either. Resolve to stick to a plain diet for a few days, and make sure you are getting sufficient exercise. Your parents may be able to give you some assistance with a financial venture you have been thinking about.

28. THURSDAY. Disquieting. It can be a challenge to get words to come out right if your thoughts are not on what you are saying. If your listeners look mystified, it should be hardly surprising. Try and pull yourself together; otherwise there is every possibility of a disastrous misunderstanding. If you are driving locally, it is vital to stay alert. Your high standards of performance are not in doubt, but other drivers are likely to be more careless than usual. Youngsters are easily bored and inclined to be tearful. Try to get them interested in games that will give their imagination something to work on. An apology to a loved one may be in order; do not attempt to pass the buck.

29. FRIDAY. Frustrating. A romantic affair may have hit a brick wall. Neither your words nor your actions may seem to please your loved one. The last thing you should do is storm off in a huff. If you can ride this one out, it will be possible to get to the bottom of the problem and sort it out. A quick glance at your finances may reveal that recent expenses have left you rather short of cash. Buying everyday items could become an exercise in ingenuity as you have to shop around for the best bargains. It is not too soon to start thinking about next year's vacation, especially since you need something special to look forward to. Just reading travel brochures can be therapeutic.

30. SATURDAY. Variable. You can get the best out of the day by devoting some time to family members who are less well off than yourself. Just knowing that you are thinking about them with warm feelings can make all the difference to someone who finds it difficult to get out and about. Finally you can put the past behind you and admit that it is good that a romantic affair is over. In fact, the way you are feeling now proves that it was doing you more harm than good. Make the most of this newfound freedom and energy to start looking for a new romantic attachment. Too much home life can be stifling; you and your mate or partner need a change of scene.

31. SUNDAY. Fair. Your finances can no longer be ignored, nor should you be tempted to live on luck anymore. Even if it takes a few hours, getting all your paperwork in order will be well worthwhile since you will then know exactly where you stand. There could be structural problems with your home that need prompt attention. As long as you act fairly quickly, you can avoid expensive repair bills and further damage. As your thoughts turn toward the new year ahead, what is most important is a better sense of security. Partly this comes from your loved ones, but basically it is an inner feeling that you have worked hard during the past year and achieved many goals.

SAGITTARIUS
NOVEMBER–DECEMBER 1999

November 1999

1. MONDAY. Calm. Following a slow, steady routine is the best way to get through the day successfully. Channel any restlessness into mental activity. Your mind may be on travel and faraway places; you could find yourself indulging in long flights of thought and imagination. The time has come to consider making some changes in your career, even a total change of occupation or perhaps pursuing a new area of study. This is a good time to start a creative project, especially one that involves writing. You are likely to come up with inspired ideas that can be put to immediate use in your creative work. Get together with friends and broaden your social horizons this evening.

2. TUESDAY. Variable. Earlier in the day you need to do some deep thinking. If you are considering changing your life pattern in some way, especially by developing new ideas which can benefit others, try to make some definite plans. Distant places may be on your mind, but this is a day for planning a trip rather than actually setting off on one. Conditions do not favor journeys connected with work. Transportation difficulties could cause you to miss an appointment, or you could arrive in a nervous, irritable mood. Later in the day think of ways to improve your image. Consider giving up a habit that annoys other people. If you are carrying excess pounds, this is a good time to start a diet.

3. WEDNESDAY. Useful. You can advance your career and your home life through your own activity and enterprise. You are in a fine position to make any planned changes and are likely to impress people with your energy and hard work. Your increased business sense is also working to your best advantage. If there are any delays involving business activities, these need not be a cause for concern; eventually things will be straightened out and get back on track. There is even a chance of advancing your career. Recognition and friendship with people who are older than you can be particularly worthwhile. Do not limit yourself in any way.

4. THURSDAY. Excellent. This is a day of opportunities. You can increase your popularity in the business world and among community activists. If your work involves luxuries or the arts, it should progress well. Sagittarius people who produce creative work, especially writing, are apt to have some inspired ideas. You are now in a good position to harness your energies in a productive way. Circumstances are just right for making significant progress and achieving a number of your goals. At home, you are likely to enjoy hosting visitors; there is a chance they will come bearing gifts.

5. FRIDAY. Fortunate. You are in the middle of an ever-changing and widening social sphere. The horizons that open up for you now are giving you more chances to develop ideas. These are sure to lead to your own personal growth as well as to the greater good of other people. Accept an opportunity to work on some kind of reform which aims to make the world a better place. Through an association with a group or club, your ingenuity is likely to be put to good use. There may be delays when traveling. A journey that is not on schedule may leave you feeling exasperated. As a result, there is a possibility you will be tempted to take risks in order to make up the time lost, but caution is necessary.

6. SATURDAY. Difficult. This is not a day to take risks with your own finances. Avoid speculation or gambling. There is a strong chance of money being wasted or lost. Also keep a closer eye on business finances and profits. Ensure that the money side of any new associations is clearly understood on both sides. Guard against a tendency to go to extremes or to overindulge in food as a way of escaping stress. Maintain a steady, quiet routine. Avoid making any changes, particularly in domestic matters. It is a time to hold back and wait to see what develops. Other people have the upper hand now; be a follower rather than a leader.

7. SUNDAY. Uncertain. You may feel anxious about home affairs because you suspect that family members are concealing something from you or that there is some kind of intrigue going on in the family. Take extra care when dealing with sensitive domestic issues. This is a favored time for holding a sale; Sagittarius business owners should advertise far and wide. You may experience an intensive flow of energy which allows you to do some good works in your community. However, this is apt to be an erratic flow, which means that nervous tension may build up. There is little point in getting anxious about obstacles in your path. Try to take such hurdles in stride; with a few deft moves you can overcome them smoothly.

8. MONDAY. Sensitive. Do not hesitate to initiate a new business activity. If you control and direct your energies well, you are likely to prosper. Be aware, however, that there are people who are working against you in the background. Stay alert for deceptive practices or promises. You could wind up working alone, and are likely to get more done that way. Even though old methods and approaches have worked for you in the past, this is a good time to review them. There is a possibility that they are beginning to hold you back, preventing you from achieving your long-term ambitions and dreams. Pay attention to health matters; consider alternative health care such as acupuncture or aromatherapy.

9. TUESDAY. Rewarding. Because you are especially mentally alert, this is an excellent time to buckle down to study. If you work on developing your concentration, you can make the most of any new interests. It is also a day to catch up with correspondence and bills. You may be called upon to give a talk to a group with which you are involved; with a little practice in front of a mirror, it should be a great success. Activities involving friends are starred. It is likely to be especially pleasurable to entertain visitors at home. This is a good time for sprucing up your image or that of your home.

10. WEDNESDAY. Excellent. Forming a dynamic association with a new contact is likely to result in unexpected financial gains for both of you. You could meet people while making a short journey who will help further your personal plans. If you are involved in business negotiations of any kind, you are likely to find people's cooperation easier to obtain than you expect. Seek new ways to use your special Sagittarius abilities and talents. You may be drawn to intriguing new subjects. Try to organize a night out at the movies or theater for a group of your friends; it should be an enjoyable get-together. This is an auspicious day for romance; an enchanted evening with a loved one can be memorable.

11. THURSDAY. Useful. This is a day when positive, constructive progress can be made in all of your affairs. Conditions favor taking up new opportunities; as a result, your financial affairs are likely to prosper. Although returns on a speculative venture may be slow, you are likely to profit in the long term. You are likely to find your social life and leisure activities particularly enjoyable. Home life should be content, with all domestic matters progressing well. This is a good time to plan a vacation with your family. Sagittarius singles are likely to find opportunities for new romance quite close to home. Accept an invitation to go out even if it is made at the last minute.

12. FRIDAY. Variable. Although partnership money matters may not look too good, you should be able to make significant gains through your own activity and enterprise. There are opportunities for advancement and for business dealings which bring you into contact with people who wield power and influence. You may be required to put in a lot of hard work, but you should reap the benefits toward the end of the year. The day's events may have far-reaching effects on your life. Concentrate on business and on developing your skills. Consider signing up for a computer class to enhance your employment possibilities. Keep a low profile in romance and social life. Play hard to get.

13. SATURDAY. Mixed. Changes for the better are coming your way in regard to money, work, and domestic matters. Your powers of concentration are at their best, making this a good day to form long-term plans for the future. However, do not expect immediate results. Promotion or other recognition for your past hard work is not far off. You should be extremely energetic, both on a mental and physical level. Channel this energy into a demanding project that requires your creativity. If you do not stay busy, you could become restless and impulsive. Guard against taking any rash action; an accident could result.

14. SUNDAY. Unsettling. Early in the day is the busiest time for your business and employment interests. Focus on plans which could bring long-term benefits in the future. Later in the day it is important not to go to extremes in personal or business financial matters. Your judgment may not be too sound; it is better to postpone making any important decisions. Blind optimism could lead to bitter disappointment. Consider all of your options. Take advantage of the creative flow which is flooding your mind with new ideas. They are likely to come thick and fast; test out the best of the lot. Do not overindulge in food or drink.

15. MONDAY. Fair. As far as business matters are concerned, this is a good day to free yourself from old ideas and outdated methods. Also throw out old papers and files. Only then will you be ready for new beginnings in fresh directions. Your imagination is active; you may come up with some very innovative ideas. If you are traveling you may encounter disruptions to your journey or unexpected changes in your travel arrangements. Sagittarius people involved in teaching or literary work can make good progress. Pay more attention to your health and diet. The reward will probably be a noticeable increase in energy. Sagittarius singles could be swept up in a new affair of the heart, but it may turn out to be only a short although sweet romance.

16. TUESDAY. Cautious. Take extra care before signing any paper or agreement. There could be some kind of deception going on; your best policy is to keep your dealings straightforward and aboveboard. There could be unexpected good luck affecting your own financial affairs, but guard against going on a spending spree until and unless all of your bills are paid. Go out of your way to cheer up someone who is recovering from an accident or operation. Consider writing a humorous letter if you cannot visit them in person. You should be mentally alert, your intellectual powers at their best. Do not hesitate to put dormant ideas into action, especially those that can help you realize your dreams.

17. WEDNESDAY. Slow. You may be longing to change your home conditions or to escape from home responsibilities. There is a possibility you will neglect tasks at home in order to concentrate on more personal matters. There could be some kind of an upheaval in domestic affairs which you find stressful even though you are not directly involved. You are likely to achieve success in your work, but only after a good deal of strenuous effort. Guard against working to the breaking point. Dealing with other employees or those working for you may prove difficult, but these upsets can be sorted out without having to get anyone else involved in arbitrating the issue. Conditions favor working on long-term goals, although immediate results are not likely.

18. THURSDAY. Rewarding. Be prepared to make some changes in your home life. If you use your energy wisely, you should be able to bring about improvements and positive adjustments in domestic affairs. You may achieve unexpected benefits through a partnership or marriage. Romance is more important than usual for Sagittarius singles. This is an important day for business activities; the work you do is likely to bring you extra benefits, such as an increase in prestige or a promotion in the future. Conditions favor starting a new venture and contacting people who could prove helpful to you. It is also a good day to invest money or to take out long-term insurance. If you are traveling to visit a member of the family or a friend who is in the hospital, the journey should go smoothly.

19. FRIDAY. Good. Sagittarius people who are involved in artistic work are apt to have some very inspired creative ideas. However, keep your feet on the ground and guard against getting carried away. This is not a day to purchase new supplies for a creative project. You are likely to feel more at ease today and able to clear out old ideas in readiness to make new beginnings. This is the start of a positive period for business commitments.

Conditions favor a new partnership. You may also feel like taking up a new sport where you have the opportunity to display your special talents and skills. Look into taking out or revising a home insurance policy. Aim to make conservative, safe investments rather than becoming involved with risky financial ventures or gambling.

20. SATURDAY. Disconcerting. Although you may be feeling unsettled and unhappy about changes at home or upheavals in family matters, guard against built-up tension leading to quarrels. In particular, do not take any unnecessary risks. Take special care when driving, especially if you are in an angry mood. There is a possibility of a disappointment in romance for you Sagittarius singles. The person you are chasing may be uncomfortable with your ardent advances and frequent phone calls. Events in your social life could cause unexpected additional expense. Quiet relaxation or meditation can help maintain your peace of mind. Enjoy a quiet evening away from argumentative friends or relatives.

21. SUNDAY. Successful. A last-minute decision to travel by a different route may lead to meeting someone who becomes important in your life; a new dynamic relationship or love affair could develop. Conditions favor business and professional activities. This is a good time to discuss your plans and ideas with others. Travel is likely to be pleasant, whether for business or pleasure. If you are driving take extra care. If you are in the market for a new car, choose one that is not too expensive to run. Tread carefully in dealing with others, especially those at home. Any changes you plan to make should be thoroughly discussed and then made openly and naturally.

22. MONDAY. Difficult. Tension is building up at home and in the workplace. It would be wise not to work to the point of exhaustion, even if you feel like pushing ahead. Your health could suffer as a result of stress. You are apt to make just as much progress by working slowly but steadily, and the chance of making mistakes will be reduced. Even if you cannot see the results immediately, success is likely to be evident later. Moving is starred, but postpone signing any paper or contract until another day. Also avoid making any journey unless absolutely essential. Plan a quiet evening and make time for relaxation. This should help restore your vitality and give you added energy for the rest of the week.

23. TUESDAY. Changeable. Earlier in the day you are likely to feel unusually enterprising. As your ambitions come to the surface and you experience an increased burst of energy, you should be able to make good progress. Plan quiet activities for later in the day; this is apt to be a more trying period when disappointments occur. A partnership deal could be delayed or blocked. Your mate or partner may oppose your ideas and plans, or they could criticize a project you started recently. Disagreements may not be easy to sort out. Even an apology may not be enough to clear the air. A romantic movie could make you starry-eyed with your loved one, but do not get carried away with dreams of a trouble-free future.

24. WEDNESDAY. Lucky. Your affairs are about to take a turn for the better with little effort on your part. Home life and relationships within your family are likely to be harmonious. Be ready to welcome visitors to your home. Any social activities you participate in should be enjoyable. Conditions favor travel and taking part in leisure activities or sport, especially if children are involved. Because you may be feeling restless, focus on new or unusual interests that are a challenge to you. If you have business dealings with people at or from a distance, you could find an opportunity or opening which brings personal benefits. An evening spent at the movies or a concert could be particularly memorable.

25. THURSDAY. Tricky. On this Thanksgiving holiday do your best to steer clear of any disagreements involving relatives or neighbors. Walk away rather than take sides. Guard against impulsive actions. Making hasty changes or a spur-of-the-moment journey can land you in hot water. Later in the day you could receive some upsetting news regarding finances; there is likely to be a dispute over an inheritance which will have to be sorted out before you receive even a nickel. As a Sagittarius you have an instinctive understanding of other people's emotional state, which puts you in a good position to support and encourage them. Participating in a team sport or independent physical exercise can relax you and improve your problem-solving ability.

26. FRIDAY. Mixed. Conditions favor making long-term plans in relation to joint finances and domestic matters, although immediate results are unlikely. Money-making activities should proceed smoothly. You can be most effective working alone behind the scenes. It is not a good day to buy items for your home despite sales. Guard against overoptimism or extravagance, especially if considering a new agreement. The best course is to postpone making important decisions until another day. There may be some problems to resolve regarding shared or group finances. Avoid extremes while exercising or pursuing other leisure interests. If a friend is having trouble, you may be called upon to lend a sympathetic ear, but do not give advice unless asked.

27. SATURDAY. Variable. This is a day to sit back and enjoy the success in your business and social life that you have worked to achieve. Conditions favor getting involved with new projects and enterprises. If you make the most of opportunities you are offered, there is likely to be little resistance in reaching your goals. If you have a special interest in science or philosophy, this is a good time to pursue independent or formal studies in these subjects. Your mind is active but also restless. As a result, you need to guard against impulsiveness and taking risks. Take special care if driving or making a short journey by bus or taxi.

28. SUNDAY. Disquieting. You may not realize you are becoming increasingly angry due to strain at home or at work. Make time for relaxation as a scheduled part of your daily routine. Guard against becoming irritable over controversies with others, particularly within your family circle. Strive for a steady, serious approach to tasks that have to be done, and do your best to take any obstacles in stride. If you are traveling, disruptions and delays are almost inevitable. It is not a good day to expect to make close connections. Conditions favor social activities and new friendships. A romance or increased social life could develop if you stay on the move and accept whatever invitations you receive.

29. MONDAY. Pleasant. Early in the day is excellent for travel and leisure activities. Do all that you can to make the most of every opportunity that comes your way. You can count on having good concentration. This is a favored time to begin studying for an exam or starting work on an all-important report. Later in the day your vitality may be lower. At that time there could be some trying events and disappointments to cope with. The latter part of the day does not favor changing your plans. Evening hours are starred for artistic and practical pursuits; your awareness of all that is colorful and delicate is especially acute. If you work in a creative area, you are likely to make a significant breakthrough.

30. TUESDAY. Fair. A quiet schedule is the best plan for today. There could be obstacles to progress or minor frustrations which cramp your style. Make no changes in your business affairs, and avoid signing any paper or contract. The key to success is to make slow, steady progress with routine work. Have faith that the results you seek will come later, bringing benefits in the future. Conditions favor all kinds of writing and keeping up with correspondence. There may be some change in your home life, possibly concerning a parent or in-law. You may have to visit or write to someone who is recuperating from an illness or accident. Your optimism and cheerful outlook improve their spirits.

December 1999

1. WEDNESDAY. Mixed. If it comes to making a choice between a social gathering hosted by friends and the requirements of your home life, the friends may win out. It is not that you do not care about your loved ones, but you are unlikely to be in the mood for domesticity. Your intuition is strong; any sort of message you receive relating to the way you treat other people and what you are expecting of them should not be ignored. Conditions do not favor a logical approach, but you can afford to back a strong hunch. Although treasured plans should be kept to yourself a little longer, they should be progressing well.

2. THURSDAY. Difficult. You may feel you are being ordered around in the office or in your community. Large, impersonal forces are having an impact on your financial affairs. You are unlikely to make much progress in this area today. Personal affairs, however, are another story. This is the time to retreat from worldly concerns and concentrate on improving your self-image. Consider going on a retreat; even a short weekend break can work wonders. Sagittarius parents may have to resolve a problem affecting a child or younger relative. Look at it from both an adult angle and a youngster's view.

3. FRIDAY. Changeable. Do not succumb to an urge to buy an extravagant item for yourself or someone special in your life. Temptation is all around, but you are strong enough to say no and to mean it. A project that is just beginning to take shape promises the success you have long wanted. Your reputation is gaining ground. Look into courses in the next school term. Signing up for one that is a little out of the ordinary can be of more benefit than taking an everyday subject that you could learn by reading a book. You may be approached to teach a short course in a subject you have been studying for years. A little flattery can go a long way to dispelling the resentment of a close family member that is due to jealousy or envy.

4. SATURDAY. Demanding. All matters connected with your home life are becoming much more hectic. You may have some difficulty keeping up with the many changes that are occurring. Not everyone is easy to get along with. You need a heavy dose of patience to cope with whiners and complainers. Even relations with people with whom you are normally on the same wavelength can be rather strained at this time. Although this is not something to be overly concerned about, greater understanding and empathy on your part might help sort things out between you. Do not hesitate to make a fast choice in a situation that is deteriorating right before your eyes.

5. SUNDAY. Unsettling. Even more than yesterday, it is vital to speak your mind. Be frank about what you consider to be very important issues. In your love life, too, avoid compromising too much or being totally self-sacrificing. Striking the right balance is a hard trick, but you deserve to consider your own wants and desires. You may have slightly unrealistic ideas. Discuss them with unbiased individuals before deciding on a definite course of action. Loved ones are willing to put themselves out on your behalf. Deal with a troublesome physical symptom without delay, even if it means going to your doctor to get the condition checked out on an emergency basis.

6. MONDAY. Changeable. People on the fringes of your life are taking on a more important aspect, especially those with whom you are involved in a business or financial sense. Although you are willing to help sort out the complicated lives of your friends, guard against taking on problems that are not of your own making. Conditions are changing quickly, necessitating a flexible approach to keep up with them. Even long-term endeavors are likely to take a surprising twist, but this should be for the better. Make your actions and reactions decisive and in a spirit of optimism. Be sure to put your good Sagittarius powers of intuition to immediate use. Guard against giving an impression of being cool or aloof in a situation where you actually feel shy.

7. TUESDAY. Buoyant. Conditions are right for you to get out and about. You have a lot to offer, but no one is going to come knocking at your door. Blow your own horn a little. Volunteer rather than waiting to be asked. A relative could benefit from your good advice, but tread carefully; you may not have all the facts. There could be a good reason why someone is acting strangely. Be cautious, too, when challenging the opinions of others. If you are working, there is a greater likelihood of inadvertently stepping on the toes of a higher-up. The approach of the festive season is apt to remind you of past merry-making and the increased popularity you enjoy among friends and loved ones.

8. WEDNESDAY. Confusing. If you want to make changes now, you have to push for them personally. You can be most effective as a trailblazer rather than a follower. Waiting for someone else to make the first move could leave you grinding your teeth in frustration. Although an older person may have good advice to offer you, they may take some time to get to the point. Guard against letting your impatience show; doing so could lead to misunderstandings and hurt feelings. You cannot rely on a promise that has been made to you, even though the intentions were totally honorable at the time it was made. Take steps to limit any damage caused by someone canceling out of a date or going back on their word.

9. THURSDAY. Good. Extra care is needed when beginning a new project, especially if you are working as part of a group. There is a greater danger of underestimating your own capabilities; you may be willing to do more than you can actually achieve. Any free time you have is likely to be gobbled up by an increased workload. Important new contacts are foreseen during lunch or a work break. Let your ideas flow freely, then jot them down so that you have them for future reference. Although some of your ideas may not be appreciated by straitlaced higher-ups, eventually you are likely to get an opportunity to show just how good they are. Staying home is favored tonight.

10. FRIDAY. Mixed. Try to team up with someone who has just the skills you are trying to develop. A new partnership forged at this time can be lucky for you in more ways than you imagine. If money is holding you back, consider seeking a loan from a relative or friend before going to a bank. Do all that you can to avoid paying a high rate of interest; an interest-free loan is ideal. If you are starting a new project, keep in mind the importance of marketing and advertising. Scrimping in these areas could lead to a disappointing outcome. Friendship and romance are likely to overlap, but tread carefully when it comes to crossing the line.

11. SATURDAY. Disquieting. Tread carefully or you may have to deal with misunderstandings later on. Guard against speaking your mind without first thinking about what you are going to say. Choose your words with care to avoid double meanings. You are entering a period in which you need to cultivate the fine art of tact and diplomacy. If you are attending a meeting, try to listen more than you talk. You can ensure success for yourself if you convince others that you care about their views and also that you know what you are doing. Do all that you can not to alienate them from you. Vagueness in the way you deal with others is likely to compound your problems and bring confusion. A surprise Sagittarius birthday party lifts your spirits.

12. SUNDAY. Variable. Current conditions are switching to put the emphasis on family ties. Far from being restricting, you are likely to find you nearest and dearest are behind you one hundred percent. You may even be encouraged to take action you had not even considered before. Even though practical matters are on your mind, find time to take into account the emotional needs of those you love. Surprises are in store socially; make the most of them as they come along. Not only can you have a good time, you can also make life more fun for those in your immediate circle. As the festivities begin to intensify, they may shape the week ahead. However, be sure to schedule work time.

13. MONDAY. Manageable. Get an early start this morning. Allow yourself as much freedom of expression as possible while also taking into account what others are thinking. Having said what is on your mind, you may have to go along with the majority vote. This is just the right time to dust off a pet project that has been languishing on the shelf. With the pressure easing on more immediate concerns, you can turn to less urgent but equally interesting matters. Good ideas that emerged earlier in the month can be put into practice; you can count on an even more successful outcome than you originally foresaw. Guard against being fooled by a smooth salesperson or a deceptive advertisement.

14. TUESDAY. Frustrating. Try to finalize your Christmas plans. Conditions are unsettled; there is every chance that arrangements you made earlier in the month have to be reorganized. Progress is likely to come in fits and starts. However, you can be productive even though constant interruptions make you wonder if you will ever finish a certain project. Do not allow disappointments caused by friends to make you deviate from the path that you have carefully chosen for yourself. Upsets appear to be minor and are unlikely to be of lasting importance in your life. Seek out new faces as a way of changing your views and broadening your outlook.

15. WEDNESDAY. Satisfactory. Reminiscing can help you learn some lessons from the past. No matter how painful or humiliating they might be, this exercise should be useful for the future. Listening to your good Sagittarius intuition is likely to give you the answers you seek. Even casual conversations may contain valuable nuggets of information. Guard against trampling on the rights and sensitivities of other people. What you want at the moment may be in conflict with plans that are already in motion. If you give a little, people are more likely to meet you halfway. There is a possibility that you may not be able to stretch your money as far as you would like; making a few gifts can help you budget.

16. THURSDAY. Tricky. You have a dilemma to resolve today. On the one hand, social occasions and the desire to be with those who stimulate your imagination are likely to be almost irresistible. On the other, there may be nothing you would like more than to stay home and get involved in preparations for the festive season. Whatever you choose, guard against letting your mind wander. Keep focused on each task. You need to concentrate fully to do justice to projects at work and at home. Taking a chance on a lottery or raffle could pay off in a small way. Keep your stakes to a manageable level; betting your shirt on a hot tip is not favored.

17. FRIDAY. Frustrating. As the momentum builds up to the festive season, it becomes increasingly difficult to keep your mind on practical matters. You are likely to be in a party mood, and no one is about to take the fun out of your life. You are likely to be in a cooperative frame of mind when it comes to hard business. Your good Sagittarius intuition and creative abilities are in overdrive, but be leery of leaving everyone else in a state of bewilderment and confusion. Not everyone is able to keep up with your frantic thinking. Keep an open mind when it comes to romance; nothing is likely to turn out exactly as you expect. The reappearance of an old flame could frustrate you.

18. SATURDAY. Misleading. If you go out shopping for presents, guard against a tendency to overspend. There is a risk of blowing your entire budget. Friends can be disconcerted by a display of misplaced generosity. Leisure and pleasure pursuits could put you in the limelight. There is no reason to stay indoors. You could be slightly at odds with a certain neighbor or friend due to a certain jealousy on your part. You will probably find it impossible to force others into your way of thinking. This is a time to go with the flow if you can; if not, go off on your own. These restrictive conditions will pass once Christmas arrives.

19. SUNDAY. Difficult. You can be taken in by a hard-luck story, which makes it all the easier for an unscrupulous person to take advantage of you. If you do decide to help someone, consider suggesting ways in which they can also help themselves, especially if it is someone you know. Offer your time to a worthy cause rather than a cash donation. Your usual self-confidence is at an ebb, making it difficult to deal with strangers. This is your mind's way of telling you to retreat into yourself a little; it will not be long before you begin to see things in a more realistic light. You may have to return a defective item to the store where you purchased it; even if you do not have the receipt, insist on an exchange or store credit.

20. MONDAY. Excellent. A combination of enthusiasm, experience, and practical common sense comprises your unique view of life. It can take you far, although your plans are unlikely to be popular with everyone. Someone who is standing in your way is probably doing so on purpose. Let them know that you have certain objectives to meet and that you will make compromises only on your own terms. Keep alert for seemingly insignificant details; these could turn out to be your main chance. Strive to get a head start on your competitors and to obtain significant support in most of your endeavors. Going out after work could keep you away from home much later than you think.

21. TUESDAY. Disquieting. Feelings of fatigue and listlessness could slow you down. Fight against a tendency to ignore a deadline. Exercise greater patience with someone who constantly interrupts you. This is not the best time to proceed with any personal plans, especially if you are in a steady relationship. Be sure to consult your mate or partner before making any major move or accepting a joint invitation. Guard against grandiose or impulsive actions, especially those that stem from a need to boost your own ego. Be especially careful about who you trust. Not everyone you meet today is reliable, although their intentions may be good at the time they make a promise.

22. WEDNESDAY. Variable. People are almost certain to argue with you, particularly when it comes to social arrangements. Stick to prearranged plans only if you feel strongly enough about them. There appears to be little point in upsetting others over basically trivial matters. Take what you hear in casual conversation with a grain of salt. Money matters are figuring quite strongly in all of your plans. This could mean that you have to juggle the family budget or make some changes to it. While this may not be easy or popular at the moment, the effort will be well worth it when the holiday bills start coming in next year.

23. THURSDAY. Satisfactory. Practical organization is just what you need at this time. Make last-minute adjustments to your plans for Christmas based on a phone call from relatives or friends at a distance who you will be seeing. The last thing you want to do is to let people down in any way, but you are unlikely to take too kindly to interference from others. If a major change is required in the routine aspects of your life, you first need to alter your way of thinking about them. You can expect some opposition but should be able to overcome it by reasoning rather than dictating. Requests are sure to be better received than demands.

24. FRIDAY. Unsettling. It may look to you that friends are living the sort of life that you would like for yourself. It could be quite difficult to separate fact from fiction when it comes to getting at the truth of a situation. You are inclined to believe everything you see, although your view could be an illusion. Your reflective, subdued state of mind could be an indication of your need to recharge your batteries. Spend time in the company of your nearest friends, even though it may be only an hour or two. Disagreements are likely this evening; few of them will be your fault. Your view of life is quite sensible and rational, even though others may fail to recognize this fact.

25. SATURDAY. Merry Christmas! The day promises to be a riot of constant activity. Surprising news from far away can help get things off to a fine start. The good cheer of those around you is likely to prove infectious, sending your spirits soaring. Although this is usually a day for family, you may feel the need to get out and about later on. Visiting friends, or helping those who are less well off than yourself, can be a welcome change. If you fly the nest for a while, you are likely to bump into someone you have not seen in a long time. Wherever you spend the day, you are sure to feel at home.

26. SUNDAY. Pleasant. Fortunate developments are foreseen on the domestic front. This is also a day for getting out and about. If you stay cooped up at home, there is a risk of getting bogged down in trivialities and petty squabbling. New acquaintances are likely to bring a refreshing change of outlook. As a Sagittarius you thrive on attention and personal popularity. If this desire remains unfulfilled, you are likely to become rather irritable and withdrawn. Today, however, you would be wise to take things at a slower pace. Do not try to force others to follow your lead. Debates with serious types may prove rewarding; you are apt to be intrigued by the diverse opinions being expressed.

27. MONDAY. Fortunate. Influential people can be surprisingly helpful. They are likely to share your vision of the future and back one of your innovative though controversial plans. Consider seeking the advice or professional assistance of a known expert in the field. This is a starred day for initiating new team ventures and cooperative endeavors. You could be given a special exemption which helps keep you from getting snarled up in red tape. Consider sending a representative to confer with others on your behalf. If someone wants to talk to you about their plans, listen with an open mind, then give full and helpful answers to their questions. In this way you can allay their doubts and fears.

28. TUESDAY. Buoyant. Even though it may be business as usual for you, partying could still be on your mind. Spend part of the morning socializing, then settle down to work. Partnership are apt to run very smoothly. Projects started earlier in the month should continue to prosper. Express yourself creatively. Your dreams could be a rich source of inspiration. A hobby can be transformed into a money-making proposition if you streamline your methods. Although a relationship with someone younger than yourself may have been going through a rough period recently, today favors calling a truce and having some fun together. A well-calculated gamble is likely to pay off.

29. WEDNESDAY. Fair. Extend your goodwill to almost everyone you meet, even though they could be in a perverse mood. Play devil's advocate in discussions being held behind closed doors so that nothing is taken for granted. Guard against a tendency to impose your ideas; doing so can leave you in a vulnerable position later on. Luck continues to be on your side, but you still must protect your cash and investments. Unattached Sagittarius people can expect romance to blossom into a deeply fulfilling relationship. Certain events may turn out to be a blessing in disguise, especially those which affect your personal ambitions. Try harder to go with the tide rather than strain against it.

30. THURSDAY. Easygoing. Colleagues and associates are apt to be openly supportive, letting you have your way with most things. What you undertake can be done with confidence, although there is a risk of being accused of trying to take too much control. Your insights are good, and you can afford to back your hunches. If there is a chance to do something completely out of the ordinary, do not hesitate to grab it. You can benefit from a change of scenery and companionship. Consider making plans to spend New Year's Eve away from your home base, even at this late stage. Other people are willing to fall in line with you.

31. FRIDAY. Changeable. You may receive some optimistic news from distant friends and associates. Apart from this, you can expect a laid-back day. Try to make the most of this respite so that you are rested and ready to welcome the new year. Social arrangements are subject to change; staying flexible and playing it by ear is the best policy. You are unlikely to be left out in the cold; as a Sagittarius you are seldom away from the bright lights and a big crowd. There may be some unresolved issues clouding your love life. Use this very special evening as an opportunity to wipe the slate clean with that special person in your life. Go into the new year arm in arm as a team.

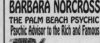